VICTORY!

FEATURING

THE WORLD'S LEADING EXPERTS
REVEAL THEIR SECRETS FOR
WINNING IN HEALTH, WEALTH, & SUCCESS
IN THE NEW ECONOMY.

Published by CelebrityPress®, Orlando, FL
A division of The Celebrity Branding Agency®

Celebrity Branding® is a registered trademark
Printed in the United States of America.

ISBN: 978-0-9886418-3-9
LCCN: 2013933308

This publication is designed to provide accurate and authoritative information with regard to the subject matter covered. It is sold with the understanding that the publisher is not engaged in rendering legal, accounting, or other professional advice. If legal advice or other expert assistance is required, the services of a competent professional should be sought. The opinions expressed by the authors in this book are not endorsed by CelebrityPress® and are the sole responsibility of the author rendering the opinion.

Most CelebrityPress® titles are available at special quantity discounts for bulk purchases for sales promotions, premiums, fundraising, and educational use. Special versions or book excerpts can also be created to fit specific needs.

For more information, please write:
CelebrityPress®
520 N. Orlando Ave, #2
Winter Park, FL 32789
or call 1.877.261.4930

Visit us online at: www.CelebrityPressPublishing.com

VICTORY!

FEATURING

THE WORLD'S LEADING EXPERTS
REVEAL THEIR SECRETS FOR
WINNING IN HEALTH, WEALTH, & SUCCESS
IN THE NEW ECONOMY.

CONTENTS

FOREWORD

By Tom Hopkins 13

CHAPTER 1

SELLING'S BRASS RING

By Tom Hopkins 15

CHAPTER 2

**UNSEEN DANGERS AND
HIDDEN OBSTACLES TO
YOUR RETIREMENT SUCCESS**

By William Geiger 23

CHAPTER 3

**THE RETIREE'S VALUE
OF ASSET PROTECTION
AND INCOME PLANNING**

By Bob Fugate 33

CHAPTER 4

16 WAYS TO SAVE MONEY ON BUSINESS ELECTRICITY AND 6 POTENTIAL REVENUE-GENERATING STRATEGIES FOR YOUR BUSINESS.

By Bob Garrett 41

CHAPTER 5

DEVELOPING A STAND-ALONE BUSINESS

By Carina Hatton 51

CHAPTER 6

SEVEN STEPS TO VICTORY AND SUCCESS

By Dave Stoltzfus 59

CHAPTER 7

TIMELESS PRINCIPLES FOR A SUCCESSFUL LIFE IN ANY ECONOMY

By David Lee 67

CHAPTER 8

THE FOUR SECRETS OF BUSINESS SUCCESS

By Elmer Davis, Jr., MBA, ALM 75

CHAPTER 9

BUSINESS DEVELOPMENT AND THE ULTIMATE CLIENT EXPERIENCE

By Dharmesh Vora 83

CHAPTER 10

**EIGHT COMMON MISTAKES
THAT EVERY RETIREE IS MAKING
IN THEIR RETIREMENT**

By Jim Byrd. 91

CHAPTER 11

**THE SEVEN THINGS DEPLETING
YOUR RETIREMENT NEST EGG**

By Don B. Bergis & Jared M. Elson 99

CHAPTER 12

**THE RETIREMENT PLANNING
BUCKET STRATEGY**

By Jack Teboda 107

CHAPTER 13

**RETIREMENT CHOICES IN
A VOLATILE MARKET**

By Jeff Mitchell 115

CHAPTER 14

**CREATING YOUR CELEBRITY
BRAND LOGLINE:** HOW TO POSITION
YOURSELF FOR SUCCESS

By Nick Nanton & JW Dicks 123

CHAPTER 15

**PLANNING IS THE FOUNDATION
FOR RETIREMENT**

By Joshua Cumrine 135

CHAPTER 16

WINNING SMILE

By Karen L. Royal 143

CHAPTER 17

**LEARNING AND PROTECTING
THE VALUE OF A DOLLAR**

By Keith W. Ellis, Jr. & Derek L. Gregoire 151

CHAPTER 18

HOLISTIC FINANCIAL DEVELOPMENT™ –
BACK TO BASICS MAKING
THE IMPOSSIBLE POSSIBLE!

By Malin Carlberg 161

CHAPTER 19

**BUILDING YOUR BUSINESS
THROUGH TECHNOLOGY:**
IT SOLUTIONS THAT SAVE
AND MAKE YOU MONEY

By Jamal Abbasi Millar 169

CHAPTER 20

**THE FIVE INSIDER SECRETS TO
GUARANTY YOU A SUCCESSFUL
RETIREMENT**

By Matt Golab 177

CHAPTER 21

PERSUASIVE COLLECTIONS –
SEPARATING PEOPLE FROM MONEY

By Eric J. Christeson, PhD 185

CHAPTER 22

VICTORIOUS FINANCIAL PLANNING REQUIRES WORKING WITH THE RIGHT ADVISOR

By Reid Abedeen...197

CHAPTER 23

SURVIVING RETIREMENT

By Todd Kim & Greg Roumpos 207

CHAPTER 24

YOUR FIVE POINT PLAN FOR RETIREMENT

By Ron Campbell 219

CHAPTER 25

FROM THE GREAT DEPRESSION TO THE GREAT RECESSION: HOW A SAFE MONEY STRATEGY REAPS REWARDS AND LIMITS RISK

By Stewart A. Miller 227

CHAPTER 26

MR. BUCKET LIST

By John Jochem & Faith Jochem 235

CHAPTER 27

GREAT RELATIONSHIPS WILL PUT YOU IN BUSINESS AND KEEP YOU IN BUSINESS

By Vanessa Nunez & Bridget Shoemaker 243

CHAPTER 28

**SEVEN STEPS TO COMPLETE YOUR
RETIREMENT INVESTMENT PLAN**

By John Convery 251

CHAPTER 29

**"DISCOVER HOW TO SELL YOUR HOME
FOR MORE MONEY...AND IN LESS TIME"
... IN THIS NEW DIGITAL ECONOMY!**

By Sasha Miletic 261

FOREWORD

BY TOM HOPKINS

VICTORY! I love the title selected for this book. And so do each of the other authors you'll read here. It has inspired all of us to write something we hope will help you on your journey to success during the developing economic recovery. A better world – whether our personal worlds or the world at large – is waiting for each of us to claim it. However, before we can claim Victory, we need to choose it, set our course for it and in many cases make a firm commitment that we will do whatever it takes to achieve it.

Victory is what we are all striving for whether it's to be victorious in the battle to gain and maintain health, wealth or any other kind of success in life. We all want to win. We want to discard the cloaks of negativity, poor habits, and defeated attitudes of the recent past. And we will— through the power of choice, dedication, persistence, and determination.

When we raise our expectations for ourselves and those we communicate with on a daily basis, we have the power to improve the outcomes not only for ourselves and those people, but everyone *they* come in contact with. It's that ripple effect we've all seen when dropping a pebble into still water. Our thoughts and actions do not exist in a vacuum. They impact the world, starting from our chosen point of origin. Be enthusiastic about what you can do to alter the course of your life and the lives of those you touch. Keep dropping those positive pebbles and you'll make a powerful impact on the victories of others who might be worlds away.

Enthusiasm for triumph and success isn't limited to athletes, politicians, and the military. It applies to everyone—in every walk of life. Parents aspire to successfully raise intelligent, responsible children. Employers strive to build winning companies that will support not only them, but also the families of the employees who make it great. Each of us aspires to achieve some level of success or victory in our lives.

Life as a whole is full of victories large and small. When exercise is important to you, you embrace your will to take the stairs instead of the elevator. When health is what matters most, you can easily walk past the snack vending machine or drive past the fast food restaurant without a glance. When saving money for something important, it's easy to skip the relatively expensive conveniences of life and maximize the use of the funds you *will* spend. When attempting to gain a new client for your company, expending extra effort on fine-tuning your presentation doesn't seem like a chore. Each of those things are small victories that you expect to win on your way to the much larger victories in life.

One of the greatest men of the 20th century had to inspire the whole free world to desire victory. The great Winston S. Churchill's word lives on to the benefit of us and future generations. "As long as we have faith in our own cause and an unconquerable will to win, victory will not be denied us."

When you grow your faith in what you desire, you too will be victorious!

CHAPTER 1

SELLING'S BRASS RING

BY TOM HOPKINS

The origin of the term "brass ring" comes from carousels in the late 1800's. On many carousels the outside row of horses were stationary. This often made them the last choice for riders who enjoyed the up and down movement of the other horses. From a distance, it might look like the carousels were not very popular. To remedy this, carousel operators added a wooden arm that would extend within reach of the outside riders. Operators would add several iron rings and one brass ring to the arm. As riders passed the arm, it became a game of skill and timing to grab the rings. Brass rings often entitled the bearers to free rides or other prizes. So getting the brass ring became a symbol of winning the highest prize.

In the field of selling, the brass ring is a closed sale. It, too, requires a degree of skill and timing to get. It's not just something you do at the end of a sale. The most effective sales professionals aim for small victories from the moment they make contact with a potential client. The culmination of a series of small victories makes the end result of the closed sale easy. Yet, if you achieve the other small victories and fail to take that final step of asking for the business – directly and specifically – you'll rarely grasp that brass ring.

What are those small victories?

Whether you're selling yourself into a job, an idea to your family and friends, a proposal to business people or a product or service to clients,

15

your ultimate goal is to get the other person's agreement. Before you can do that, you have to 1) get their attention, 2) build their curiosity about what you're offering and 3) demonstrate what's in it for them when they go along with you.

To get people's attention, you must first be likable. People like to hang out with or do business with other people who are like them. Having similar interests, needs and goals brings people together both for enjoyment and to do great things in life. To understand how to get people interested in what you're doing, put yourself in their shoes and see the world through their eyes. When you can "see" what is important to them, you'll be able to determine the right approach for getting their attention.

For example, if you sell beauty products, you'll want to understand how your potential clients live their lives. Do they spend a lot of time outdoors so the sunscreen SPF factor might be important to them? Do they go for glamour at events nights and weekends where more dramatic make-up might be used? What's their age group? Are they more concerned with acne or wrinkles? If you have the same concerns they do, it will make your job of helping them understand the benefits of your products much easier. If you're younger and your clients are older, it would be wise to reference other clients you've worked with who have used your products successfully. The same applies if your clients are younger than you. They have to feel that you understand their wants and needs before they'll listen to your advice.

If you're seeking a win in a situation such as getting a new job, to get attention, you would need to study the business itself. You need to determine the culture of the company and if it's something you would like. You want to know exactly the skills and talents the company is seeking so you can figure out how you might fit into their plans for growth and development. Once you understand that, you can feed back their information as it relates to your skills and abilities. It's critical that you learn to ask a lot of questions that get the interviewing parties talking about the company and the job. After all, not everything can be covered in a job description posted online or in an ad. When you ask questions specific to their needs, they'll recognize you as a potential match and you'll go farther in the interview process than someone else who doesn't understand how to sell themselves into a job.

Rather than going in and interviewing to get information about the company and the job itself, it's always better to think of your communications with a potential employer as a sales presentation. Discover their needs, present your talents, and then, if the match appears to be a win-win, close for your start-up date of employment. I know it's a different approach than the interview-and-hope strategy that most people use but if you're applying for a sales or marketing job what better way to be victorious than to use your skills to sell the "product" you know best – yourself?

To make that final close for a job, you could simply smile and ask, "When would you like me to start?" It may seem a bit brash but would you rather say, "Well, thanks for your time. I'll wait to hear from you." Those who call for or expect victory don't play the wait-and-see game. They are proactive and assumptive about their success the same way a professional salesperson is when closing on a product or service.

WHO WILL TAKE THE NO'S?

When selling products and services, how well you and your family eat and live may very well depend on your ability to close sales. In sales, you are in essence in business for yourself. It's up to you to constantly learn and adapt what you're doing to your clients' needs. It can be exciting and invigorating to operate in that realm. It can also be ridiculously frustrating and frightening. How it goes for you boils down to one thing: how well you do your job. In selling, your income is a scoreboard reflection of the level of service you provide to your clients. If you're not making enough money, you're not giving enough service (or providing service to enough people or companies).

Most salespeople have this fear of hearing the word "no." It's a normal, natural fear of rejection. What they don't understand is that they are being told "No, not your product." Or, "No, not now." Or, "No, not that color/size/shape/style." They're not being personally rejected as in "No, I would never do business with you because you're a horrible person." There's a huge difference in the meaning of those words but not in how the hearer of them feels, unless and until they learn how to turn those no's into victories.

Sales professionals are wise to employ strategies to keep themselves going on those days when they hear a lot of no's. Since the no's are inevitable in the world of selling, invest in programming yourself to respond positively to them, as well.

One strategy is to think about your loved ones. Who would you rather have accept some "no's" in their life? Your spouse who has been planning a wonderful family vacation as soon as you can afford it? Your kids who will soon enough be grown and gone who have set their sights on attending that special sports camp? Or yourself? Most people will opt for taking it on themselves in order to provide nice things and experiences for their loved ones. If you decide to do that, also decide to learn some strategies to deal with those "no's."

Here's one of the most popular strategies among my students: Let's say it usually takes you 10 client contacts to close one sale. If that's the case, you have to get through nine no-sales in order to close that 10th one, right? So play a game with yourself that those nine rejections are each taking you one step closer to your one closed sale. Think of them as stepping stones to your desired result. Each one is providing you with 1/10th of the income you'll generate from the final sale.

This strategy turns each no sale or rejection into a small victory toward the sale you will eventually make. It makes it much easier to take those no's from potential buyers. After each non-sale, you can genuinely smile and say "thank you for the opportunity to talk with you" and walk, drive to, or phone your next potential client feeling positive about being just that much closer to a sale.

Without implementing a strategy like that, it's possible you will carry the negative weight of each rejection into your next sales call and make it harder to give your next presentation with your highest level of enthusiasm. And if you aren't presenting at your highest level, your potential clients will be less likely to buy. It's a downward spiral you can avoid by learning how to shake off the negative effect of hearing the word "no."

THE CLOSED SALE

I mentioned about getting people's attention and building their curiosity in your presentation or demonstration. Each of those aspects of selling is important and generates small victories. But the biggest victory of all in sales is that closed transaction. And the number one reason people who spend their time learning about a product and participating in presentations don't buy products is because they were never asked. Yep, the salesperson stopped doing their job after the presentation. They didn't ask for the sale.

Unfortunately, too many salespeople think the presentation is the fun part of selling so they spend most of their time there. They involve people in pushing buttons, spinning wheels, watching slide shows and videos and putting on great presentations that knock people's socks off. Then, they expect the buyers, who have obviously enjoyed themselves during the presentation, to reach for their credit cards or checkbooks and buy.

That's like having a football team work their way down the field and never attempt to cross into the end zone. It sounds silly but it's so true. Too many people act as if the "show" is the sale and if people don't jump up and down and scream, "I want it," that their job is done—that there is no sale to be had. In reality, they're only part way through the sales process.

Once the presentation or demonstration is finished, that is when true sales pros start asking more questions. After the presentation, at the very least ask, "John, how are you feeling about all of this so far?" Encourage John to tell you something. He will either say, it's great and you ask him how soon he'd like to get started. Or, he'll have questions that need to be answered that allow you to keep the sale moving forward. Or, he'll object to something from your presentation, which gives you the opportunity to clarify or fine tune what you've told him. Any of those things are great because you and John are still involved in the sales process and you will have an opportunity to circle back and ask for his business again.

As a salesperson, your main job is to ask for the business. Never assume. Never hope. Never wait-and-see. ALWAYS ask, clearly and specifically for the order. "Mrs. Jones, with your signature right here, we'll get that fancy new set of presidential china shipped out to you today." "John, what purchase order number should I put down for the new office copier?" "Kate, all it will take to get your new life insurance policy started now is a voided check and your approval here on the paperwork." "Will that be cash, check or charge?" See how easy those closing questions are? The point is that you have to ask them.

Never ask, "Do you want it?" It's too easy for buyers to second guess themselves and say "no." Your closing questions or instructions have to be more engaging than that and, when appropriate, include a specific action for the buyer to take.

Asking for the business shouldn't be stressful for you. You're not sticking these people up with a gun to their heads. You're not reaching into their pockets or purses and stealing money. Too often, people in sales stop short of asking the final, all-so-important closing question. The reason for that is that most of us have been taught that it's rude to ask people for things. It's especially rude to ask people to give you money. But in sales, you're not just asking for their money. You are offering them a victory – the benefits of your product or service – in exchange for your own victory – the money for those products and services. It's nothing more than an exchange. And, since childhood we've all known how to trade – baseball cards, lunches, clothes and more. In selling, you're just trading products and services for money.

Few people on the planet would fail to understand that products and services cost money. Most people expect to be asked to pay in order to satisfy their wants and needs as they relate to products and services. So, as a salesperson, you need not fear it.

Just like grabbing that brass ring, selling involves both timing and skill. It's a daily challenge with great rewards for those who develop their skills. And the best part is that you can test and try new things every day – improving constantly. Make selling your hobby. Watch how others succeed in getting their brass rings. Then, modify their strategies for your particular selling situations. You'll achieve greater success in selling and in life.

About Tom

Tom Hopkins is world-renowned as The Builder of Sales Champions. He is a master at helping sales and business professionals learn the communication skills necessary to educate clients and assist them in making wise buying decisions. The primary focus of Tom's training is to eliminate the stereotype of the pushy, unscrupulous salesperson portrayed on television and in the movies.

Tom wasn't born to wealth and privilege. In fact, he wasn't always successful. An average student, he started his working career in construction. The hours were long. The work was grueling especially in the heat of Los Angeles summers. Married and with a child on the way, he knew there had to be a better way to earn a decent income for his young family.

In his early twenties, Tom entered the field of real estate. He failed miserably his first six months in the business. His only suit was a band uniform he had from high school and his only mode of transportation was a motorcycle. To top that off, even though he was 20, he looked like he was closer to age 15. Clients would come into the real estate office and upon seeing him, ask if his dad was in.

After observing what the more successful real estate agents were doing, he started a learning process that involved selling skills, psychology, time management, and self-development. By the age of 27, he had achieved millionaire status through the use of his selling skills – helping 1,153 families with the great American dream of home ownership.

Upon achieving such great success, Tom was often asked to speak. The talks he gave about what he did and said with clients developed into the legendary sales training programs he has taught worldwide to millions of sales professionals since 1976. Tom teaches the foundational training upon which millions of successful careers have been built at live events, through video and audio recordings and in the 17 books he has authored. His strategies and tactics have proven successful in a wide range of industries and through all sorts of economic cycles.

Tom's books include the million-plus-selling *How to Master the Art of Selling,* the award-winning *Selling in Tough Times, Selling for Dummies™, Low Profile Selling* and *Sell It Today, Sell It Now,* which was co-authored with Pat Leiby and *The Certifiable Salesperson* co-authored with Laura Laaman, as well as industry-specific tomes for the real estate and financial services markets.

Selling is Tom's hobby and his passion. His life's goal is to shorten the learning curve of those who choose selling as their career. He makes selling easy to comprehend. His teaching style is entertaining and memorable.

Tom Hopkins understands both sides of the selling equation. He appreciates the fears of both buyers and salespeople. Buyers don't want to be "sold" anything. Salespeople fear failure. The selling skills and strategies that Tom Hopkins teaches reflect an understanding of how to communicate with buyers so they feel confident in making wise buying decisions.

Tom Hopkins International, Inc.
7531 East Second Street
Scottsdale, Arizona USA 85251
www.tomhopkins.com
info@tomhopkins.com
480-949-0786
800-528-0446
Twitter: /TomHopkinsSales
LinkedIn: /TomHopkinsSalesTrainer
Facebook: /TomHopkinsSales

CHAPTER 2

UNSEEN DANGERS AND HIDDEN OBSTACLES TO YOUR RETIREMENT SUCCESS

BY WILLIAM GEIGER

UNSEEN DANGERS

If you're feeling confused about planning for retirement, or wondering how the wild swings in the financial markets will affect your wealth...

If you're questioning whether you're making the best possible decisions with your portfolio or not...

You have good reason... *Nothing is as it was.*

If you're approaching retirement or have recently retired, you face five unseen dangers that you may sense but can't quite define. If so... *You are not alone!*

An extremely volatile stock market, a bond market that is on the edge of a massive bubble, taxes that are moving inevitably higher, personal inflation rates greater than the averages and constantly increasing personal longevity is putting your future financial security at great risk.

How will you plan for a comfortable retirement that may very well be longer than you anticipate…**and not outlive your money?**

HIDDEN OBSTACLES

Let me ask you, what would you do if you knew for certain that the advice you've been given over the last 30 years no longer worked?

You might search for better solutions, but if you're locked into the investment rules of yesterday – the myths of today – you might miss better, more effective strategies and tools that are now available.

These investment myths are pernicious.

Even in the face of vast contrary evidence, many wealthy Americans, perhaps like you, are clinging to advice that tells you to "… *stay the course, don't panic, you're doing everything right, the market will bounce back – it always does.*"

Perhaps these words are coming from advisors that you've trusted for years, professionals who you believe are attentively watching and managing your wealth.

Nothing could be further from the truth.

These myths reflect what may have worked at sometime in the past and conveniently support the fee and commission generating structures of major brokerage firms, mutual fund companies, discount brokerage firms and fee-only investment advisors.

They are myths that work well for advisors and their firms, but not necessarily for you as you try to prepare for a successful and comfortable retirement.

MYTHS, HALF-TRUTHS AND LIES

"Putting all (or substantially all) of your wealth into the market (using individual stocks, bonds or mutual funds) is the best way to prepare for your retirement."

Maybe, but then again, maybe not. *Do you want your family's retirement to depend upon <u>hoping</u> that the markets do well in the future?* I wouldn't.

"A well-diversified portfolio of mutual funds or stocks will reduce your risk (while one fund goes down the others go up) and provide a conservative path to and through your retirement."

Not really true, in 2000, 2001, 2002 and then again in 2008 and 2009 we saw everything go down.

"Adding bonds to your portfolio (as you approach retirement) will reduce your risk of losing money."

Not now; the next time interest rates start to go up again virtually all bond portfolios will suffer substantial losses in value.

"You can use and depend upon a mutual fund portfolio to provide you income during retirement and never really worry about running out of money."

Absolutely untrue. We will be discussing a real, live couple who suffered tremendously from this myth.

"Don't worry, you have a conservative portfolio and besides, I am watching it closely."

Wrong, wrong and wrong.

"Your *fees are negligible.*"

Really? How is it that your brokerage firm, mutual fund company or discount brokerage firm can afford the rent on a nationwide complex of offices, staff and massive amounts of advertising?

"Everyone out there is so incompetent/dishonest that I am better off managing my own portfolio." ("I've made a lot of money in my life, I'm a smart guy, all I need to do is use the Internet to figure this out.")

I'm a pretty smart and successful guy too, but I would never dream of learning brain surgery on my own, it's not where my unique ability lies.

"We've been in business for 100, 150 or 200 years so we really know how to help you manage your money and we are here for you."

In the last few years we have seen major Wall Street firms such as Merrill Lynch, Smith Barney, the Hartford and others *so mismanage their own money and risk* that they needed to be bailed out and merged with other firms just to stay alive. How many firms and advisors actually protected their clients during the crashes of 2000 and 2008? Did yours?

MARK AND CATHY

Recently on my weekly radio show, we discussed a retired couple that suffered tremendously from some of the unseen dangers and hidden obstacles (myths) that we've been discussing. They had heard our show last summer and called to ask for a second opinion on their portfolio as well as for us to prepare a financial plan for them.

The couple, we'll call them Mark and Cathy, were 77 years old and told us the following story:

In the summer of 2000, when they were 65 years old, they sat down with their broker at a major Wall Street firm to discuss how they might retire and how to get an income when they were no longer receiving a paycheck. Mark and Cathy had been good savers, were fortunate to have large gains in their portfolio in the late 90's, and when they met with their broker they had a portfolio consisting of a million dollars of mutual funds.

Their question to their broker was how do we do this, how do we retire and receive an income when we're no longer working?

Their broker, according to Mark, said "We are going to set up your account to withdraw 5% or 50 thousand dollars a year to supplement your social security. You can count on your portfolio growing at the 75 year average of around *10% over time so even though you're withdrawing money, your portfolio will continue to grow and you can get raises in the future to stay up with inflation.*" (Even though the 75 year track record for the market was an *average* of 10% that may be irrelevant to them for their time frame in which they were retiring. There is an old joke about an economist who drowned while standing in a river with an *average* depth of 4 feet; he happened to be standing in a 10-foot hole.)

Mark and Cathy withdrew 50 thousand dollars (*only* 5%) from their portfolio in the summer of 2000, both gave up their jobs and began to lead a life of leisure. Almost immediately thereafter the market began correcting and their portfolio began to lose value. Mark called his broker and was told not to worry, this was just a temporary correction. Mark and Cathy said ok and went about their lives. By the next summer

(2001) after withdrawing another 50 thousand dollars to live on Mark and Cathy found their portfolio to be worth less than 750 thousand dollars (resulting from a combination of portfolio losses and withdrawals to live on). Now they were worried.

Mark and Cathy sat down to review their plan with their advisor and told him how upset they were becoming. Their broker told them "Don't worry, stay the course, this is normal to have ups and downs, I know what I'm doing." They left this meeting feeling a little bit better and went back to their day to day lives, after all, their advisor worked for a major Wall Street firm.

Two years later, in the summer of 2003, their portfolio had dropped to just under 500 thousand dollars. Cathy told me that at this time they were in a full-blown panic and quite upset. She told her advisor this and he told her and Mark that the firm's Senior Economist was saying that the correction was just about over. Mark and Cathy told their advisor that they wanted to sell everything and put their money into CD's just to protect it. Their advisor became upset and basically told them not to be idiots, that only small, unsophisticated investors "get out at the bottom." They had come this far so they listened to his advice and hung on.

Although the firm's economist was finally right (even a broken clock is right two times a day), and the market went up for the next five years, Mark and Cathy's portfolio was only breaking even with their withdrawals. Then between 2008 and 2009 their portfolio dropped to 237 thousand dollars. Even though the market recovered well after 2009, again their portfolio was too small to sustain their withdrawals.

When Mark and Cathy came into our office in the summer of 2012, their portfolio was a little over 184 thousand dollars! They were 77 years old and would run out of money in 3 to 4 years at the age of 80 to 81 years old. They are in good health (they have longevity on both sides of their family) and they will run out of money before they run out of life.

At this point they are too old to go back to work, they will have to sell their home at a depressed price and hope that the money they receive will last for them or they will have to depend on their children to live out their days. As sad as their situation is, what is even sadder is that it did not have to end up like this for them. They (and their broker) did not understand the unseen dangers of stock market volatility and its affect on withdrawals in retirement nor did they understand the myths that their broker was depending upon.

The *huge* mistake that Mark, Cathy and their broker made was using the market (a *growth* investment) to try to create a dependable *income* for their retirement. They were using the wrong tools.

IT DOESN'T HAVE TO BE THIS WAY

I have a Craftsman tool set at home that has served me well over the years. If I have a Phillips head screw that is loose, I reach into my tool-box for a Phillips head screwdriver. That doesn't make the hammer a bad tool; it's just not appropriate for this job. If on the other hand I have a nail that needs to be driven, the hammer is a perfectly appropriate tool. There is no such thing as a bad tool; it is either appropriate or not appropriate for the job at hand.

Mark and Cathy were using the wrong tool to create income that they could depend upon; they were using a tool that is designed for growth over a very long time period. Mutual funds are not bad: they're just designed for another job. Let's look at an example of what Mark and Cathy could have possibly done differently.

JOHN AND SARAH

John and Sarah called into our radio show recently and came to our office for a second opinion and a financial plan to prepare for their retirement. They are both 55 years old and want to retire in 12 years at the age of 67. They have had mutual funds being managed for them at a major brokerage firm by a third party money manager.

John, who is a successful physician, told me that their portfolio was worth 1.5 million dollars. Their problem he said was it was worth 1.5 million dollars five years ago and after riding a roller coaster in the markets it is still basically the same value. He said, "We are five years older, five years closer to retirement and we haven't made any progress."

Their goal he said was to hopefully have a six figure income when they retired but he was worried about everything that is going on in the economy, the markets and the world and had no idea if they would be able to reach their goal.

We showed them how they could divide their portfolio into two different parts with 500 thousand dollars being used in a managed mutual fund portfolio (a growth tool) and one million dollars being allocated to a retirement income annuity (an income tool). A retirement income annuity (RIA), which is owned by them and can eventually go to their kids, has a rider that will provide income for John and Sara when they retire. In fact, John and Sarah's million dollar RIA will provide a minimum income for them of over 126 thousand dollars when they are ready to retire in 12 years, guaranteed by a multi-billion dollar insurance company.

This minimum guarantee along with the couples projected social security payments will add up to over 170 thousand dollars of income at the age of 67. And, they have a half million dollars in a managed mutual fund that given enough time (without being reduced by income withdrawals like Mark and Cathy's portfolio) should provide them with good inflation protection. In addition, John and Sarah will be free to save more towards their retirement while they sleep well at night with the assurance that their retirement income goals have been provided for.

OUR STORY

Life is great

Today we help select individuals prepare financially for their retirement with the assurance that they will be able to live comfortably with income guaranteed for their lifetimes – without worrying about every bear market that occurs throughout their days. We tremendously enjoy working with successful individuals and learning their stories. We are committed to their ongoing success in life and helping them to move forward into retirement with confidence.

IT hasn't always been this way

After working in strategic planning for a major Washington, DC bank I began a career in financial services as a stockbroker in my mid 30's. I was excited to be able to use my planning and financial skills to help clients to prepare for comfortable retirements. I worked for several major firms over the next 10 years but was continually disappointed. I watched as poorly trained "financial advisors" were pushed to sell products to their clients that they (the broker and the client) didn't understand. They were given quotas of product that they were expected to sell to their clients with the underlying goal of producing income for the brokers' firms with only lip service being paid to their clients' goals.

In 1995, I was working for Kidder-Peabody, an old white shoe Wall Street brokerage house that was then owned by General Electric. They had not managed the risk in their own portfolio, they blew up financially and were forced to merge with another firm.

A NEW AND BETTER PROCESS

At that time I was managing Kidder's Private Wealth Management Group in their Washington, DC office and decided that if I ever wanted to serve my clients in a truly client-centered environment that focused on preparing them for a safe and comfortable retirement, I would have to create that environment myself. In 1995 I formed my own firm and developed a proprietary retirement planning process we call The Retirement Navigator. This process uses different tools for producing income and growth so that our clients can effectively plan out their retirement income irrespective of which direction the markets move.

THE RETIREMENT NAVIGATOR PLANNING PROCESS

The Retirement Navigator planning process has made a huge difference in both our clients' lives and our practice. We are now able to plan 5, 10, 15 to 20 years in advance for the income our clients will need for retirement and both the clients and we sleep well at night. This has made all the difference.

About William

Bill is the founder and president of Geiger Wealth Management, a Registered Investment Advisory firm that specializes in retirement planning and portfolio management for select individuals in their 50's and 60's, with portfolios in excess of $500K.

After serving in the United States Air Force he received his Bachelors Degree in Economics from the University of Maryland, as well as an MBA in Finance from the Kogod School of Business at American University in Washington, DC.

He produces the weekly radio show *Saving Financial Lives* appearing on WIOD, WFTL and WGUL and is an author, an economist and a financial coach. He has been featured in *Newsweek, USA Today, The Wall Street Journal, The Washington Business Journal* and *Medical Economics* as well as numerous other publications. He has appeared on ABC, CBS, NBC and Fox television and is frequently featured on several major financial websites.

Mr. Geiger lives in south Florida with his wife Maytte and their two dogs, Nana and Holly. He and Maytte share five children and five grandchildren.

He can be contacted at: (800) 544-0102
Or: wgeiger@geigerwealth.com

CHAPTER 3

THE RETIREE'S VALUE OF ASSET PROTECTION AND INCOME PLANNING

BY BOB FUGATE

I want to share a story with you about two of my clients. For confidentiality purposes, I will call them Mary & John.[1] This couple attended one of my educational workshops in the fall of 2007. After the program was over, I was visiting with each guest when Mary and John told me they had an interest in finding out more about me with some special questions as to how my work would apply to them.

They had recently moved from southern Michigan to a lakeside home in Tellico Village. The auto industry had been good to them and they wanted to enjoy the fruits of their lifelong labor around the lake, in the hills, and along the golf courses of the warmer climate of East Tennessee.

Their lifelong savings pattern, including a noticeable 401k accumulation and their seven figure after-tax investment accounts, had them feeling financially secure until they attended my workshop. They had been through the 50% market loss from 2000 through 2002 but attributed that to the "tech bubble burst" and the "effects of 9/11." Their thought was that the economy had returned to the 1982 to 2000 boom time that had allowed them to accumulate a very nice retirement nest egg. Their lifestyle dreams would be easily served with a similar market they believed had returned for them to enjoy.

Mary approached me very inquisitively with real concern on her face and with a worried inflection to her words, wanted to know what I meant when I asked the workshop group if they thought history repeated itself and, in particular, if stock market history repeated itself. She didn't catch all that I had said, but she did remember that, historically, most "zero growth or bear market periods" were noticeably longer than "boom or bull market periods."[2] Mary also remembered that our last boom market from 1982 through 2000 lasted about 17 years and that we were only seven years into the current zero growth market. She wanted to know how long I believed this zero growth market would last and, furthermore, if it would necessarily follow historical patterns and last longer than the 17-year boom market. Mary told me their former advisor's plan did not include any zero growth periods for their accounts and certainly did not account for any losses.

Of course I told Mary that I did not know the future and that the past 100 year pattern of market performance did not indicate the future.[3] I told her it only gives us flags of what could happen and that good planning should account for all reasonable scenarios. I suggested that she and John bring all their materials and meet with me confidentially in my office.

Following appropriate questions from me during our evaluation visit, Mary and John shared their lifestyle goals, the purpose of their move to East Tennessee, the real value of their investment assets, and the purpose of their money for their lives and the lives of their children and grandchildren. About two weeks afterwards, we held a strategy meeting where I suggested options for accomplishing their goals. They reacted with questions and comments as I supplied verbal and written education for their analysis.

A week later I presented an implementation plan that Mary and John believed would reduce the risks of unforeseen market losses, high fees, and the lack of uncorrelated asset allocation to handle unforeseen but expected variations in returns. As a CERTIFIED FINANCIAL PLANNER™ Professional, I liked the plan and they adopted it and signed all the paper work to put it in place.

About two weeks later John called. I could tell he was very disturbed. His former insurance broker with whom he had placed a variable annuity product with a current value of $720,000 had called and really upset John. The agent told John he was really making a mistake by transferring out of the variable annuity. He reminded him that the market had given him great returns in the past and that he needed to remain 100% in the market to continue receiving those beneficial gains. When John asked about the 4.2% total fees I had shared with him from a third party Morningstar report, the agent told him all products had fees and what he currently had was better than anything available.

John told me Mary was also very upset. The Michigan agent and his wife had been good friends of theirs and they trusted them. John told me they still believed that my plan was better suited for their needs but didn't know how to leave their friends in Michigan. I suggested we only move half of that variable annuity and leave the other half where it was. They agreed and seemed much more comfortable. Although I knew they had not yet completed the total plan they needed and wanted, they were more secure now than before we began working together.

Mary and John transferred about $360,000 and left $360,000. When we met a year later for a progress report, there was about $403,000 in the half transferred by our company and about $220,000 in the half that remained in the variable annuity. The 2008 market collapse combined with the high variable annuity fees had cost them over 38% of their previous value and they were 45% below the value of the half we transferred. Asset protection became a real retirement value when they felt the tragedy of market losses and high fees.

Soon after the 2009 meeting, Mary and John transferred 100% of their assets to Retirement Financial Solution's Team Management. They have uncorrelated asset allocation: some in absolute return investments with guaranteed growth for income benefit and some in some risk instruments that historically have had very little loss and are repositioned for no market losses regularly. They have had no market losses since 2007 and have sustainable income planning in place for the rest of their lives.

In 2003, I left the "one company captive brokerage world," where my fiduciary responsibility and legal obligation was to serve my company rather than my clients. I completed my Certified Financial Planner™ designation and opened my own independent company with my fiduciary responsibility to my clients. Since that time, I have added 369 clients and, except by death, have lost only two. Just like Mary and John, none of my clients who followed our planning approach have lost money in their total accounts they invested with me from 2003 through October 2012. This is why my clients are happy and don't leave. There is always a home at my company for clients who not only want a stable and prosperous retirement, but also want to be in involved with a group of people who actually care about them. For those who don't make their way to our doors...here are 5 things to look for when choosing a Financial Planning Company.

1: MAKE SURE YOU ACTUALLY LIKE YOUR FINANCIAL PLANNER AND THAT THE COMPANY SPECIALIZES IN YOU

Sounds intuitive, but make sure you like your financial planner. That he or she treats you with respect and kindness and truly understands your goals. That's first and foremost. Second, find out what the planner's specialty is. Do they specialize in YOU? For instance, my specialty is those people near retirement who are 50 years old or older with investment assets of $250,000 or more. Our primary focus within this group are people who want to preserve their assets, make sure their income needs are satisfied today and for the lifestyle they want until they are 90 to 100 years of age, and then want to transfer whatever they have left to their children and other heirs – with the control they want and with the least tax erosion possible.

2: MAKE SURE YOUR FINANCIAL PLANNER HAS A STRONG TEAM

Whatever value I have, it is certainly time limited and constrained. Being originally trained as a broker, I found that I neither had the expertise nor the adequate time required to be all things for even a small, select group of clients. When I became independent, I evolved to the team approach. I am the managing director of relationships. My job is to meet people, tell them our story, ask the real questions to find out what they are deeply interested and dedicated to doing, and then respond in an educational and non-pressuring manner to give them positive options. I do all of this in a fiduciary and ethical manner as a Certified Financial Planner™ Professional. The remainder of the process is conducted by five highly-qualified, hand-picked associates. This is "The Team."

In addition to my in-house team, my clients also receive advice from the financial planning team of my SEC Registered Investment Advisor, Global Financial Private Capital, LLC, which provides advanced advice, and risk analysis which adds to what I provide my clients from our local office. They add value not only to my clients, but also to my team as a whole.

You get the point, the "team approach" to your financial future is a winning strategy. That said, a team is only as good as the players and the coach. Make sure when you're looking for a financial planner that you learn about the entire team. If there are other people in the office who will be handling your finances, meet them and get to know them. Your retirement is too important to be impersonal about it. Make sure your team is solid.

My job is not to do all things but to "quarterback" or direct these professionals who are the best in a particular area of expertise, and my clients benefit from this immensely.

3: MAKE SURE YOUR PLANNER IS IN COMPLIANCE

For consistency in our compliance standards we are part of Global Investment Practice Standards (GIPS). This is the "police" that watches our security investment standards. These standards are adopted by 34 countries around the world. GIPS is required for institutional investing practice. Our Registered Investment Advisor does about 500 million dollars of institutional investing and takes the experience and education of that to our individual clients. Only about 6/10 of 1% of financial advisors in the United States are GIPS compliant and, because we are, our clients benefit from it.

4: LOOK FOR UNCORRELATED ASSET ALLOCATION FOR ASSET PROTECTION

The University of Tennessee prepared me for life as a broker with training in "Modern Portfolio Theory" and the "Efficient Frontier." Harry Markowitz helped develop these systems in the 1960's and was awarded a Nobel Prize for his introduction and work on them in 1990.[5] Early on in my broker career, I followed these theories, as do most brokers today. A simple explanation is that there are combinations of stocks and bonds that will give an investor the most return for the amount of risk the investor is willing to take. The theory worked great from 1982 through 2000 when stocks were the highest yielding investments available and, over that time frame, had only short-term losses.

From 2000 to today, the theories (or at least the way brokers have practiced them) have not worked for a client's positive gain. From July 1, 1999 through June 30, 2009 the S&P 500, an indicator of stock returns in the United States, lost 2.2% per year.[6] Bonds would have had to have made up much more than the theories suggested to have been competitively beneficial to those using them. During that same time period, Harvard's Endowment Model returned a positive 8.9%, Princeton's Endowment Model returned a positive 9.7%, and Yale's Endowment Model returned a positive 11.8% each year.[7] When Harvard's results were compared to a 60% stock, 40% bond portfolio (which may not have been on the modern portfolio efficient frontier but would have been comparable), it outperformed it 250% from July 1, 2000 through June 30, 2010.[8]

My contention and assertion is that modern portfolio theory is not diversified because it is only in stocks and bonds. Look at your 2008 portfolio results. They all went down. Now look at your 2009 results. They all went up. Each investment owned went up or down differently but they all went in the same direction. They are highly correlated. How could modern portfolio theory protect any portfolio in 2008? Our clients who followed our total planning approach did not lose with what I directed because of uncorrelated asset allocation – that did not allow the account to have total account losses.

David Swenson, Chief Financial Officer for Yale University Endowment Fund, founded the endowment model in 1985. His model lost money only one year since 1985 while the S&P 500 and Dow Jones lost money in six different years. We copied his model and applied it to our client's desires, needs, and tolerance of risk. We apply the diversification using the endowment model that has proven to perform better than modern portfolio theory and most broker and advisor programs. Retirement Financial Solutions financial team will have a different endowment type diversification model for every client to install true diversification that meets their specific needs within their desired level of risk.

5: MAKE SURE THEY CAN PROVIDE INCOME PLANNING WHEN NEEDED

When income planning is needed or requested, our company meets basic needs from absolute return investments, such as fixed index annuities which have no market risk, with guaranteed growth for income benefit...and yours should too. We also use 100% liquid investments that historically have not lost money and returned a positive growth. An income generator that is often recommended are non-traded commercial Real Estate Investments Trusts, REITs, that are currently returning noticeable dividends and are positioned for potential capital gains. There is the potential for both principle losses and dividend changes with these non-traded REIT investments.

If assets are left after providing for basic income needs, then we recommend either planning for the largest and most efficient transfer of assets to others or investments with the most potential gains for special desires if market conditions turn out mostly positive. Often we do a combination of both to better meet a client's desires.

References

1. Mary and John are only used to indicate people. The real names are withheld for reasons of privacy.

2. Source: Ritholtz, Barry. (January 9, 2006). "Cult of the Bear, Part 2." Retrieved October 16, 2009 from TheStreet.com website: http://www.thestreet.com/comment/investing/10260656.html

3. Source: Ritholtz, Barry. (January 9, 2006). "Cult of the Bear, Part 2." Retrieved October 16, 2009 from TheStreet.com website: http://www.thestreet.com/comment/investing/10260656.html

4. As of January 2012 and October 2012.

5. en.wikipedia.org/wiki/Harry_Markowitz – last updated 9/24/2012.

6. Source: 2009 Annual Financial Reports for Harvard, Yale, and Princeton. Historical returns are not indicative of future performance.

7. Source: 2009 Annual Financial Reports for Harvard, Yale, and Princeton. Historical returns are not indicative of future performance.

8. Source: 2011 Harvard Management Company, Inc.

About Bob

Bob Fugate is a CERTIFIED FINANCIAL PLANNER™ Professional that left the captive brokerage world in 2003 to open his own independent company, where his fiduciary responsibility would be to his clients rather than to any product or company. Through January of 2012, Bob had added 369 new clients and except by death, has lost only two.

In 2005, Bob adopted the endowment model of diversification established by David Swenson, CFO of Yale University's Endowment Fund. Bob believes in the diversification of this endowment model and he uses it with his clients. Since 2005, the clients that used this approach - Swenson's endowment model - have seen little or no negative returns in their total account value, including 2008 which was a hard year for many investors. This, plus the individual personal attention that Bob and his seven licensed staff members provide, continue to keep his clients happy.

Bob has been recognized as one of the ten most dependable wealth managers of the southeast United States by *Forbes* magazine in September of 2008. He has received the designations of Chartered Financial Consultant (ChFC®), Charter Life Underwriter (CLU®), and Life Underwriter Training Council Fellow Recipient (LUTCF®). Bob helps retirees or those near retirement to protect their assets and provides sustainable income planning.

Bob has been featured in *Newsweek* magazine as a Financial Trendsetter and recently filmed an upcoming episode of the Consumer's Advocate TV Show, shot by an Emmy Award Winning Director to be seen on ABC, NBC, CBS and FOX affiliates across the country.

To receive important information for your retirement life, call 865-392-4260 or 888-938-6492 or visit: www.RetirementFS.com

CHAPTER 4

16 WAYS TO SAVE MONEY ON BUSINESS ELECTRICITY AND 6 POTENTIAL REVENUE-GENERATING STRATEGIES FOR YOUR BUSINESS.

BY BOB GARRETT

With 38 years in business as of this writing, and 10 of them as an energy consultant, specifically in the field of "electricity," I've discovered 22 strategies and options that have saved my friends and customers tens of millions of dollars, mostly for COMMERCIAL ELECTRIC BILLS. While some of these strategies "may" apply to RESIDENTIAL electric bills, I am primarily a commercial expert.

My strategies are a condensation of ten years of experimentation, re-engineering and whittled down to 2500 words or less.

So, let's dig in and see what the strategies are. Before we begin, I'd love to share a philosophy with you. It's guided my life for decades.

Here it is:

All people, when contemplating doing a "thing" (anything), they ONLY do the "thing" for 1 of 2 reasons:

1. The prospect of gain.

2. The avoidance of loss.

As I pondered and internalized that, I realized that's it very true. To illustrate... I'm writing for the prospect of gaining credibility in my industry, to be seen as an authority on the subject. Some will SKIP this chapter as they may view it as "a loss to avoid" even if they don't know what's IN this chapter. So, each "thing" that crosses our sights is decided upon; based on those two criteria.

I hope this helps the next time you are convincing anyone to do anything. If you hit either of those "hot buttons," you will succeed far more by talking to them "where they live."

With 22 numbered hot buttons in this chapter, there are 16 savings strategies and 6 REVENUE strategies.

SAVINGS STRATEGIES

1. **Bill audits** – I'll take my customer's electric bill and rip it apart, making sure that it's accurate, no mistakes, the rate class is correct, they either are or are not paying sales tax. One customer years ago was accidently paying state sales tax for his manufacturing firm. Once corrected he got a check back, after a little red tape, for $40,000 plus. Needless to say, this can avoid mistakes and have prospects of big gains.

2. **"Bill Stretch"** is what I call this one. Most get a bill and it will say "due in 10 days." Little do customers know, in "some states" with "some electric providers," this is a negotiable item. If you can stretch this from 10 days to 15, 20 or 30 days, CASH FLOW is pumped up, in your favor. You can use your money a little longer. In large companies with electric bills in the hundreds of thousands annually, this can be a pretty hot ticket item. Again, the prospect of gain is at play. It does help to have a navigator who knows the ropes and can find the provider who's willing to do this, or that the consultant may have some leverage with.

3. **"Blend and Extend"** – if your business is in a deregulated state, typically Texas, Illinois, Maryland, New York, Ohio, New Jersey, Pennsylvania and Washington D.C. , you have the option

of being on a deregulated electricity contract. If you are in a longer list of states in which NATURAL GAS offers choice, you will be on a contract as well. Those contracts can always be "shopped" or looked at well in advance of their expiration dates. Then the consultant shops for bargains, market dips or unique products and attempts to PRE-LOCK a rate well in advance of those dates. If done correctly in the right market, those rates may DROP and begin with an immediate effect. Hence the terms "blend and extend." Another potential gain for the one paying the bills.

4. **Contract Assist** – This is a service we offer a customer in which we negotiate unique contract language such as being able to add or delete one or more meters from a contract, by pre-arranged agreement with the retail electric provider. Some are more lenient than others when it comes to adding or dropping energy load that's already been hedged on the front end of the contract.

5. **Contract Tracker** – I'll track a contract belonging to either a customer or a non-customer in which we simply read the document; discovering rate, product type and more. Then we put it into our watch software and attempt to catch a market dip along the way, thus providing a "first strike" capability. Again, another way to save money for the customer or prospective customer.

6. **Discount Locks** – We have the ability to look into the crystal ball and based on market conditions, we can sometimes pre-lock your rate 12-24 months before your contract expires. This is yet another way to save money, sooner than later, simply by being engaged with the client, on an exclusive basis, so that we can afford to track a customer's opportunities so they can attend to their business while we do what we do best.

7. **Electricity Procurement** – We offer wholesale, retail, fixed, flex, index, block & index, tranches or hybrid products. Some products are actual wholesale rates based on the price of the fuel used to generate the power. In Texas, a natural gas based index is used to act as a monthly settlement price on which the rates are based for that month. The rates may fluctuate but most of the time remain below a normal hedged fixed price. Again,

another chance to reduce the overall bill. If you reside in a non-deregulated state, it never hurts to ask your electric provider if they offer an "indexed" product. Some very well may, even though the market is referred to as "regulated."

8. **Legislative Guidance** - We keep up with all the laws and tariffs so that we can effectively deal with things such as Nodal Congestion, RUC, CSAPR, PUC rate caps being lifted. We also track fuel prices such as natural gas, weather and other supply issues. Then and only then can we pinpoint the best TIME to strike, the best PROVIDER to strike with and the correct PRODUCT and strategy to deploy.

9. **Market Track** – Our customers who work with us on an exclusive basis are entitled to year-round energy alerts, weather alerts, product price strikes, rate locks for the peak seasons, and a monthly touch newsletter. An informed customer is a happy customer.

10. **MicroReader** – this is nothing more than dissecting a customer's contract and literally reading every line of what is sometimes a 10 or 15-page legal-sized single spaced document. Once we have analyzed all the components, we can offer any number of improvements. It's the exception when we can't find some aspect of the customer's current or future options to improve upon.

11. **RepTracker** – We keep a large spreadsheet that tracks some 20-25 characteristics of 20 or more REPS (Retail Electric Providers). We know which ones do what, which ones take credit cards, which ones have certain bandwidths and which ones to steer clear of. This is the best way to actually play cupid between the customer and the provider. Its taken years to assemble all the information, so our clients consider us a valuable part of their team. Any time you have a team member that watches your back, saves you money and actually generates extra revenue for you, we are often elevated to the same status as a financial officer or trusted advisor.

12. **Residential discounts** – This is an arrangement we have made with several REPS. it simply offers discounts to all our cus-

tomers, their friends, family and employees. We like to help all those we come in contact with. After all, if you can save a few dollars, it's all the more value we drive for our customers.

13. **Power Factor Correction** – The best way I can describe this is to have you imagine a mug of beer, with foam on top. Energy is just like the beer, in that it's a commodity, put in a grid, transported and delivered to your "door" which is your meter. Along the way, some of the power is lost, and some is actually BILLED to you, yet you may not actually CONSUME all of it. This would be analogous to the "foam." Power Factor Correction is nothing more than capacitors that can be installed by qualified personnel that basically removes the foam" before you get billed for it. This in turn RAISES your Power Factor efficiency and LOWERS your delivery costs. This can be done for a business or even at residential meters. Most energy consultants have relationships with engineers who can do this for a very reasonable fee.

14. **Team National** – Once in a while, something very unusual comes to my attention. There's a great company in Florida called Team National. They have ingeniously assembled an incredible website with around 225 name brand companies' websites – ALL ON ONE WEBSITE. It's so easy to use it's almost embarrassing in that you just look, click, and save. We paid $2500 for the access to this site and I now offer the "link" for free to a customer who works with me and only me. Benefits include things like specials, great savings, free shipping and more. To me, I just like the time savings. I don't have time to keep 225 websites on my computer, but I do have time to click on one site and get anything I need delivered to my door. While not related to energy, it's yet another way I drive extreme and unexpected VALUE to my clients. My sole objective is to be the only energy consultant they will ever need and go beyond ANYTHING my competition would ever dream off.

15. **Triage** – An "energy" triage (I got this term from the TV show M*A*S*H) is nothing more than a deep analysis and "doctor room" snapshot of the current situation. We look at the market, the company, their needs and objectives, the current rate, the

savings, all the ancillary services from my list of 22 that might apply to this particular client, and do a full report with the findings. As odd as it may sound, with regard to their energy needs, we're actually in the role of "the doctor." We are duty bound to be loyal to the client, do what's best for the client, yet allow the client to make all the decisions. If they listen to our advice yet make the final call, then down the road, it's always their decision. We never "sell," "push" or take the role of "salesy." We're actually compensated by the electric companies, so we're literally a zero out of pocket cost to the client.

16. **Perpetual Utility** – As opposed to something that sounds like it "doesn't exist"; this actually does. We want to be a full service consulting group for our clients. So, we ask that they simply call US for any and all problems, issues, questions, or concerns. We'll handle it. After all, if you have ever called a major utility and tried to get a "fast answer"... good luck on getting them to even pick the phone up. Your time is money and no one wants to waste time on hold or fishing through someone's website and sending emails to who knows who. They want answers. They want them fast. And they want results. That's a "Perpetual Utility" and the reason we renew nearly 90% of our clients when it comes time to renew a contract. If you work with Bob Garrett – there's no need to talk to a utility company ever again.

REVENUE STRATEGIES

1. **Exclusive Client Benefit – Free & highly-prized *Texas Energy Referral Association Membership (TERA).*** Each exclusive client I work with is given a "credit card" for all who want one. The card comes with privileges and is free. Let me explain. Our business is highly... and I'll say that again... HIGHLY competitive. When going head to head with another firm, I took a page from a very famous NFL quarterback who became a very successful commercial realtor. His unique approach was to sign footballs for his prospects and sometimes offer a percentage of his FEE, back to the client. Example; a huge law firm wants to move. It's a huge long term deal with massive lease terms and sizable commissions for the broker. If a portion of the fee goes back to the client for moving expenses for example, and no one else offers that; guess

who would win the business?

Our slant on the same scenario is to give out the TERA cards and offer a percentage of our fee back to either the client, his or her company charity or if their ethics won't permit fee acceptance, I can give it to my organization of choice; BYO Musicians. BYO is a charity band that plays Classic Rock and Roll for all kinds of charity groups. This allows us to give back and enjoy music while truly helping our community. We have worked with Habitat for Humanity, Komen Breast Cancer, the Make-a-Wish Foundation and many more, raising hundreds of thousands for their worthy causes.

2. **Demand Response** – With rising power needs nationwide and shrinking power reserves, a great way for states to access more generation in the power grid during peak times of the year is to literally "pay" customers for "shedding part of their load during peak energy spikes, typically during a hot summer or a super cold winter. The customer has equipment installed by a qualified and state approved vendor. Then with the flip of a switch, when needed, power can be diverted so that homes and businesses don't lose their power. This avoids rolling brownouts or blackouts. This method is more cost effective than building a billion dollar power plant and is only used when needed. A large food chain, for example, might allow every other row of overhead lighting to be "shed," while leaving all the computers and cash registers running as always. So, the "power grid pays you" may be an option.

3. **Electricity Sales Tax Audits** – Fund *recovery for* any overpayments & to avoid future overcharges.

4. **Energy Assessments** – Energy efficient systems like *lighting upgrades, HVAC* or *roofing* - leading-edge product innovation and design. Saves money, improves the environment and saves on maintenance.

5. **"FreeFly"** – This is the creative use of paying a corporate electric bill with a credit card. Then, by using the card's *air miles*, company airfare costs are offset. Overlooked by nearly everyone, this is a money saver and a GREAT employee perk for a job well done if the company can't use all the air miles.

6. Referral Revenue – TERA membership assures an ongoing *fee-share for all future referrals* – funds often applied to all or some portion of your electric bill.

So, for any of 16 <u>Savings</u> strategies or 6 <u>Revenue</u> strategies, just seek the counsel of a qualified and experienced energy consulting professional.

About Bob

Bob Garrett, also known as The Texas Energy Guy, is a best-selling author and energy expert who's helped thousands of business owners save tens of millions of dollars. Bob's first book *$100,000 Selling Anything by Phone* is in the Top 10 rankings in his space on Amazon. Bob is known for his *Victory 22 – 22 ways to Attack Electricity Bills and how to Force Your Electric Bill to Pay YOU.* Bob deploys 16 attacks on an electricity company's rate structure and 6 creative revenue-generation strategies for his clients. More than 95% of what he does costs his clients nothing out of pocket, as he's paid by the Fortune 500 electricity providers his clients select.

To date, he's the only energy consultant who offers all 22 strategies and virtually eliminates his competition in his space. Six of Garrett's strategies were literally created from scratch and don't exist anywhere else, other than through *Victory 22*. There's no more comprehensive way to take apart an electricity bill than using the *Victory 22* method. Power companies hate him, but his customers love him.

To learn more about Bob Garrett, The Texas Energy Guy and how you can receive the FREE Special Report: *Victory 22 : 22 ways to Attack Electricity Bills and how to Force Your Electric Bill to Pay YOU,* visit: www.Victory22.com or call 214-718-7376.

Bob may be reached at: info@victory.com

CHAPTER 5

DEVELOPING A STAND-ALONE BUSINESS

BY CARINA HATTON

My name is Carina Hatton. I own four businesses with my husband, and I am a realtor. We also own several investment properties. I have always had a plan for my life. I am an entrepreneur at heart. I have wanted to own my own business since I was little. When I was five years old, I went door-to-door selling wrapping paper and cards out of a small magazine. I made $8.00 in one day, selling eight items at $1.00 per item. That was my first, but definitely not my last, foray into selling things. I was always looking for something to sell. Each Christmas, I would ask for a cash register from the old JC Penney catalog. That was my dream – to own my own store someday. I dreamed about having long lines of customers and getting to ring each one of them up on my own cash register (electric, of course, not the manual kind). It had to have a working register tape.

Those were the days.

When I turned fourteen, I went out and got my first job. I was a cashier – my dream! I worked hard to be the fastest cashier at the lawn and garden shop where I worked. I had a system, and would start ringing the next customer up before the one I had finished had removed their bags from the counter. I took pride in what I did. I learned from my superiors that I needed to stay busy at all times. Never let the boss see you standing around. I took their advice, and learned all of the different departments in the store. I bagged grass seed, did inventory, sold flowers and bushes, and recreated all of the signage in the store. I couldn't figure out why they wouldn't consider me to be the manager. I knew that place inside and out. Forget the fact that I was only fourteen!

As I grew older, I started making plans to get started with my own business. I didn't know what I would sell, but knew it would be retail. I had previously sold lots of different things with businesses you could get into for a small price - mostly multi-level marketing companies. I learned selling techniques with each different company that I hadn't learned before. I read every manual I received cover to cover. I went to all of the training classes that were held. I listened to the teleconferences. I read every book that was listed as suggested reading.

I started college at 19, and decided to get my degree in computers because that was the hot thing at the time, and I thought I could make some money at it. The week after I received my undergraduate degree, I started on my Master's degree in business. I was so excited! I took all of the marketing and entrepreneurship classes I could, and read every book on leadership, management and selling I could get my hands on. Halfway through my Master's degree, I ended up in the class of a man who was very passionate about what he did. He was an insurance salesman who called the local McDonalds his office. He told the class that not many people are able to own their own business due to their inability to get a loan to get started, and their lack of capital to inject. I learned that it was usually easier to buy a business that was already running than it was to start one from scratch. You need credit, experience and capital to get a loan to buy a business that is already running. The business has to cash flow enough to cover the loan and pay you a reasonable salary. That was all I needed to know. I had a plan.

I started researching online to figure out my options in the town I lived in. I was mainly looking for a retail business to buy. Meanwhile, I was laid off from my computer programming job. I used the extra time I had to my advantage, and worked for two months straight every day – to get my business plan completed to purchase a franchise donut shop that was for sale in town. I made sure to follow all of the advice I had received in all the ventures I had been in when creating my plan. I looked at every business plan example I could find. When I went to the first banker I knew, he said it was the best business plan he had seen. I was approved in a few short days. I was so excited!

I worked at my donut shop seven days a week for two and a half years to learn the business. I used all of the skills I had learned over the years. I must have hired and fired 300 people in those first two years. I would hire anyone and everyone that applied. No one was turned away! I learned many things about people during that time, and how to work with them. I mostly learned how to better read an application, and to be a lot pickier in my hiring practices. As time went on, I kept reading as much as possible. I tried many hiring techniques, and learned which ones worked and which ones didn't very quickly. I tried my best to make the store a positive place to work and shop. That was the most important thing in retrospect. I quickly fired anyone who appeared to have a negative attitude. Negative people cannot be empowered very easily. They can't easily be trusted with important tasks, and aren't likely to volunteer.

It took lots of patience, but when I found the right person with a positive attitude that did not specifically have the skills I was looking for, I trained them. Once they were trained, I let them run at their position, coaching them as needed. This turned out to be the greatest thing for my business. I didn't have to micromanage the staff. I let them use their own brains! It gave me more time to work on the business, not in it. Our sales increased, our customer counts increased, we were nominated as Small Business of the Year by the local chamber of commerce. I kept at it, giving them items to do, but not telling them how to do each step specifically. Years later, I am an off-site owner, with a dedicated long-term staff that treats my store like it is their own. I also show appreciation to my staff on a regular basis. I empower them, then I tell them what a fabulous job they did on the task. They LOVE working there because they know they are so appreciated.

What I did is something anyone can do. The key is to find the right people to work with, people who possess positive personalities. Everything else is teachable.

One funny story that happened a couple of years ago was when the lady who manages my donut shop asked if she could hire a particular woman who had wandered into the store looking for work. She really liked her personality, and "she really needs a job," she told me. I told her that from my vast experience (smile) I didn't think she would work out. She appeared to be a job hopper from her application, and had several misspelled words, which told me she had little care for how she represented herself. I told the manager if she wanted to hire her, she could, but I would not personally hire her. The wonderful, new lady lasted for two weeks, and didn't show up for work on the busiest day of the week, leaving my manager shorthanded that morning. She called me laughing, knowing I was not going to say, "I told you so," but had every right to. I laugh thinking about it now. I told her why I would not have hired the woman, and we laughed and laughed. She is such a positive person that she took this as the learning experience it should have been. She will never forget what happened with that woman she hired, and I am sure she learned a lesson that day. I am not saying I know everything about hiring people. I just had been through it before and figured the outcome would be about the same. Most times, I have found when a person who applies for a job is desperate for a job – they don't work out.

Another time, my store manager asked if I would teach her to do the inventory. I had been doing it for years, and was reluctant to give up the enormous responsibility. I was very worried she would mess it up until I really thought about it. The worst thing that could happen was she would put down the wrong inventory, and I would not order enough ingredients from the supplier. I worried about having to drive downtown (45 minutes) to pick up an item we were short on. Then I got a great idea! If she put down the wrong inventory, and I ordered the wrong items or shorted the order somehow, SHE would be the one to drive down and pick up the items needed.

It worked like a charm. In the first few months, she made many long trips down to the supplier's warehouse. Then like magic, she started to get the inventory right! She made sure she had the amount on hand correct, knowing if I ordered the wrong items, she would be the one to pick them up. Problem solved! Not only did I teach her to do something that helps the business, it helped me because I didn't have to do it anymore!

Most people like to feel like they are doing their part, they feel good about a job well done. I have learned to delegate things to those who I can trust to do them. If the person is not fully trusted yet, I simply keep the item on my own to-do list until I am sure it is done. Once I get that trust built up with the person, I start delegating more important items to them. If I delegate items and they are not getting done, I have a talk with the person about whether or not I can trust them to get things done. It is then their decision whether or not we move forward with them getting more things to do. I make it clear to them that if I cannot trust them to do the items correctly they will not get anything to do anymore. I have found that most people like to have the responsibility.

This is where the choice of being empowered is given to the person you want to empower. They get to decide if they want to be responsible for certain things that need to be done. If they show they can get things done, they get more responsibility. They key is to let them decide how to do the task themselves. Never, ever tell them how to do it unless they ask. I get joy out of seeing how they get the task done. Most times, I find they work harder at it than I would have, and do things a totally different way than I would have done it. It then teaches me something! I learn about how others think, and how they handle things! It makes me a better leader.

The biggest mistake an employer can make in terms of empowering their employees is telling them exactly how to do something. This can turn into the horrible thing of micromanaging. Micromanaging is really death to a business. When you micromanage people, they stop using their own brains, and then no one wins. Then it is your fault if things don't go right because you have not given any authority to your staff.

If you have read any of Napoleon Hill's books, he talks about the MasterMind. This is two or more people working together to solve problems, and come up with ideas. The whole concept is built on two or more people working together to solve problems, each using their own brains. It is an awesome thing that will make your business grow.

Whenever important business decisions are made in my businesses, there is always more than one person involved in the decision. This is mainly to make sure we are not overreacting. It takes a lot of patience to work with others and lead others effectively. Delegation and empowerment adds a whole other level to it. You have to essentially keep track of what you have delegated to someone, or empowered someone to do, until you are comfortable with the fact that they will do the job effectively. This can be a tedious job at first, but well worth it in the long run.

You will see that your business starts running like you would run it, only you don't have to be there all of the time. The employees know their opinions matter, and they have the authority to work things out on their own, so they take great pride in their jobs.

You have to show your employees you trust them, and that you value their opinion. You do this by empowering them. You empower them to make decisions that affect the outcome of the company. You hire people you know you can trust, then let them run with it.

About Carina

Carina Hatton was born in Merriam, Kansas and currently lives in Olathe, Kansas, with her husband, Jeff and three children; one teenager and two preschoolers. She makes a habit of putting her family, God, and then business first in her life. She grew up in the Catholic Church and attended a private school – Mass six days a week (cringe!), which, among other things, gave her a great education and a faith in God and the power of prayer. Her parents raised her to have integrity and a strong work ethic. She was born the eldest of six children, where she knew from an early age that if she wanted something, SHE had to work for it.

She is an avid believer and participant in the Arts and organized sports; a tradition that she has continued with her children. She believes it makes you a much more rounded individual who can easily transition into someone that can take responsibility for their own decisions and actions.

She showed signs of early inquisitiveness, intelligence, and leadership at an early age. Her mother said that she was reading at age 2, which was sometimes embarrassing. She once read a poster in an auto parts store to her grandmother that made her laugh, and they immediately exited the store to return to the car!

She maintains a positive attitude, is a self-starter, and surrounds herself with positive and ambitious individuals; which of course makes her a driven personality and a perfectionist. Determined to go to college, she paid for it herself through student loans and first going to a local community college – then she attended a Technical college and received a degree in Computer Information Systems in order to have a high demand job to fall back on. (She noted to herself: Backup Plan.) She pursued her Master's Degree in Business immediately, so that she could get on to her first and real "Plan."

Carina is an avid reader with an insatiable urge to learn every detail of a business and its personnel. She takes advantage of every opportunity to learn from seminars, books, CDs, DVDs, peer interaction and long discussions into the night with her husband. She enjoys a good-natured competitiveness with her husband and a few others. It keeps her grounded.

She believes in transparency with co-owners and employees, as well as a "need to know" basis when appropriate. She delegates as much of her workload as possible to her staff. It gives them a feeling of self-worth and satisfaction and leaves her to pursue the more important issues that a business or businesses can present.

She has a strong belief that positivity in the workplace is the key to hiring and retaining employees, and relying on them to handle your business responsibly and to treat it as if it were their own – that is her goal. Her ultimate goal has always been to have a business that stands alone with an off-site Owner – due to proper staffing, an appreciation of employees, work well done, and praise offered when a job is handled in a proper and professional manner.

Observation: As owners, her husband and herself are joined by only a handful of their peers who reward their employees, both verbally and tangibly by using praise, increase in responsibility, awards, frequent lunches brought in, cash and other incentives. And yes, they do still give out Christmas bonuses! In the end, Carina says it is a personal choice whether an entrepreneur is best suited for a single business venture or diversified interests and investments, as she does.

CHAPTER 6

SEVEN STEPS TO VICTORY AND SUCCESS

BY DAVE STOLTZFUS

AN EARLY START

There's a picture in my mind of a small Amish boy in Lancaster County, PA, maybe six or seven years old. Their family is large – he is one of five boys at that point, and he has eight sisters. He finds a rare moment of peace in his father's shop in the bottom of the tobacco shed on their farm. A row of large windows looks out on the countryside, and a bright sun shines.

The boy searches the shop for small scraps of wood then uses a band saw to make straight cuts. He gathers nails from the old bins, and his hammer makes an uneven sound as he struggles to force the small nails straight into the wood. He strikes his fingers almost as many times as he strikes the head of the nail. But he is determined and persistent.

In the end, there it is: a birdhouse with a red roof, not exactly how he had pictured it. Nothing fancy, nothing refined. Just a small box with a roof and an entrance. He compares it to the mailboxes his father makes, and he tries to figure out how to perfect it.

But the Amish boy is not caught up with the imperfections of his project. To him, the birdhouse represents the path to a dream, the tools toward an investment. He sees a way of making money that will afford him all of the nice things he's been looking at in the catalogues. He had circled $200 worth of toys not too many days before – way more than his family could afford to buy.

In his mind he begins scheming and planning. How can he market this product? How can he get the word out? How can he increase the production and the supply, if needed? He figures that if he can sell 100 birdhouses at $2 each, he'd get close to having enough to buy all of the things he wanted.

Perhaps you've guessed it by now: that little Amish boy was me. My entrepreneurial side developed at a very early age. I wanted to create things and market them and sell them. I don't think I sold any of those birdhouses when I was six or seven, but that never discouraged me. I was determined to figure it all out.

I was determined to strive for victory.

GETTING INTO BUSINESS

When I was 16 years old we moved off of the farm and my dad focused more time on his craft business. He mostly built small items like shadow boxes, but he also experimented with things like magazine racks and letter racks. I worked for him and learned all that I could.

I bought my dad's craft business at the age of 19. It was a big step for me, the first of many challenges I would take on in my life. Soon after the purchase, I changed the company's direction and focused more on custom woodworking and cabinetry. There seemed to be a bigger market in those areas, so we pursued them. We made adjustments. We pushed forward.

For 14 rocky years I ran that business, and I made a lot of mistakes. I overextended myself financially and emotionally. By the end of those years I was burned out and discouraged. As a young family man, my stress level was too high. My family buckled under the pressure, so I sold out, and at that point I didn't think I would ever experience true victory. It felt like I was walking away from all of my goals in life, and I wasn't sure how to get back on to the right track.

It would have been easy to quit at that point. It would have been easy to walk away from my calling as a business man and take an easier road. For a time, I did. I spent six months in the construction industry putting up steel buildings as an hourly worker. I knew the owner of the company and he paid me well, but it just didn't fit. I couldn't imagine that God would have had me run my own business for fourteen years only to have me spend the rest of my days working for an hourly wage. I thought there must be something else out there. Then came the phone call.

A CHANGE OF PACE

A friend of mine who knew I had sold my business checked in to see what I was up to.

"How's work these days?" he asked me.

"Well," I said, hesitating. "I'm in construction, but I'm keeping my options open."

In other words, I'd take anything I could get.

"I've got a position opening up over in production if you're interested," he said. "It's for a moulder operator. I know you do good work."

"Sure," I said. "We should talk."

I scheduled an interview, but I wasn't sure what to think. I had owned my own business for my entire adult life. I wanted to have another shot at running my own thing, and it was hard for me to accept that I would be working for someone else. I felt like all of my goals hinged on me owning a business.

During my first interview I met with two of the owners of Country Lane Woodworking. It felt strange sitting on my side of the desk, answering the questions I had always asked when people came to me looking for work. But I shared my experiences and my strengths. I told them where I had come from and where I wanted to go. I explained to them that I was an entrepreneur at heart, but that I was also willing to do anything they wanted me to do.

After I answered one of their questions about customer service, the two men looked at each other.

"I think we're interviewing him for the wrong position," one of them said.

That comment caught me off guard, but the second owner agreed.

"What do you mean by that?" I asked, my curiosity piqued.

"We're also hiring for a sales position right now. You might be just the person for the job."

The idea intrigued me, but I had never felt like sales was my strength. When I owned my own business, I had been so caught up in all of the other areas. In fact, one of the reasons I had to sell was because I just couldn't land enough work. Still, we scheduled another interview for the sales position. I went away feeling very uncertain but also slightly excited and optimistic.

I was beaten down by life. I lacked confidence. I wasn't sure of the way forward. Yet they saw my potential. They knew that I had a lot to contribute to their business. The second interview came and went. Two weeks passed.

Then they offered me the sales position along with the potential to manage that division within a year. Their confidence in my abilities surprised me. After all, I felt like I had failed in my business, but they still saw something in me that was worth taking a chance on.

Their risk paid off. In my first year our sales division grew 78%. At the time of writing this, 2012 sales for the division I'm in are up 40% over 2011. That is a sales growth of 148% in two years.

SEVEN STEPS TO SUCCESS

Victory isn't easy to find. It doesn't put itself out there for just anyone to grab hold of. No, it takes perseverance and determination and a willingness to experience defeat and failure without giving up. Here are seven things that allowed me to achieve victory and have success after some very difficult times.

1. **Always keep learning.** One of the biggest ways I continue to learn is through reading: books, blogs, magazines, and newspapers. I'm always trying to expand my knowledge base because nearly every great opportunity I've ever had come as a result of me trying to learn something new. Be willing to learn from your friends and your competition. Be willing to learn from your mistakes and your successes. Never assume you know enough.

2. **Face reality but keep pushing forward, even after hard times.** There came a day when I had to face reality and sell my business. It just wasn't working anymore, and I was out of ideas. At that point, it would have been easy for me to look back at my fourteen years of being a business owner and come to the conclusion that I hadn't succeeded at anything. But now, when I look back on those days, I realize the mistakes that I made were preparation for where I am today.

3. **Re-evaluate everything.** Pursuing excellence and victory in all areas means constantly evaluating everything you are doing. Do you feel like you are a competent communicator, that your emails and correspondence are "good enough?" Never say, "This is working. I'm not going to change it." Too many times as a business owner I took on the attitude that a product or procedure was "good enough." That became a hindrance to meIf you strive for excellence and constantly evaluate everything, it will become evident to your customers, and they'll appreciate the products and services you supply.

4. **Do not overextend yourself.** The problem with overextending yourself is that you become ineffective. After arriving at Country Lane and growing sales by 70%, someone asked me how I could do that for Country Lane but could never do it at my old business. It's because I was overextended at my old business, trying to do everything and succeeding at nothing. Allowing others to help you on the journey to success will keep your life in balance.

5. **Train yourself to care about your customers and it will be easier to do business with them.** As a society we are becoming more and more disconnected, and it's leading to a lack of compassion. I contribute some of my success in sales to the difficult times I experienced and how they help me to relate with those I do business with. Are you willing to walk away from a sale if it becomes evident that it's not the right thing for your potential customer? Until you can say yes to that question, you'll never be completely victorious.

6. **Have a mentor.** Or multiple mentors. Determine to learn from the best. If you can find other men and women who want to see you

succeed as much as you do, it will change your life. But there's a difference between someone telling you what to do and someone helping you to discover what to do – the latter is so important. A mentor may at times give you some good action points, but they will not attempt to control you.

7. **Set goals for yourself in the areas where you want to improve.** Over the years I found myself slowing getting more and more out of shape. I couldn't find the time for exercise because I was running a business and raising a family and trying to succeed. But I knew it was important. Eventually I set a goal to run a half marathon, which I achieved in September of 2012 when I finished my first half in a little over two hours.

I am a blessed man. When I was at a low point, Country Lane was willing to give me a chance. I came to realize and appreciate these seven things while working there, and they've set me up for a successful run as a sales person.

Victory is attainable, no matter where you've been, what you've done, or how you feel you've failed in the past. But it's not easy. It's not something that will come easily. You have to commit to the process and push through difficult times. You have to persevere and find others who can come around you and support you.

About Dave

Dave Stoltzfus is a sales manager at Country Lane Gazebos where he manages the retail and non-stocking dealer sales division. He is in charge of sales, marketing budgets, sales and tracking systems, and home shows, but his real passion is getting to know his customers and potential customers on a personal level.

Dave Stoltzfus lives in Lancaster, PA with his wife and four boys.

To learn more about Country Lane Gazebos or to connect with Dave Stoltzfus, Visit: www.gazebo.com or call him at 717-351-9250.

CHAPTER 7

TIMELESS PRINCIPLES FOR A SUCCESSFUL LIFE IN ANY ECONOMY

BY DAVID LEE

suc·cess /sək'ses/ noun
  1. The accomplishment of an aim or purpose

According to the definition above (source: dictionary.com), success is the accomplishment of an aim or purpose. I concur. I am convinced that God gifts each person on this earth with unique abilities. True success that brings lasting fulfillment is the result of finding and using our gifts to benefit the world around us. Allow me to share my personal "success story" before laying out what I believe are seven principles for achieving success in any economy.

From the time I was five or six years old, I dreamed of becoming a pilot. And I didn't just want to be any kind of pilot—I wanted to be a fighter pilot! Flying was all I could ever think about. I spent much of my free time on flight simulators on our home computer. I was fortunate to have parents that believed in the same success principles laid out in this chapter, so when my mother noticed my love for flying, she encouraged that gift to blossom. I had always been an "A" student throughout my schooling, but in Junior High I began to associate with some bad influences. My grades began to suffer, and my parents began to worry. Knowing of my love for flying, my mother offered me the opportunity to take flying lessons when I was age 13. I took one flying lesson and I was hooked! After taking that one lesson, I told my mother that I wanted to go to the United States Air Force Academy and become a fighter pilot. Her response: "You'd better get your grades up!" And so I did. I realized that the best chance to become a fighter pilot was in the Air Force, since they had more fighter cockpits than any other service. Through research, I had learned that getting accepted to and graduating from the Air Force Academy would virtually assure me of a pilot slot. So, I made it my goal to be accepted to the Academy and become a graduate of that institution. I worked very hard throughout my high school career to make good grades and be involved in extra-curricular activities. I graduated Valedictorian from my high school and was accepted to the Academy. After four grueling years, I graduated and went on to pilot training and eventually became an F-16 pilot, fulfilling a childhood dream.

I served on active duty as a T-38 instructor pilot and an F-16 instructor pilot, accumulating multiple "Top Gun" awards during various flight-training programs. I also had the privilege of protecting the President of the United States on several missions in the months preceding 9/11. After serving on active duty for almost nine years, I decided to leave the active duty military while continuing to serve two additional years in the Air National Guard in order to give my wife and our children a more stable lifestyle. Even though I was doing what some would consider "living the dream" of being a fighter pilot, my priority was my family. I decided to take the road less traveled and exit the military for the benefit of my family, not knowing exactly what God had in store for me. I simply stepped out on faith, trusting that God would provide a new opportunity.

Before leaving the military, I did a lot of self-evaluation, trying to determine what I would enjoy doing for my second career. I decided to go into the financial planning business because I had always enjoyed managing my own investments and evaluating companies for investment opportunities. Even though I had no idea what I was getting into, God provided a path before me, and I ended up being mentored by Chuck Beale, who had been my parents' financial advisor for over forty years.

It was truly a blessing from God to be mentored by someone with so much experience in the field. Chuck was also a believer in the same success principles laid out in this chapter, having achieved a great deal of success himself in the business world. Chuck retired a few years after

I entered the business world, but through his mentorship I was able to develop a successful financial planning practice. Since 2005, we have helped hundreds of retirees and near-retirees protect their investments in a very unstable financial world.

Achieving success truly is "the accomplishment of an aim or purpose." I have had some success by achieving my aim of getting accepted to and graduating from the US Air Force Academy. I achieved my objective of becoming a fighter pilot—an achievement many dream of, but few achieve. And I achieved my dream of starting and growing a successful business that would give me the quality of life I desired, allowing me to control my work hours while earning an income I could never imagine was achievable.

Given the successes I've had both in the public and private sectors, I'd like to share with you some timeless principles for achieving success, regardless of what the world throws at you. These principles are not necessarily all-encompassing—there are many variables to success. These are simply seven of the ones that I feel are the most important. So here they are:

1. Get to know your Creator – He wants to know you!

If success is the accomplishment of an aim or purpose, then no one can be a true success without knowing the reason they're here on this earth to begin with. God put you here for one reason: He wants to have a relationship with you! This is the reason we're all here—to know and love God and to be used according to His purpose. How can you know the purpose you were created for if you don't know the Creator who created you for a purpose? One day this life will end, and eternity begins. Any measure of "success" that you achieved in your short time here on earth will be soon forgotten, so you need to have an eternal perspective on success.

You can only get to know your Creator by knowing His Son. John 3:16 says, "For God so loved the world that He gave His one and only Son, that whoever believes in Him shall not perish but have eternal life." Knowing Jesus as your personal Lord and Savior is the foundational step to eternal success that brings lasting fulfillment!

2. Develop a positive self-image and think positive thoughts.

You are made in the image of God—act like it! Psalm 139:13-14 says: "You formed my inward parts; you knit me together in my mother's womb. I praise You, for I am fearfully and wonderfully made."

Think of that—the Creator of the Universe also created you! He created you just the way you are, and He is proud of you! You need to not just develop a positive self-image, but also develop the *discipline* of thinking positively. Philippians 4:8 says: "Whatever is true, whatever is noble, whatever is right, whatever is pure, whatever is lovely, whatever is admirable...think about such things." Why is this so important to achieve success? It is because we tend to become what we think about most. If you are constantly thinking positive thoughts, you will tend to attract people and things that reinforce those thoughts. The opposite is also true. So, think positively!

3. Know and use your unique gifts.

Ephesians 2:10 tells us: "We are God's handiwork, created in Christ Jesus to do good works, which God prepared in advance for us to do."

Is there something at which you are naturally talented? Chances are, that is your gift to use! I wanted to be a fighter pilot from a young age. I was good at it, as evidenced from the natural affinity I had for it and the awards I accumulated. Once you know God, you will see that He uniquely gifted you. What are your unique talents and skills? To be successful and fulfilled, learn what God uniquely gifted you to do, and then use that gift to benefit the world around you.

4. Set Goals and Dream Big.

Setting goals is extremely important! It has been said, "What the mind can conceive and believe, it can achieve." I believe that is true. Jesus told us in Matthew 17:20, "Truly I tell you, if you have faith as small as a mustard seed, you can say to this mountain, 'Move from here to there,' and it will move. Nothing will be impossible for you." Why is goal setting so important? When you write your goals down on paper, and you constantly review them, it is like programming your mind for success. It is almost magical! When you know the Creator, and you live with a deep conviction that He has gifted you in a unique way to benefit the world around you; and when you start to dream big and put those dreams to paper by formulating specific, measurable goals while realizing that He is able to accomplish far more than you can even *imagine*, it's amazing what you can accomplish! My favorite verse in the Bible is Ephesians 3:20:

"Now to Him [God] who is able to do *immeasurably more* than all we ask *or imagine*, according to [God's] power that is at work within us."

If the God who controls all the resources in all the world is able to do far more than we can even ask or imagine, then dream big with big goals; and watch how God uses His infinite resources to accomplish His will in this world!

5. Surround yourself with the right people and influences.

"Blessed is the man who does not walk in the counsel of the wicked or stand in the way of sinners or sit in the seat of mockers. But his delight is in the law of the LORD, and on His law he meditates day and night. He is like a tree planted by streams of water, which yields its fruit in season and whose leaf does not wither. Whatever he does prospers." Psalm 1:1-3

Did you know that we tend to become like the people we are around the most? Do you want to become successful? Associate yourself with those you want to aspire to become like! Spend time with them, and over time you will become like them, too!

6. Trust God when things don't go your way.

Romans 8:28 tells us: "We know that in all things God works for the good of those who love Him, who have been called according to His purpose." Once you know your Creator and have a personal relationship with Him, then you have the confidence to know that He wants what is best for you. In Jeremiah 29:11, God tells us: "For I know the plans I have for you...plans to prosper you and not to harm you, plans to give you hope and a future." This knowledge gives me great confidence to know that any setbacks I face are only temporary. God uses setbacks in my life to prepare me for something better in the future, and to strengthen my faith in His ability to provide and to work out all things for His glory and my ultimate benefit.

7. Persevere!

Hebrews 11:1 says: "Now faith is confidence in what we hope for and assurance about what we do not see." I am convinced that most failures in life occur due to lack of perseverance (or, faith). Many people quit when the going gets tough. They trust in what they can *see*, instead of having *assurance about what they do not see*. I believe there is much more going on in this life than meets the eye. There are supernatural forces at work all around us, all of the time. I am convinced that the struggles we face are really just tests of our character and our faith. When you see life as a series of tests to be passed, it helps you cope better with the struggles.

So, there you have it! Those are my principles for success in life in *any* economy. It is going to be very important to have a set of *principles* you live by in the coming years. I believe the coming years are going to be economically challenging—and it is not just the US that is facing difficulties. The entire world is now linked economically, and I believe we are facing a global depression. The future will bring great challenges for investors looking to protect capital and grow their wealth. However, as I believe we are now seeing, wealth is very fleeting. King Solomon said it best:

"Do not wear yourself out to get rich; do not trust your own cleverness. Cast but a glance at riches, and they are gone, for they will surely sprout wings and fly off to the sky like an eagle." Proverbs 23:4-5

Wealth can be very deceptive. Don't put your faith in a number in a bank account or a brokerage account, where it can be taxed away, inflated away, or made worthless by reckless monetary policy. If you follow the principles laid out here, you will not be caught in this deceptive trap.

Success in any other area of life (marriage, children, finances, health, etc.) is much easier once you accept and commit yourself to these principles. There are many folks out there that will give you their secret formula to success in investing, or tips for better health, etc.; but without a knowledge and commitment to these basic principles, none of the other tips will work; or they won't bring you lasting fulfillment. Everything in this life is temporary and fading. The only things that are truly important—that bring true success *with* fulfillment—are the things that transcend this life. My hope and prayer is that you will focus on what makes you "eternally successful," and not just temporarily so.

True success and fulfillment in life is to find and use our gifts to benefit the world around us. I believe God gifted me with a desire and ability to fly airplanes, as well as with a desire and ability to develop a successful business. Because true success begins with knowing and loving God and living life according to His principles, my desire is that as many people as possible will come to know Him throughout the world. My goal for the coming years is to use my gift for flying combined with business success to fund and fly aircraft around the world for missions so that more people may come to know Him.

About David

David Lee is the President and CEO of Beale, Lee & Associates – an investment advisory firm in the retirement community of Bella Vista, Arkansas.

David is a 1996 graduate of the United States Air Force Academy. After serving nearly a decade in the US Air Force as an F-16 fighter pilot, David entered the business world seeking a more stable lifestyle for his family.

Since 2005, David worked diligently to protect the retirement savings of hundreds of retirees in the area. By focusing his practice on conservative investments with minimal risk, combined with laddered retirement income strategies dubbed "sound investments, structured to last," David skillfully piloted his clients through the 2008 financial crisis, catapulting his practice to new heights in the years since. David is a sought-after speaker in the community on retirement planning issues, co-hosting a regular TV segment and a weekly radio show, as well as frequent speaking engagements with local community groups. David's goal for the coming years is to train and mentor ex-military personnel in the financial business and to provide them a "turnkey" business opportunity for those looking for a second career outside the military.

David currently resides in Bentonville, Arkansas, where he actively serves the community as Vice Chairman of the Bentonville Airport Commission Board as well as the Bella Vista Library Board; and gives back to the community via several charitable organizations such as Samaritan's Feet.

David and his wife Jennie are the parents of two children, Faith and Connor. He can be contacted at: david@bealelee.com.

CHAPTER 8

THE FOUR SECRETS OF BUSINESS SUCCESS

BY ELMER DAVIS, JR., MBA, ALM

Humor me for a moment, and try to think about what makes a strong business.

Are suits and brief cases involved? Or long hours peering over excel sheets? If so, that's fine. I've been in consulting for a long time, and I've helped all sorts of businesses grow more robust by tinkering with things few business owners ever think about.

Some of my clients run mechanic shops; others make products for wide distribution and large profits. But many, many more businesses like them lose money every year, because they take certain things for granted, or feel overwhelmed by financial mumbo jumbo that separates them from their money.

Fine-tuning your business is about as useful as it can be confusing, and in my line of work, I've found that the smaller steps are usually the best. I've condensed my advice and experience down to what I call **The Four Secrets to Business Success**, and I'd love to share them with you.

I want to write about a few things you may not have imagined. Specifically – what happens at the cash register, and what happens at the bank. More often than not, I begin working with clients to save them money on credit card transaction costs – each time they process a credit card payment from a customer, they pay a fee.

There are a number of ways to keeps these fees low that business owners have no idea about, but which I'll explain here.

Let's get started!

1. COST MANAGEMENT

When I started working with Jim, I couldn't believe how smart he was. Jim's business was in automotive repair, and he was a bona-fide mechanical engineer.

I like to think I work with good people, but it's not everyday that I get to bounce ideas off of such a well-educated guy.

One thing, though – there's a difference between knowing your craft and knowing the minutiae of your business. That's where I come in, every time. I like to say that no matter how good you are at what you do, there will always be something you can fix about your business.

In Jim's case, it was his cost management. In our first meeting, he told me that he charged competitive rates to stay afloat and get new clients. He regularly checked what his cross-town competitors charged, and always took that into consideration.

Sounds like a good strategy, right? Well, only to a point. I helped Jim turn around and look back at his own business first, before trying to compete with the other guy.

What Jim didn't consider was that he knew almost nothing else about those other businesses. He only saw what they charged – not how many people they employed, what they made each year, or what their rent was.

His competition could be owned by a wealthy family that aren't out to get the profits he is. They could be government-owned. The fact is, I told him, he didn't know their business.

But, naturally, he knew what his staff and financial numbers were. Why not charge clients based on what makes sense for him and his business? Then, we got to work.

We looked at his various costs – his labor costs, his rent, his electricity – and figured out how much it cost for him to open his doors everyday.

From that price, we found what he could charge to find his break-even point, or how much he has to make to stay even.

And from there, we also considered what he and most of my clients do when they work with me. We began to lower his non-cash transaction costs. Whenever a customer used a debit or credit card, the bank charged Jim a certain amount. Depending on whether the customer used a debit or credit, a Visa or Master Card, Jim was faced with different fees. We decided that he would implement certain strategies to lower those fees, some of which we'll look at in the following steps.

2. HUMAN RESOURCE PRODUCTIVITY

Let's consider another of my clients – Dr. Grey, the Dentist. Dr. Grey's staff ran a very efficient business. However they, like Jim, overlooked how much banks charge with each non-cash payment.

I sat down with Dr. Grey to look at exactly what she was charged, and when. She, just like Jim, assumed that non-cash payment fees were fixed, like taxes, or like subscriptions. When she saw the different amounts (some of which were unsettling high) banks charged, she wanted help. To the uninitiated – which can be most people – the amount banks charge on non-cash sales may look random.

But they are far from it!

I began to explain – these fees should be carefully considered. They vary by way of how the transactions are processed, where the customer is, what the customer does, and so on. Certain things, like whether or not the customer enters their secure pin number, make the difference between the business being charged 3% of the transaction or just $0.35. When you're running a dental office that offers technical and expensive services, 3% of a sale is often much, much larger than $0.35!

I can often save clients 45-50% on their non-cash transaction fees by helping them conduct their transactions in a safer way. There is a way to make the charges appear less random, and in many cases my clients can learn to keep their transaction fees at $0.35 virtually every time. The key is in how they conduct themselves with customers, and how they handle each transaction.

You see, banks want security. They don't like risking money on loose spending.

If someone gives their credit card number over the phone, or emailing their zip code, security number and expiration date, it can be easily stolen or miscommunicated. These lazy transaction practices lead to more faulty transactions, which costs the banks more, which inclines them to charge more on the outset to protect against potential losses.

The goal for the businesses I work with becomes: *make the real-time moment of payment secure in as many ways as possible.*

I worked directly with Dr. Grey's staff on everything from their hours of service to what they can say at the time of payment, to make the transaction more secure in the eyes of the bank. Security, in Dr. Grey's case, meant a pin code. Sometimes customers won't voluntarily give them, but will if they're asked. Dr. Grey's staff now asks for a pin code each time the customer hands them a credit card.

But instead of going into a speech about why they need them, Dr. Grey's staff keeps it simple: they say they'd like the customer to input their pin *for security*. That's all it takes, most of the time.

The customer wants their finances and identity to remain secure just as much as Dr. Grey. The business owner wants the transaction to be streamlined, so that each payment is conducted in such a way that minimizes risk in the eyes of the bank, who decides how much each transaction will cost the business owner.

The banks, ultimately, want to trust that the payment will go through without a hitch.

The key takeaway for Dr. Grey was this: miscommunication loses money. Ask customers to give a little more. They'll protect themselves, the banks will feel assured, and you – the business owner – will save money.

Another example of this is what happens in restaurants across the country, all day everyday. Customers don't want to pay with cash, and trust their servers with their credit cards for up to a few minutes while they process their payment in the back.

Banks don't like that and yet, for the time being, restaurants don't get it.

The clients I've had that run restaurants now take payment devices to the table, and slide the card in front of the customer, who usually signs off on the transaction on an electric device. Think a mobile phone or tablet. The server brings the device to the table – they don't take the customers property to some corner register.They swipe it in front of them, and watch the customer sign off on it.

The card never leaves the table – it won't get dropped, it won't get lost, and a less-than-honest employee won't copy its information when no one's looking. Banks like it and customers don't mind it. It will drastically lower non-cash transaction costs and all it takes is a little interpersonal management.

3. CASH FLOW

One of my clients runs a candy company. Their business is sweet – over the holidays, they can make half-a-million a month. And while that sounds like they've got it all figured out, there was a problem.

They couldn't get their money on time! There's something to be said about getting money, whether it's a small or giant amount, on time and when it's useful. Just because the records show your business is robust and making large profits doesn't necessarily mean that you can get your hands on it. My candy company guys had such a problem.

With a group as large as they, one of my first approaches was to help them get their money quickly. You see, there are simple things one can do to get the money, say, a day sooner. And sometimes there are easy fixes that transfer money to the business owner two weeks earlier than their initial, default agreement with the banks.

There's nothing wrong with changing the often-ignored details of money transfers. If your bank decides to collect your transaction information at 4 a.m., even if you close your doors at 5 p.m. the day before, you won't see your money for at least two days.

However, if you ask the bank to receive your business day information an hour after you close, at 6 p.m., you'll get your money the next morning. In this case, the trick is to reconsider how you work with your bank. Their habits are not set in stone, and you won't cheat anyone by asking for them to work with your schedule.

You want a 0-day hold on your money. Why accept anything longer than that? There's a lot you can do with half a million in one month, and there's little to argue against this simple fact: the sooner you receive the money you've made, the more you can do with it.

Think about the time value of money, which means the potential investments you could have made with that extra day or two with your money. What if the market skyrockets and you didn't get your money invested in time to cash in?

Also, for the safer investor, what is a day worth if you're invested in a bond or annuity? If your profits are in the millions, a day or two without your money could mean thousands lost.

4. ASSET MANAGEMENT

For my last point, let's consider what a business can do with their money once they've received it, and how they can make the most use of their earnings.

First, consider those transaction fees that we worked to lower by way of streamlined staff-customer interaction. With each check and credit or debit card transaction, there will be a bank fee that will be deducted while your money is being processed. There's something to consider here: when will the bank deduct this charge?

Many business owners shrug their shoulders, thinking that banks will take the money when they will, and that there are forces at work that they cannot understand that determine when the fees are taken. That's just not true. Part of my work with businesses is determining when the banks take these fees. In the same way that we can determine when the banks give us our money, we can determine when they deduct their fees.

In the interest of keeping things simple, the most preferred method is a one-time, monthly deduction of all transaction fees. That way, you don't see bits deducted everyday. You see what you have to work with in its entirety at the first of each month.

We'll keep the same philosophy as we did when I told you to ask for money when it's most convenient to you – the sooner you get it, the more you are able to do for your business. Only difference here is the later you pay those transaction fees, the more time you have to invest that money. So, preferably you'd like to pay your one-time monthly fee at the end of each month.

Until then, you can take interest on it, and many of my clients have begun trading in markets and making further profits, and haven't been thrown off by daily fee deductions.

My large businesses fine-tune their money so they know just how much they have at all times, so they can make more of it through other avenues.

FINAL THOUGHTS

Whether you're thriving or just starting, your business could use some work. It's just a fact of life. But that shouldn't dissuade or intimidate you – it should ready you to make your business work *for you*, and not for anyone else.

My four secrets aren't really secrets at all; they are good ideas, from simple to complex that help a business grow for the owner specifically. I help my clients grow according to their needs, and to run their business for themselves, without hurting themselves because banks ask for inconveniences.

Therefore: know your expenses, streamline your time of sales, collect your money when it works for you, and ask the bank to work at your pace and schedule. It's as simple as that! The complexity comes from your wants and needs, which we can make happen with a little hard work!

About Elmer

Elmer Davis, Jr., MBA, ALM has over 25 years of experience in marketing and finance, including working with private and non-profit organizations, as well as Fortune 500 corporations.He began his business career in marketing with Bristol-Myers in Washington, DC in the early 80's, then moved on to work for industry giants like Mobil Oil.

He was a partner with Anderson, Philips, Davis, and Hoffmann in Washington DC, NYC and Los Angeles, and served as Executive Vice-President and Chief Diversity Officer for Financial Dimensions, Inc.

A graduate of the Florida A&M University School of Business and Industry, Mr. Davis holds a Bachelor of Science in Marketing, as well as a Master's of Business Administration from Howard University. He also recently earned a Master's of Liberal Arts from none other than Harvard University in Operational Management.

He has conducted leadership-training forums for clients in numerous industry segments, including the public and private sectors and major Universities. Elmer has also written several articles, including *Understanding the Communication Environment, The true costs of miscommunication, Effective strategies for business growth, Financial management for cash flow and profits,* and *Embracing Workplace Diversity and Eliminating Employment Discrimination.*

He was chosen as a Mortgage Bankers Association National Diversity Champion in 2005 and a Heritage Who's Who in 2004.

Elmer is well regarded as a facilitator of crucial information and trainer having worked with organizations in various industries providing specialized training to maximize profits through human resource productivity, asset management, pricing, and expense control. Elmer is a natural communicator and was a recent guest on MIT University radio WMBR.

His current company, TBK Ventures, Inc., has helped to control the costs and increase profits for businesses in the Pittsburgh, PA area and around the country. If you would like more information about how Elmer can help you or your business reach that pivotal next level, visit his site at: www.elmerdavisjr.net or call 855-293-0877.

CHAPTER 9

BUSINESS DEVELOPMENT AND THE ULTIMATE CLIENT EXPERIENCE

BY DHARMESH VORA

Early in my career I was like most young entrepreneurs. I wanted success. I was constantly on the go – educating myself in order to tell potential clients how much I knew, attending conferences to learn how to speak to my potential clients, reading self-help books – anything and everything I could get my hands on in order to impress people who may or may not need what I had to offer.

Business was doing well, but I felt that something was missing. People weren't beating down my door even though I was quite knowledgeable. I expanded my client base with public seminars, I was on the phone and I was doing what every other advisor was doing. (hmmmm.)

Then, one day, all of that changed. I was given a book, *Raving Fans*, by Ken Blanchard. I immediately read it. And re-read it. Blanchard wrote, "If you really want to 'own' a customer, if you want a booming business, you have to go beyond satisfied customers and create Raving Fans." YES! That is what I wanted!

That was the easy part.

I had been in business for about sixteen years at that point. Now that I knew what I wanted for my *clients,* I had to figure out what *they* really wanted and how to deliver.

Around that time I started feeling under the weather, nothing serious, but enough that I had to see my doctor.

So, I called my doctor's office, had to press several buttons to get the receptionist who promptly put me on hold. Once she came back on the line, I had to answer a myriad of questions prior to being granted an appointment.

I showed up for my appointment at the requested time – fifteen minutes early – was handed a clipboard, asked for my insurance card, told to sign forms and have a seat. I then waited for thirty-five minutes prior to being led into the examination room.

A nurse came in and took my vitals and then hustled out, stuck my chart on the door and there I sat waiting, once again. I was not surprised. This is what I had been conditioned to expect. This is what the vast majority of us had accepted as the norm.

That was my experience as a client. My eyes were wide open. Now I had direction.

I had to create an atmosphere that was unlike the "norm," what we had all been conditioned to accept. I had to rebuild my practice from the inside out. I needed a mission statement, a business plan and an end result.

My first step was to speak with several of my long term clients. I wanted to know what *they* wanted. I asked them for their candid input on everything, including their first impression of my office when they walked in and their experiences with my staff. It was a real eye opener, and quite humbling, as well.

I needed to develop a process for each aspect of my business – from hiring staff to filing paperwork. Every aspect of the practice needed to be addressed.

First and foremost, I had to start with my staff. I had been hiring staff in the same manner as most businesses. You know the routine: I placed an ad, reviewed resumes, interviewed the applicants that looked like what

I wanted (at least on paper), hired the one that answered your questions the best. It was basically a throw-it-against-the-wall-and-see-if-it-sticks method.

The first step I made was to define each position. This included duties and responsibilities: skill set needed, outcomes and the work atmosphere of the position. Keep in mind that job descriptions will flex as business expands, but the foundation has to be set first.

What I found, once I had identified each role I needed filled, is that I was short-staffed and my current employees were not working efficiently. That was not their fault. The office was running on auto-pilot. The phone would ring and if the receptionist was on another call someone else would answer. The client on the other end would have questions and the person who answered would try to help.

When an office is running in this manner, the client becomes confused as to whom they should speak with, and the administrative staff is running in circles trying to be a jack-of-all-trades.

Creating job descriptions is a MUST.

Now that I had clearly defined roles for my staff, I needed to figure out if the people I had employed were well-suited in their roles.

At this point in my process, I did some research on how to effectively hire staff. There are numerous resources available and one that I chose was the Kolbe Index Test. "The Kolbe A Index measures a person's instinctive method of operation (MO), and identifies the ways he or she will be most productive. It need only be taken once, since these innate abilities do not change over time." (Resource Kolbe.com)

So, we all took the test. And it was accurate. I did let one staff member go and moved another into a position that suited him. I hired more employees and tested them all. The atmosphere in the office was changing.

Each employee had a defined role and plan. Our clients knew exactly who to contact depending on their need. Then I took it one step further...

All of my clients received a DVD of the staff. Each team member gave a brief introduction and defined his role to the client. It was a personalized touch and a great experience for our clients.

So at this point, I was feeling pretty confident that the office was running like a well-oiled machine. I not only changed the location of the office but I also changed the aesthetics. I created a warm and inviting atmosphere. Clients felt comfortable enough to stop in just to read the paper and have a cup of coffee.

Even though I was making these changes and creating processes, clients were not beating down my door. I was missing something…

So I started thinking about my experience at the doctor's office. The receptionist, the nurse, the doctor - the referral to another doctor…. Ah ha!! I would not get the answers I needed until I saw another specialist and that would only be after the two doctors spoke…

In essence, that is what I was doing with MY clients. They would come in for their scheduled appointment, we would create the base for their financial plan, they would have tax returns and brokerage statements and statements for debt, etc. Once the base plan was created, we would have to contact their CPA and their broker in order to ensure the integrity of the plan.

CRAZY!!! I am sure my clients weren't too happy about it, but since that was the normal experience, it wasn't questioned.

Now that the office was running smoothly and all employees knew what was expected of them, and the clients were getting communication "touches" once or twice a week, it was time to expand!

I wanted to create a one-stop shop. My vision was to bring everything in-house. I had to diversify in order to create the unique and meaningful company my clients deserved. I found that what people really wanted were answers. They want an advisor who listens and communicates and cares. I wanted to provide clear and concise information to my clients.

So, I left the Broker/Dealer world and started my own RIA firm. I hired in-house portfolio managers (Co-Chief Investment Officers). One is a Chartered Financial Analyst (CFA) and the other is a Chartered Market Technician (CMT). Collectively, they have approximately forty-five years of experience managing money.

My clients now have total transparency as to the performance of their holdings, how much is billed for fees, how much each trade costs – there is nothing hidden. I have the ability to protect their portfolios in bad economic conditions by taking a cash position – a whole new world has opened up for all.

I hired a tax advisor who also has the licenses necessary to be a financial advisor. (Keep in mind this is a new role that required defining, and taking the Kolbe test and passing the interview process.)

I hired an in-house marketer. This specialized position handles all correspondence with our clients and potential clients – from the personalized videos to birthday cards and invitations to client events and seminars.

I rented out one of my offices to an Estate Planning Attorney. Again, I did the necessary research and "interview" process to ensure that this was someone I wanted to work with my clients.

As new staff was added to the firm, clients would receive introductory videos of the newest member and the role they fulfill.

At this point, the office was running without a hitch, client satisfaction was up, we were opening new accounts every day, we were setting ourselves apart from the other firms in town – Life was good, but there was still a component missing.

The missing piece was the financial plan for the client. That *is* why they come to see us. What every client needs to know is what their financial future holds, are they on track to meet their goals, do they need to make subtle changes, and have they taken on more debt, or even paid off some debt? I was STILL like every other advisor out there when it came to this – the most vital aspect of what advisors do. Basically, when sitting with the client, after plugging in numbers and spending a few hours together a couple times a year to create the financial plan, the plan is outdated as soon as the print button is hit.

I needed to provide MORE – THEY deserved more! A living breathing financial plan.

Software, databases, programs and financial platforms are vital to our industry, not just for our reporting and recording, but also for compliance and regulatory entities. Fortunately, there are also programs designed specifically toward client experiences. These programs range from just basic information to fully interactive and dynamic programs.

After exhausting research and what seemed like at least a hundred demos, I chose an interactive, comprehensive program that gives real-time market results. Each client now has his own log-in and password and a living, breathing financial plan at his fingertips 24 hours a day, 7 days a week. Once the client is set up, we link all of his accounts to the program for data aggregation. The best part is that it is not solely related to brokerage accounts. This software truly creates the "ultimate client experience."

Mortgages, bank accounts, credit card debt, open credit lines, brokerage accounts, insurance accounts and retirement accounts are all linked in one spot. Personal financial statements instantly change as debt is paid down, or as the market is moving throughout the day. I now have the ability to see assets that I do not manage. I am now able to collaborate with my clients on-line! A simple question can be asked and answered in seconds or minutes rather than in hours or days.

In addition, clients have a personal vault in which they may upload important documents, pictures and statements. Any paperwork they have the ability to scan may be uploaded into their secure account.

Within months of having this program up and running, we saw the true value in what we were providing to our clients. A recent fire on the side of a mountain in our town had destroyed several hundred acres. That summer when the monsoons came (rainy season), the bare mountain was not able to contain the water and the result was a community that was ravaged by flood waters.

Many families were evacuated with very little notice. One of those families happened to be clients. Two days after being evacuated they stopped by the office. They still could not return to their home – but they needed a copy of their homeowner's insurance policy that we had uploaded to their "vault" on-line, just two weeks prior. It was pretty powerful.

I have skated the surface, in very general scenarios, on how I have structured my practice. I had to have a plan of action, as do you.

1. Write a mission statement and a business plan. Read *Raving Fans*.

2. Create a process for EVERYTHING and put it in writing. Make sure all employees have a copy. You should literally be able to take this "book" to a new location and duplicate your office painlessly. (Or at least minimally.)

3. Listen to what your clients need, and deliver.

4. Seek advice from professionals: Align yourself with companies that are out there to help take your business to the next level, including compliance firms, marketing firms and consultants who will help reorganize and restructure your business WITH you.

5. Brand yourself through effective marketing.

6. Use social media, video and DVD media, any means available to communicate with your clients.

7. ALWAYS be open and honest with your clients. Even when a trade goes bad, or something happens that wasn't planned for, do not run. Pick up the phone, schedule an appointment and hit issues head on.

Obviously, it is impossible to squeeze everything into one chapter. There is so much more detail involved in creating and implementing the things I have outlined. It has taken me years to get to where I feel my clients are finally receiving an experience which they deserve. Don't get me wrong, I am not finished, there is always room for improvement and my next phase heavily involves new methods of client communication.

One final note: During this process, the restructuring and growing of my practice, I started to think differently. I know in this chapter I kept referring to "clients," but as I was growing mentally I started to realize that they are not my clients. The people whom I work for are truly my bosses. They have hired me to do a job and I must deliver.

About Dharmesh

Dharmesh Vora is the Owner and Founder of the Vora Financial Group PLLC, Vora Wealth Management PLLC, and Vora Tax PLLC. Born and raised in India, he moved to the United States at the age of 13 and has been a resident of Flagstaff, Arizona since 1989.

Dharmesh has been in the financial services business for over 20 years. He specializes in working with retirees and individuals nearing retirement. His areas of expertise are in reducing taxes, asset protection, asset preservation and increasing income during retirement. He has served clients through out the country. Along with estate and tax attorneys, Dharmesh hosts a series of seminars on investment strategies, tax reduction, asset preservation, and estate planning.

Dharmesh is a member of the Million Dollar Round Table and Top of the Table, the Premier Association of Financial Professionals. Million Dollar Round Table's Top of the Table is an exclusive forum for the world's most successful life insurance and financial services professionals. Top of the Table members are committed to providing exemplary client service while displaying the highest standards of ethics and professional knowledge. Dharmesh is also certified by the Life Underwriter Training Council as a Life Underwriter Training Council Fellow (LUTCF) and has certification from LUTC for Life Insurance, Personal Insurance, Employee Benefits, Disability Income Insurance, and Business Continuation Planning, and has also served as moderator for the LUTC.

Dharmesh currently serves on the Flagstaff Chamber of Commerce Board of Directors. He has served on the executive boards of Habitat for Humanity and is a charter member of Childhelp USA, Flagstaff Chapter. He was previously the Chairman of the Board for the Junior Chamber of Commerce (Jaycees). Dharmesh also served as a past President of the Northern Arizona Association of Insurance and Financial Advisors. Additionally, he has served as an Ambassador for the Flagstaff Chamber of Commerce. He is a member of the Better Business Bureau and has been an active member of the Rotary Club since 1993.

Vora Financial was voted "Best Financial Services" for the Best of Flagstaff 2010 and has recently been featured in the April 9, 2012 issue of Forbes Magazine in the Arizona Financial article.

Vora Financial office locations include Flagstaff, Sedona, Scottsdale, Prescott, and Peoria.

CHAPTER 10

EIGHT COMMON MISTAKES THAT EVERY RETIREE IS MAKING IN THEIR RETIREMENT

BY JIM BYRD

In conducting in-depth planning, you have got to look at three areas of tax planning, investment planning and legal planning. And in doing this planning with people, I have found that there are eight common mistakes that every retiree is making in their retirement.

What I found is that many retirees throughout this country wake up every morning worried about their money and it is not uncommon for the typical retiree to unknowingly throw away thousands of dollars every year through unnecessary taxes and expenses. It is not that they are ignorant, they aren't aware that it is happening and you can't fix something if you don't know it is broken. I found several different common financial mistakes that retirees routinely make with their finances.

#1. <u>**The first mistake**</u> is thinking your tax preparer is a tax planner. This is a very common mistake and one that can cost you each year. It is not time to do a lot of planning at the point when you see your tax preparer during tax season. Your CPA or accountant simply is doing his best to get the right numbers in the right boxes and make the IRS happy. This is the key question, does your accountant call you in May or June to schedule a time to review your tax return line by line and make certain that you are taking advantage of every tax opportunity you can?

Most CPA's do not do that. Why not? Because they are tax preparers not tax planners. Tax planners review your return annually and provide guidance as to what moves to make to improve the numbers the next time around. They do it every year as a matter of course, not just when asked. I have found some common areas on the tax return where people may be paying more to the IRS than they have to. First, it is tax on phantom income, paying tax on income that you don't use. You can actually look on your tax return and see this. Taxing Social Security income, you have already paid tax as it went into the system and now you have to pay it again as it comes out. There is double tax on IRA distributions. There is phantom tax on municipal bond interest and, you know, this was supposed to be tax free! There is tax on non-retirement income accounts, which can often be structured to be 90% tax free. These are just some of the areas where we have found mistakes that people are making on their income tax returns and most of the time, they are not aware of this.

#2. **Number two** is investing as though you are still working. I think this one would top our list. If you are like most people, during your working years, you invested for your future retirement through some type of retirement plan like a 401(k) or 403(b). In most cases, these plans had a menu of investment choices and the menu was probably comprised of a variety of mutual funds and stocks. You could select a stock fund, bond fund, some type of money market or interest-bearing fund or even invest in company stock, sometimes at a discount. Think about this structure for a moment. Your plan was probably with a large financial company like Fidelity or one that is similar and you probably interacted with this company for 20 or 30 years and have become very familiar with this institution. Then you retire. What did you do? If you are like most people, you made few if any changes in your portfolio. At the most, you may have positioned more money in bond funds and less in stock funds but odds are good that you didn't even do that.

Retirement represents a fundamental change in your life and doesn't it make sense that your portfolio should fundamentally shift as well? Going from one mutual fund to another doesn't cut it. It is like buying the same car but in a different color. A Chevy is still a Chevy regardless of the wrapping. You are retired now and it is time to look at your investing in a whole different light. What was appropriate for building a portfolio while you were working may no longer by appropriate now that you are preserving and distributing in retirement.

#3.<u>Number three</u> is not protecting your nest egg from significant market drops. I am seeing people come in every day and they are worried about losing money in the market. They are not aware that there are safe alternatives out there. Have you ever heard of the rule of 100? The financial rule of thumb is taking your age and subtracting it from 100. The result tells you how much of your portfolio should be at risk. To put that into perspective, let us say that you are 65 years old. If you subtract 65 from 100, that is the amount (35%) of your portfolio that could be placed in a higher risk fund. The other 65% should be invested in safe money, but it could vary based on each individual.

Instead, take the 35% and put it into safe money. I find there are a lot of discrepancies out there; a lot of brokers don't understand what "safe" money is. An example would be bonds. Bonds are not considered as safe as people were once lead to believe. Bond Funds do not mature so rising interest rates would cause bonds held in the fund to fall, negatively affecting total return. Also, some of the fixed index funds are now showing disfavor with brokers. Look back at the market, particularly those nasty years of 2000 – 2002 and the 1½ year stretch of October 2007 through March 2009. A lot of people lost a significant amount of their portfolio. They were scared and didn't know what to do. The fact is they have less time to earn it back! So what is safe? What we may have been told was once safe may not be safe anymore. Bonds, corporate stocks, utilities are all not as safe as they used to be; however, an independent financial planner can provide you with advice and alternatives.

#4. **Mistake number four** is not guaranteeing your basic income needs. This is probably the most heartbreaking mistake you can make. So let's imagine you are cruising through retirement, not a concern in the world. You do what you want, when you want. Life is good. Then the unthinkable happens. The economy turns, the market plummets and your retirement portfolio is evaporating in front of your eyes. And to compound matters, you are also taking money out at the same time. What happened? Considering you have a higher chance of being hit by lightning than winning $500,000 in the lottery to fund your retirement, you realize that there is a serious need to become realistic about your retirement planning.

When it comes to your retirement income, it shouldn't matter what the current market conditions are. Your income should be guaranteed and come to you for life. So, exactly how do you protect and guarantee your retirement income? You simply put enough money into a guaranteed product that will deliver to you a base level of income that you need for retirement. It is fine to use assets for extras in life but your base level income needs to come from these guaranteed products.

There are safe vehicles available that will guarantee lifetime income without compromising your principal. Independent financial advisors whose main focus is on retirement planning are very familiar with these products. Do not confuse Independent advisors with stock brokers as they are market driven and do not understand what vehicles constitute "safe" money. I am seeing people every day who are trying to fund their retirement with traditional stocks, bonds and fixed income markets and they are losing money. I call it thinking outside of the box. You have got to look at something different that focuses on retirement planning through an independent financial advisor.

#5. **Number five** is thinking your traditional IRA or other retirement account is always a good thing. I remember when IRAs were introduced in the '80s and how popular they were as a retirement savings alternative for people who wanted high interest and a tax shelter for their retirement savings. But as you know, every dollar you take out is taxed and withdrawals often force you to pay more tax on your Social Security income. You are required to take withdrawals at age 70 1/2 whether you want to or not and all growth in your account increases your future tax liability. The idea of being in a lower tax bracket at retirement no longer holds true. The tax shelter that you use to build your retirement turns into a perpetual tax liability once you do retire. In my opinion, it is the worst asset you could leave your surviving spouse from a tax perspective.

#6. **Number six** is not paying attention to all of the portfolio costs. The investment world is full of hidden expenses. Mutual funds top the list but they are certainly not alone and it doesn't matter where you invest your money. Odds are good that you are paying hidden fees and expenses that you may not realize. There is a good article on this that was put out by *Wall Street Journal* in 2010 talking about mutual funds and the hidden costs. It shows that the hidden fees in mutual funds are often the same as, or more than, the fees that they have to disclose. Hypothetically, if you have a mutual fund that shows a 1% annual fee in the prospectus, you could be paying 2% after accounting for the "hidden" fees.

Let's put in real numbers so we can see what that means. If you had $500,000 in a mutual fund portfolio with a 2% fee, it would cost you $10,000 a year. If you hold that mutual fund for 10 years, it would cost you $100,000 in fees. To those who had significant gains that would be okay, but what if you didn't make anything? You still have to pay the fees regardless of any gains or losses. But don't get the impression that this only happens to mutual funds. You'll find the same thing going on with closed-end funds, REIT's, variable annuities and bonds. Big games are played with bonds when you buy and sell them.

While an investment portfolio is a great way to build wealth, many investors are unaware of the variety of fees that are part of just about every investment one can make. When was the last time you've had a truly objective analysis on your portfolio expenses? Don't you feel as though you deserve to have this information? That is just one of many services we offer to our clients.

#7. <u>Mistake number seven </u> is not knowing how much liquidity or how much money you actually need in retirement. Financial media tells you that you need liquidity during retirement, so this mistake isn't your fault. Much depends on age and what your current assets will allow as well. It used to be that a safe withdrawal rate was 4% to 5%. However, with the current economy, those rates are decreasing to between 3% and 4% and could be set to decrease even further as the state of the economy declines.

There are three features in all investments that you must consider. They are: Safety of Principal, Growth Potential and Liquidity. What does this mean? Well, it means that every investment option out there gives you two of the options at the sacrifice of the third. You must recognize that you have a trade-off.

For example, a mutual fund is liquid and it has growth potential but how much safety from market loss does a mutual fund provide? None. On the other hand, a bank CD provides safety from market loss and is liquid even though there is a penalty to liquidate it. But it is liquid none the less. However, a CD has very little growth potential. So, there is a trade off...

So which of these features should a retiree give up? The financial media says you need liquidity but you also know you need safety from market losses. So, does that mean you have to give up growth potential? Before you do that, think about why you need liquidity.

Let us imagine that you have $500,000 in your retirement portfolio. Ask yourself, how much of your portfolio value do you really need to access at any single point in time and what do you need it for? If you're like most retirees, you want income. You may like the idea of protecting your core nest egg and living off the earnings it generates. In fact, a lot of the people want to preserve their principal for their heirs and their children.

My years of working with retirees have taught me that they want more than their regular income for three types of circumstances. They want to purchase something sizable, normally a new car or maybe even another home. Retirees want to help their children out with college funds or a financial crisis. Unexpected healthcare costs generally increase as people get older and it is the #1 need for liquidity. Your core nest egg is money that you don't need to live on. Once you recognize this, you can sacrifice liquidity to some degree so you can enjoy safety of the principal and more growth potential than you otherwise would not have realized. I educate people that there are very good products out there offering safety and high returns. You need to work with a financial planner that is not just market-oriented but can look at other alternative products and vehicles that can give you a guaranteed lifetime income.

#8. **Mistake number eight** is not utilizing the benefits of life insurance. Americans are living longer than ever before. Health care costs are rising including long term care costs, but only 50% of Americans have long term care insurance. What if you could take your "liquid" money that is in an account earning a low interest rate and provide life insurance and long term care insurance without any out-of-pocket cost? The "new" single premium whole life insurance policy will allow you to deposit a single amount into the policy leaving your principal liquid. It earns a minimum of 2% interest rate and is indexed to the market, currently paying 5% tax deferred. You will receive for your deposit a health benefit that can be used by the beneficiaries to pay taxes on an inherited IRA, estate taxes or provide extra needed income for the spouse. It also can provide a long term care benefit up to $7,500 a month depending on age and the amount of money deposited. All proceeds go to your loved ones probate and federal income tax free!

I always tell my clients that procrastination is the thief of your tomorrows and you can't fix something if you don't know it is broken. Unfortunately, most people spend more time planning their vacation than they do planning their retirement. In this economy and this environment, you have got to think differently.

About Jim

Jim Byrd is a fee-based Investment Advisor Representative and owner of Safe Harbor Financial Services. A fee-based advisor is paid to provide non-biased options on products, strategies and tax solutions. He is currently enrolled in the Charter Financial Consultant Course (CHFC). Only the top 1% of advisors in the country acquire this designation, which represents enhanced education toward retirement planning – enabling them to better assist clients to reach their retirement goals.

Throughout his career, Jim won numerous management awards and other various awards such as: Leader's Conference, President's Conference as well as industry honors including Top of the Table Million Dollar Round Table and Court of the Table. Jim has also held a number of positions with civic organizations including: President of Airport Metro Kiwanis, President of Mobile Association of Life Underwriters, President of General Agents and Managers Association, Chairman of the Board and Ambassador of the Year for the Eastern Shore Chamber of Commerce. Safe Harbor Financial also has the honor of winning the Small Business of the Year award for 2012.

Safe Harbor Financial Services, LLC is a member of the Better Business Bureau and the National Ethics Bureau.

You can find more information about Jim on Facebook or hear him on his weekly radio show on WABF 1220 AM and Talk Radio 106.5 FM. You can also see him on Fox 10 TV, "Studio 10" every other Thursday, between 8:00 and 9:00 a.m. or you can watch his shows on www.fox10tv.com. Click on "Studio 10" then "Dollars and Sense".

For more information, please visit our website: www.safeharfin.com
Or email: jbyrd@safeharfin.com.

CHAPTER 11

THE SEVEN THINGS DEPLETING YOUR RETIREMENT NEST EGG

BY DON B BERGIS & JARED M ELSON

What comes first: the chicken or the egg?

Well, the way we see it, in the world of retirement, estate and investment planning, it's not a matter of what comes first, it's what comes last that matters most. And in today's world, too often we see people whose nest eggs come first, followed by a lo-o-o-o-ng list of takers and taxes that leave you as the very last person on the list.

Let us introduce ourselves. We are Don Bergis and Jared Elson. We are business partners, friends, and together we are Regent Wealth Management. We have known each other 30+ years and have more than 20 years of combined experience in this field of retirement financial planning.

But let's get back to you.

Planning for your retirement may seem overwhelming, unapproachable, or downright impossible. Depending on the stage of life you are in, that might actually be the case. But that is where people like us come in.

There are three stages of life when it comes to financial and retirement planning. The first stage is the learning stage where you are in your 20's, basically learning how to invest and trying to save what you can.

By your 30's, 40's and maybe even 50's, you have moved into the accumulation stage—climbing the career ladder, filling your garage with tools and toys, chauffeuring kids to soccer practice and piano lessons. In a nutshell, you are busy, busy, BUSY. It's in this stage of life we often see people making the most mistakes. They don't have enough time. They don't have enough money, so they hand what they do have over to Wall Street. We don't have to tell you how that's been going for the last decade. What we're finding is that after the last 10 years, folks have been adding to and saving in their retirement accounts while they're working, but they're not managing them and haven't gotten real growth to show for it. This time, in theory, should be about accumulating, right? Unfortunately for many, it's been just about trying to stay even.

But we get it. We've been there. Our clients have been there.

When you are in the accumulation stage of life and the market is down, you, in theory, still have time for the market to go back up and recover losses. But once you have moved on into retirement or the preservation stage of life, there is no longer room for your money to fluctuate up and down. You are no longer adding to your nest egg; therefore, you cannot invest with the same mindset you had while in the accumulation stage of life. The last thing you want to have happen is to run out of money before you run out of life.

Ever hear the phrase, "Your lack of planning does not create my emergency?" Well, let's take that one step further. Your poor planning when it comes to retirement, does not just create an emergency situation financially. It can affect your health, your family and their health, and your dreams of spending your golden years in retirement, even your legacy after you have passed on.

Here's a true story.

James Verone, who was a resident of Gastonia, North Carolina, was 59 years old. He had not done a particularly good job of saving for retirement and found himself in the event of not being able to have any reliable income. So he discovered at 62 he could take his Social Security. Well, James wasn't working, he was 59, and he had no means of reliable income. So, he decided to rob a bank.

James robbed the bank and walked outside, handed the money to the guard, and waited to be arrested. He hoped to be put in jail for three years where he would receive a square meal, a safe place to sleep, and consistent care so that at the age of 62 when he got out he would able to collect his Social Security and have health care.

As we say, it isn't the plan that we would have necessarily chosen, but at least it was a plan.

The reliable source of income that James was missing is what we like to call "mailbox money." Back in the 50's, 60's and 70's, the term mailbox money was used to describe the monthly checks retirees received from their pensions, investments or both. While electronic fund transfers have replaced the days of hard copy checks in the mail, the result should still be the same—retirees spending with confidence because they know the money will be there every month.

But it's not the same. Not anymore.

In 1978, companies started offering IRAs and 401Ks instead of pensions. Good intentions; bad results. With the transition away from pensions, employees were held responsible for having to save the money themselves. Very quickly retirement planning and your mailbox money went from being a guarantee to becoming a hope and prayer. When it comes to the preservation cycle of life, you have to have guarantees. No longer did hard working employees have the security of knowing everything they had saved in their IRAs and 401Ks would be there for them when they retired. Yes, it would be there, but how much of it?

That's where our list of the seven things depleting your nest egg come in and how we can help you avoid losing too much of it before it gets to you.

THE SEVEN THINGS DEPLETING YOUR NEST EGG

1. **Taxes, State, Federal, plus the Affordable Health Care Act:** First and foremost, the first thing that comes out of your nest egg is taxes. And it is not news that taxes are going up. But it might be news to some of you that even if you have saved inside a 401K or IRA with pre-taxed dollars, you will have to pay taxes on those when you come into retirement.

Even more surprising to some of you, those taxes that employers and government promised to be "lower in retirement" may very well not be. If you were successful in your career, followed all the rules, and then add your Social Security income with the grand total, you could end up in the same tax bracket you were in when you were working, and pay 35% to 45% or more in taxes. That is why we say 401Ks are not tax-free; they are tax-deferred. If your employer offers a match, put enough in to get it.

Let's also not forget the new Affordable Health Care Act which adds a whole other slew of taxes taken out of your portfolio.

Here's the good news. With a proper strategy and the right products, we have been able to cut those taxes for our clients by nearly 50%.

2. **Fees and/or Commissions:** Let's be real. No one can predict the stock market. No one. The stock market is not really an investment; it's more like a speculative event. Too often we have clients come to us in the beginning of their retirement and show us their portfolio from their accumulation stage of life. Too often we see that they have left their money management in the hands of Wall Street where brokers get paid astounding fees and commissions— out of your pocket nonetheless—to ride the roller coaster with someone else's money. What's worse is that many of these fees are hidden. You don't even know the money you are losing. In this case, we would definitely say ignorance is NOT bliss!

3. **Volatility**— When Ronald Reagan was debating Jimmy Carter on television, Jimmy Carter said at one point, "I don't know why my competitor is telling me the stock market is so unreliable, we've just had the largest daily gain today. The market went up 30 points!" Now that was 1980 but the idea remains—one day it's up, the next day, who knows. Life is a rollercoaster enough as it is, and while volatility may not be as much of an issue during the accumulation stage of life, once you have hit the retirement or preservation stage, you cannot risk riding that rollercoaster. If something goes down 50%, you need it to go back up 100% just to break even. Not being exposed to those ups and downs while in retirement is key.

4. Inflation—It is what we like to call the 300 pound dead pig in the living room. MIT conducts and reports a daily study on inflation. It's more than 3%. If you are on a fixed income and inflation continues to go up but your nest egg does not, in a nutshell, that's a big problem. Your money is going to run out faster than it should. We have strategies that guarantee income and a 2-3% annual income growth. Even if inflation increases to higher than that, our clients say at least they're here 'to live and fight another day.'

5. Medical System—As you near the retirement age, it's also likely that you will be nearing the stage of life where you have more healthcare needs. Let's face it, there's nothing affordable or accessible in the Affordable Healthcare Act. Not only is it doubling the number of people that will have to be served, but general practitioners are leaving their U.S. practices, creating a supply and demand problem. Having access to medical care when you need it will become a tremendous problem. As a result, the medical tourism business is the fastest growing segment of the international tourism business today.

Then there is the issue of long-term care. If you or your spouse have an accident or a long-term illness, where you may need the assistance of a nursing home facility or in-home care, the cost of these services can be tens of thousands of dollars . Even if you have long-term care insurance, the additional costs of that will come off your nest egg.

6. Estate Tax/Estate transfer—Who doesn't want to leave something for future generations? Even after we have passed on and transferred our valued assets onto the people we love most, it is sad to say that the "tax man cometh" anyway. While this is much more of an issue for a high net worth individual, it's still a real problem when it comes to keeping your money for you.

7. YOU—Finally, we get to you. You can be one of the factors that can deplete your financial goals to retire with confidence. It is crucial to have a sustainable plan that is comfortable for the lifestyle that you want to live in throughout your retirement. YOU worked hard to earn it, YOU scraped it together, YOU saved it, invested and planned for it to last you through your later years. When your money finally—FINALLY—make its way into your hands, how will you protect and manage your golden nest egg?

While scary, this list is not to frighten you. It is to arm you with information and motivation to help you make smart choices today. We want to help you to keep more of what is rightfully yours to live the retired life you rightfully earned. When you enter retirement, you are entering it for the first time, the only time. Being financial advisors, this information comes out of experience from seeing these seven things present themselves every single day in our practice. We've seen the same scenario with all our clients and we can tell you, these seven things are fact and this is what happens.

Make sure you have an accumulation advisor that you trust, that you manage them while they are managing your money. Make sure you have a preservation advisor that is making the most out of your nest egg and guaranteeing you your mailbox money every month. Most of all, make sure you are informed, invested and engaged with your nest egg so you can spend with confidence during retirement. After all, the egg must come first if you want a safe, secure and confident future to come first, too.

About Don & Jared

Don Bergis

Jared Elson

Don Bergis and Jared Elson have been helping clients with their financial goals for the last ten years. They take a practical and personal approach with their clients, assisting them with numerous strategies. These various strategies focus on the fundamentals of implementing tax efficient programs, income building, income distribution, and legacy concepts. As trusted professionals, Don and Jared specialize in retirement and estate planning. They believe in thoroughly educating their clients about the advantages and disadvantages of every financial decision they make, and then help them to accomplish and execute their personal financial plan to retire with confidence.

Don and Jared have enjoyed being the trusted authority for hundreds of clients, friends and associates throughout California. Don and Jared are both members of the National Ethics Bureau.

Don is a graduate of Cal Poly University with a successful background in the high tech industry. He was raised in Los Alto Hills, California, and resides in the foothills of Gilroy with his wife, daughter, son and their three dogs. Don enjoys living in the country, horseback riding, fishing, music and reading a good book. He is involved in his church and several community groups.

Jared is a graduate of San Jose University with a degree in Communication and Business. He also has a background working in the high tech industry having spent nearly a decade taking on multiple roles with Yahoo! prior to working as an investment advisor. Jared offers investment advisory services through Global Financial Private Capital, an SEC Registered Advisor. He has lived in the south county area all his life. He was raised in Morgan Hill, California and he and his wife call Gilroy their home. Jared enjoys playing amateur ice hockey, outdoor activities, reading, and spending time with his family and friends.

Jared M. Elson is a Registered Investment Advisor. Investment Advisory Services are offered through Global Financial Private Capital, LLC, an SEC Registered Investment Adviser. Don B. Bergis is not registered with Global Financial Private Capital, LLC. Insurance products offered through Regent Financial & Insurance Services, LLC.

CHAPTER 12

THE RETIREMENT PLANNING BUCKET STRATEGY

BY JACK TEBODA

The shortest distance between two points is a straight line, but some of us sometimes take a more circuitous route. This was the case for me. Here I am, a financial planner for thirty-plus years, but I started out with a bachelor's degree in education.

I thought I would be a teacher in a school system somewhere for a while, then move into an administrative position as a principal for a local high school somewhere in this great country of ours. I graduated from Iowa State University as a scholarship athlete in 1972. In my four years at ISU, I thought about emulating my high school coaches; that education would be a great career path. If it was good for them, it had to be good for me, too.

I got a teaching position right out of college not far from my hometown and dug in, in what I thought would be long career in education…five to ten years as a teacher; the remaining years as a principal.

In my fourth year of teaching, a former baseball coach I'd had the summer of my junior year in high school stopped by to say 'hi' while I was in the middle of teaching a gym class. He asked how I was enjoying my teaching career so far, and also asked if I'd given any thought to a career change. I'd heard rumors that he'd left teaching to sell life insurance, and a career change was not on my radar screen.

So I replied, "Coach, thanks, I appreciate you asking, but I truly love working with these kids. In the time I've been teaching, not one day has ever seemed like work to me, I enjoy it so much." Coach responded with something very profound—he said, "You'll still be working with kids, they'll just be a little bit older."

My wife Babs, who was teaching at a local elementary school, and I had been discussing starting a family, but we were concerned with making ends meet on just my salary, so I joined with coach and began selling insurance part-time. Within two years, my part-time gig paid more than teaching and coaching (knowing teacher's salaries, not a big surprise), so I left teaching and began working full-time in financial planning in 1978.

The industry has seen a lot of changes since that time. I went from life insurance to getting my securities license and selling stocks, bonds, mutual funds, and variable annuities—all wonderful vehicles for people who plan to be working for many years. But I began to realize that they weren't so good for retirees and people getting ready to retire. They didn't have enough time left in their jobs to make up for market losses, and I saw many people devastated by the recent economic downturn. There had to be a better way to plan—and live—a safe retirement with a secure income that would last.

Sometimes the simplest thing on paper turns out to be very difficult in execution. Anyone that's tried to assemble a prefab backyard shed or install a wireless printer knows this.

On paper, you work for a living, earning and saving money until you retire, and then you live comfortably the rest of your life on the pension you got at your job, Social Security and your savings. And…how's that working out for most Americans right now? Pensions have mostly gone the way of the dinosaur and Social Security—who knows?

The way I see it, you worked hard for your money, so when you retire, make your money work hard for you. Too many people put their nest egg in one basket. I recommend keeping your nest eggs in buckets instead.

This strategy takes your money and puts it into several different investments that are designed to grow and pay an income at designated times in a person's retirement. Some investments will pay immediately; others will grow and pay out later, providing a continuous income.

When I meet with a client, we thoroughly discuss their lifestyle, current expenses, projected expenses, current income—everything and anything that will help me determine their future income needs. I also discuss their risk tolerance, because that will help me determine which vehicles I will use for their buckets. Here's how the strategy works:

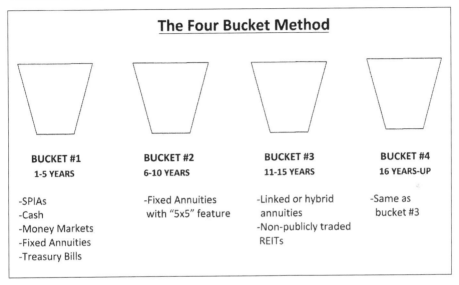

The Four Bucket Method

BUCKET #1	BUCKET #2	BUCKET #3	BUCKET #4
1-5 YEARS	**6-10 YEARS**	**11-15 YEARS**	**16 YEARS-UP**
-SPIAs	-Fixed Annuities with "5x5" feature	-Linked or hybrid annuities	-Same as bucket #3
-Cash		-Non-publicly traded REITs	
-Money Markets			
-Fixed Annuities			
-Treasury Bills			

Typically, I set up Bucket #1 to pay an income for the first five years of a client's retirement. There are many different vehicles that can be used—I like SPIAs (single-premium immediate annuities), but fixed annuities, U.S. Treasury bills, CDs, money markets, cash equivalents (or good old cash itself) can be used, as well.

When Bucket #1 is empty, Bucket #2 kicks in. I usually recommend fixed-indexed annuities, which have a "5x5" feature, enabling them to be annuitized (pay out) after five years, for five years, taking care of years 6-10.

Bucket #3 is for years 11-15 of the plan. Some advisors like to use stocks, but I'm a "safe money" guy, so I usually use fixed indexed annuities with guarantees, non-publicly traded REITs (real estate investment trusts) or other long-term investments that could weather market swings in years 1-10 of the investment. Bucket #4 is more of the same, slated to pay out at five-year intervals. You can use fewer buckets for longer periods of time, and the strategy will still work well; the four-bucket strategy is a personal preference.

Some advisors will set up systematic withdrawals for their clients, where a set amount is withdrawn from one fund continually. Although this is a pretty simple method, it doesn't always take the client's short-term and long-term goals into consideration. Plus, it's easy for clients to understand that each bucket has a specific purpose for a specific time. And, if a bucket isn't meeting its earnings projections, you can take steps to adjust it before it's too late.

A sidebar with the bucketing strategy is that some clients may need emergency funds over and above the income they are receiving. We often get requests for withdrawals from accounts in Buckets 2, 3, or 4, and that's okay. However, we tell clients that a withdrawal may affect their future income adversely. This can be frustrating for both the client and me, such as when it's time to take income from that account and it isn't as great as projected due to the lowered amount in it.

Many people seem to be pessimistic about their longevity, too, and don't realize that the longer they live, the longer they're more *likely* to live. If they're using systematic withdrawals, they're more likely to run out of money than with the bucketing method, where funds are set aside for specified times.

Let me tell you about my clients, two brothers named Jim and Jerry, to illustrate my points.

Jerry had been my client for several years and I was meeting him and his wife for a review. His 92-year-old mother had recently died, and Jerry told me a disturbing story. After the funeral at their hometown downstate, Jerry was at Jim's home. They were sitting at the table, having a cup of coffee, and talking about family matters that needed attention since their mother's passing, when Jerry noticed that Jim had a stack of unopened mail. There were several envelopes sitting in the pile from Smith-Barney. Low-key as always, Jerry asked Jim about the unopened mail.

"No need to open it," Jim said. "It's all bad news."

"That settles it," Jerry said. "You need to come up and see my guy."

So that's how I got to know Jim—I am Jerry's "guy."

Jim lived about three hours away, and we met at a restaurant about half-way in-between. He told me that he had lost his wife about a year and a half ago and, ever since then, he felt like his finances were all scattered. With his inheritance from his mother and his other accounts, Jim had about $250,000 on which to live the rest of his retired life. He also noted that when his wife died, he lost her Social Security of $941 each month (when a spouse dies, the survivor keeps the higher of the two Social Security checks). "I'd like for you to pay me $941 every month out of the $250,000," he said. That, he said was number one on his "wish list."

"Number two," he continued, "I don't want to ever be afraid to open up a statement ever again."

After looking at his statements, it was obvious that Jim had way too much money at risk in the stock market for his age. All the losses mounting up—his wife, his mother, his money—took away all of the pride and courage he'd accumulated throughout his life. Jim felt old and powerless, especially now with more bad news: his daughter's husband had abandoned her and their baby, so Jim now had to take care of them. So his goals included, number three, growing his money and four, protecting it so he could provide for his descendants.

The first thing I did when I got back to the office was design a plan to rebalance Jim's portfolio to eliminate the market risk. We repositioned it so that his assets could work more efficiently and, more importantly, safely for him. We created a four-bucket strategy for him. From the original nest egg of $250,000, we created the following:

Bucket One: $45,000. This bucket will produce an guaranteed income of $1,000 per month for the next five years, replacing the income lost to Jim when his wife died. While this bucket is paying out, it will also be earning interest.

Bucket Two: $45,000. This bucket will grow, untouched, for five years and then, after bucket one has paid all its money out, will begin paying out $1,000 per month for another five years.

Bucket Three: $35,000. This bucket will also be allowed to grow, untouched, for 10 years while buckets one and two are doing their jobs. Starting in year 10, this bucket will pay out the $1,000 per month.

Bucket Four: $125,000. This bucket will produce for Jim a guaranteed lifetime income of $1,000 per month, and has plenty of leeway for inflation and contingencies. Depending on how long Jim lives, this bucket will produce a legacy for his daughter and granddaughter.

Add up what the buckets contain and you will get $250,000, working hard for Jim in just the way he wanted. Using the money's "time value" to produce interest, while at the same time providing income guarantees and making sure that whatever is left in the buckets (after they have finished growing and paying out) is left to his heirs, is a plan that we all—especially Jim—can live with.

On top of all that, because of the way we structured the $1,000 per month payout, 95%, ($950) was tax free. In accordance with IRS rules, the payments represented a payback of initial investments instead of capital gains. Over the first five years, Jim will be paid $60,000, but he only has to pay taxes on $1,800 of that. For bucket two, we adjusted for inflation and 84% of his income from it will be tax free. Not bad!

When my wife, Babs and I were young and raising our kids in Elgin, IL, we used to read to our kids each night at bed time. One of the children's favorite stories was *The Goose That Laid the Golden Eggs.* It's simple for even a child to know that if you have a goose that is providing you with golden eggs, you not only don't want to kill that goose, you want to protect that goose from any and all dangers. That's what the buckets do, and that's why I recommend using them to ensure your nest egg is golden, not rotten.

About Jack

Jack Teboda is president of Teboda & Associates in Elgin, IL, a complete financial planning organization with experience in all aspects of retirement planning. Over the past 30+ years, he has gained the knowledge and experience to help others attain financial independence through conservative strategies.

Fast facts about Jack:

- He has a Bachelor's degree from Iowa State University and a Master's degree from Northern Illinois University.

- He and his wife, Babs, have three children: Blakely Petersen, a personal trainer; Kylee Schroeder, a teacher and Trace, who is attending the University of Wisconsin-Whitewater.

- He is a Certified Estate Planner (CEP) and a member of the National Council of Certified Estate Planners.

- He is a Certified Elder Planner.

- He is an Investment Advisors Representative, a Registered Representative of ProEquities, Inc., a Registered Broker-Dealer, and a member of FINRA and SIPC.

- Teboda & Associates has an A+ rating from the Better Business Bureau. (http://www.bbb.org/chicago/business-reviews/financial-services/teboda-and-associates-in-elgin-il-12007113)

- He is an avid golfer and exercise enthusiast.

- He and his family are active members of the Harvest Bible Chapel in Elgin.

CHAPTER 13

RETIREMENT CHOICES IN A VOLATILE MARKET

BY JEFF MITCHELL

Over the next chapter I'll be sharing some great ideas with you, and many reading this might say to some of these lessons, "Yeah I've seen that before" or, "I know, I know"; but the true exercise of this chapter is to ultimately get yourself to ask:

"AM I REALLY DOING IT?"

At the end of the day, what you're really answering to is *your* Peace of Mind. With the worries of today's stock market, the turmoil in the world, and unexpected medical expenses, retirees must look to two places for improving their Peace of Mind: <u>Their Health and Their Wealth</u>. We need to make sure when you lay your head down on your pillow at night and feel that cool cloth on your cheek, the last thoughts keeping you from a peaceful sleep are those of your life savings. Your life savings should be protected regardless of what the markets do day after day.

I would like to tell you about one of my clients, the Melfords.

We met at one of my educational workshops. They came because they were interested in planning for her upcoming retirement, though he had been retired for about 6 years. They wanted to get a second opinion.

When he had retired, they had gone to your 'run-of-the-mill' financial advisor. This advisor used a combination of "different" investments in order to diversify his portfolio, and help minimize their risk. What they found out when the markets began going down was that these supposedly diversified investments really did not react differently like they were told. Instead, all the investments seemed to be losing money.

They decided they would go to this advisor and ask him about Mr. Client's losing investments. During the meeting they were supposed to be eased by the Advisor's cookie-cutter response, "Don't worry about it, the markets go up and markets go down, but they always come back. You are in this for the long haul aren't you?"

The problem with this is that your long haul has gotten a lot shorter, hasn't it? On-top of this, you are no longer working and contributing to your life's saving. You cannot make up for any loses and as a result they compound any spending from these losing investments.

This couple was 68 and 62 and had worked and saved for over 40 years, their long haul had now gotten a lot shorter. Typically, a couple at those ages, according to numerous studies and the Life Mortality Table, have 20 to 25 more years left. Do they really need to put this money at risk? But do we need to plan for them just in case they live to 95 or 100? Definitely.

The #1 relief to the "Pillow Test" when planning for your retirement is to have a lifetime of income; one you can never out live, even if you live too long.

What should your income plan include?

SOCIAL SECURITY, PENSIONS, AND INVESTMENT INCOME

Social Security is a topic that I could write more than one book on, so I will keep this very simple. Social Security is something that not everyone is entitled to. And with the problems this country is faced with, it might not cover what we think we have been promised. That's why the best plan includes the possibility of both outcomes.

As for your pension, if you or your spouse is lucky enough to have one, we need to be very careful with them in today's financial environment. We need to look at your pension and understand it.

Is it coming from a private corporation, a teacher's association, a state, or federally-funded pension? Which leads us to the next question: How safe or guaranteed are your pension payments and can your pension plans take away benefits that you believe you are entitled to?

I believe planning for the unexpected should be part of your plan. So one way to have that peace of mind and to sleep well at night is to have your own self-directed pension plan. This is a plan you can control, where you decide how it is invested, how much you take out, and how often you would like to take it out. This is a self-directed pension plan that you can make changes to, you can stop your payments and then restart them at a later time. You can change the amount you are receiving, or take a lump sum out if you really need to. And once you and/or your spouse have lived a lifetime on your self-directed pension plan, and if there is money still left in it, it will be passed onto your choice of beneficiaries.

It is very sad to hear the stories of somebody after a lifetime of work, retiring and starting their pension payments, only to pass away after a short time of collecting those payments. In most cases all that money that was put away for their lifetime pension is now lost to any beneficiaries – except maybe a potion to their spouse if they chose that option. With a self-directed pension plan, if you live too short of a time, the balance of all your hard-earned retirement is then passed on to beneficiaries that you get to name.

A lifetime annuity can be sold in many different ways. ***You need to be very careful and understand how it works and all the costs involved!!!!***

You can buy an immediate annuity that pays you a lifetime of income. One choice could be to start your payments right away and guarantee yourself these payments for a period of time (say 10 or 15 years), while another choice could be to take the payments out over your lifetime (stops paying when you die), or a choice could be a combination of say 10 years or your life time whichever is longer. The biggest challenge right now with an immediate annuity is that the interest rate environment that we are currently in is at historical lows. So this would put your payments at some historically low rates too.

There is another choice in payment and that would be with a deferred annuity. There are then basically three types of deferred annuities to choose from: Fixed, Variable, and Fixed Indexed.

THE FIXED ANNUITY

A **fixed annuity** is a fixed rate of return for a fixed period of time. Some may have upfront bonuses, which may lower your rate of return or increase your surrender charges. But, we are currently in a very low interest rate environment, so I think now is probably not the right time to be sold one.

THE VARIABLE ANNUITY

A **variable annuity** is usually a group of mutual funds held in an account tied to an insurance policy. Some may have upfront bonuses, which may lower your rate of return or increase your surrender charges. The one thing that confuses the people that I meet with are all the fees.

I have never met with a single person that has understood what all the fees are and how they benefit the owner. The fees range from 2% to over 4%, and include Administration, Mortality & Expenses, Riders, and Sub-Account Fees.

This would be a good exercise for you if you own a Variable Annuity: call the company, (not the broker that sold it to you, their typical response is something like, "Don't worry the fees are built in.") and ask the company if your policy has Admin, M&E, Rider, and Sub Account Fees and what are they? It is really hard to get a good return on your money if you have 3% coming out every year in these types of fees, regardless of if your account is going up or going down. Remember, if the insurance company is taking 3% out each year and your investment return is 6%, you're only keeping 3%. This may not be the best choice of investments for retirees.

THE FIXED INDEX ANNUITY

A **fixed index annuity** is a guaranteed contract with an insurance company. Some may have upfront bonuses, which may lower your rate of return or increase your surrender charges. They do not invest your premium directly in the market. This allows you to not be exposed to the down side of the market index. Fixed Indexed Annuities are simple in nature, but take care to understand the specifics of any contract because there are certain variables called caps, spreads and participation rates.

For example, if the annual point to point cap was 3.5%, this means if the Market index credit was up 10% or 20% you would receive 3.5% credit. In turn though if the market index is down -10% or -20% your credit is 0, not negative. There are some very good Fixed Indexed annuities out there, but my word of warning would be talk to more than one advisor and ask each advisor which one they sell the most of, why they feel that product works so well, and what are the names of the companies the advisor works with. Then, have the advisors call the companies and ask the questions!!! **This is your Life Savings.**

Some deferred annuities Fixed, Variable, and Fixed Indexed have lifetime income riders. They have all sorts of marketing names to them. Here is what you want to know:

• What is the guaranteed interest rate that the income account will grow every year and for how many years?

• Can I withdraw from my account and will the income account still grow at the guaranteed interest rate?

• If I do take a withdrawal and it does not grow that year, will it continue to grow in future years?

• When I do start using my guaranteed income account at what rate will you pay out?

• Does that rate increase every year that I wait to start lifetime income?

• Will that rate ever increase or will the payout ever increase in future years after I have started my lifetime income payout?

• Will my beneficiaries ever receive my guaranteed Lifetime income account (most cases NO)?

• And last but not least - What is this costing me and how is it figured?

There are some great lifetime income riders out there in the marketplace; you just need to ask the right questions. Don't ever be afraid to ask the questions. If you don't get a straight answer or you get the runaround, get up and leave. This is your life savings, and there are plenty of good advisors, giving good advice for all the right reasons.

Once you are sleeping comfortable because you have a guarantee of lifetime income plan, you need your "Fun Account." This is the second part of your "Pillow Test." This account is for when you have peacefully fallen asleep and now you can dream. What have you wanted or wanted to do, but you thought you could not afford?

We have you covered with a lifetime income, so now lets spend some. The "Fun Account" should be for those vacations you have always wanted to go on, that new car, a kitchen or bath remodel. Or, maybe there are family members you would like to help, college for grandchildren (I know how expensive college is these days), help buy a home, or churches or charities you would like to donate to.

The beauty of the Lifetime Income Plan is it opens up a world of possibilities with the remainder of your life savings. Maybe you just did'nt know you could afford to do this and still have a comfortable life. One of my greatest pleasures is helping my clients to give these financial gifts now during their lifetime, while they can see all the enjoyment these gifts bring.

So take a few minutes right now and grab a piece of paper and start dreaming. Remember these are your dreams, write them down. Maybe over the next couple of weeks, keep a pad of paper and pen next to your bed so when you wake up you can write down those dreams. Then I would ask you to go to your current financial advisor and ask them how they are going to help you "make your dreams a reality."

Now I know some of you give yourself advice, or maybe it is your spouse, or somebody else; if you can't make those dreams real, I will tell you it is time to get someone else to help you.

About Jeff

Founder of Monolith Financial Group, Jeff Mitchell, has dedicated nearly three decades of his life to educating and assisting retirees and pre-retirees with the goal of planning for the protection of their financial future. Monolith Financial Group serves the retirement needs of Northern California residents, and their professionals provide unbiased counsel and comprehensive financial solutions for each client. An advocate for comprehensive financial and retirement planning, Jeff ensures that all components of a client's financial affairs work in collaboration, producing the best possible outcome. He specializes in identifying potential loopholes within financial, accounting and estate plans, and detects where unnecessary monies are "falling through the cracks." Jeff instills in his clients and community a true understanding of the disadvantages of an unplanned retirement and the costly mistakes that could arise from lack of preparation and attention to detail.

It's a well known fact that the U.S. population is aging. As a result, the number one concern among retirees is out-living their money. Thus, many of the financial and estate planning techniques that have been used for years need to be revisited. It has been estimated that if you reach the age of 65, you are likely to live past the age of 85. This leads to making a plan to ensure the wealth you've accumulated remains secure, while not forgetting about taxes and advantages in the laws which can work for you rather than working against you. Monolith Financial Group takes a holistic approach to retirement planning with the security and flexibility to develop a custom retirement portfolio.

Jeff is a member of the Million Dollar Round Table's — Top of the Table — exclusively for the world's most successful life insurance and financial service professionals. Earning both the Certified Senior Advisor (CSA) and Chartered Senior Financial Planner (CSFP) designations, Jeff has shown his commitment to continuing to provide the best advice to his clients. As a fiduciary, Jeff is responsible to act solely with the clients' investment goals and interests in mind, free from direct or indirect conflicts of interest.

To schedule a time to discuss your financial future contact us at: info@monolithfinancial.com or call us at: 800-248-9122 today! www.monolithfinancial.com

CHAPTER 14

CREATING YOUR CELEBRITY BRAND LOGLINE:
HOW TO POSITION YOURSELF FOR SUCCESS

BY NICK NANTON & JW DICKS

So the head of the hip, cutting-edge ad agency was stymied. His client was just beginning to turn around his company's staid image – and was counting on the agency's new group of TV spots to complete its return to greatness.

And the head of the agency was very pleased with the work his creative team had done. He knew the spots would break through the clutter and deliver the message the company desperately *needed* to deliver.

The only problem was that the agency couldn't think of what *words* to use to deliver that message. It had to be a catchy, simple slogan that brought together all the different commercials with a powerful unifying vision.

Now, it was almost midnight and the agency head was beginning to panic. They had to have the slogan in place tomorrow to show the client. So he paced around at home trying to think of something - *anything* - that might work.

And for some reason Norman Mailer came to mind.

He had recently read Mailer's Pulitzer Prize-winning book, *The Executioner's Song* about the murderer Gary Gilmore, who Mailer had gotten to know when the convict was on death row. And he suddenly remembered what Gilmore's last words were before they flicked on the switch of the electric chair where he was seated.

"Let's do it," Gilmore had said.

The agency head remembered those words and how brave they had seemed to him, even coming from the mouth of a ruthless killer. It was a strong statement. And it seemed to him like it was exactly the kind of statement they needed.

But "Let's" was wrong. Everything wasn't a group activity.

It should be "Just." *"Just do it."*

He thought that just might work for Nike.

Believe it or not, the above is a totally true story. Dan Wieden, one of the partners in the innovative Wieden Kennedy ad agency (the ad agency's work propelled Nike to be named "Advertiser of the Year" twice at the Cannes Film Festival, the only company ever to have that honor), was completely stuck for a Nike slogan – until he remembered Gary Gilmore's last words.

SUMMING YOURSELF UP FOR SUCCESS

Even though the words came from a very unusual source, "Just Do It," of course, became one of the most well-known advertising slogans of the past few decades. Trying to sum up the appeal of a brand can be very tricky, difficult business; even though you only need to come up with a few words, they have to be the *right* words in order to convey the uniqueness of your brand to your existing customers and, more importantly, potential leads.

One of the first steps in the powerful process that we call "StorySelling" (a topic that's the basis for a new book we're writing) is to do what Nike did – and find the right words to define your brand. We believe you do that by creating your "logline."

If you don't know what a logline is, it's a short one-to-three sentence encapsulation of the plot of a movie or TV show that's used to quickly sum it up – a little longer than an advertising tagline like "Let's Do It," but just as vital to defining what your Celebrity Brand is all about.

If you ever visit the movie and television indexing site, IMDB.com, you'll find millions of examples of loglines. Here are a couple of examples:

The CBS comedy *2 Broke Girls*: "Two young women waitressing at a greasy spoon diner strike up an unlikely friendship in the hopes of launching a successful business - if only they can raise the cash."

The Leonardo DiCaprio thriller, *Inception*: "In a world where technology exists to enter the human mind through dream invasion, a highly skilled thief is given a final chance at redemption which involves executing his toughest job to date: Inception."

As you can see in both of the above cases, a logline defines the main character(s), the situation – and the challenge. You need to do something similar with your logline to attract customers to who you are and what you're all about.

THE OBITUARY TEST

So - how do you go about figuring out what the right logline is for your brand? Don't worry, we're here to help.

We've discovered an incredibly useful exercise that will help you narrow your story down to its most important elements; it was created by author Klaus Fog and it's called "The Obituary Test"[1]. It's best summed up by the lyrics in Joni Mitchell's classic song, "Big Yellow Taxi" – *"You don't know what you've got 'til it's gone."*

In other words, what would your clients and customers miss the most about you if you were suddenly no longer around? By considering what your absence would mean to the people who buy from you, you can more easily uncover what's important about your story – because you're forced to identify what elements are the most crucial and compelling about your personal brand. This, in turn, helps you immensely in creating your StorySelling logline.

The exercise itself is simple – just write your "obituary," as if you were no longer with us (maybe get somebody to send you flowers to put you

---

1 Klaus Fog, *Storytelling: Branding in Practice*, (Springer Heidelberg Dordrecht 2010), p. 72

in the mood). As you do so, keep in mind the following questions:

- What's the biggest thing your business will be remembered for?
- What about the way you ran your business will be the most missed?
- Which customers will miss you the most and why?
- How were you different from others in the same business as you?

Most importantly, be *honest and factual* when you write your obituary – only write what your customers and clients *would actually know and remember* about you. And don't be embarrassed - nobody else has to see it except you (although it would be great if you shared it with people you trust and who know you well, to get their honest reactions).

You should also put some effort into creating the correct *headline* for your obituary – the first thing customers would write about you, based on your professional image. Because *that* is going to be your "Just Do It" moment.

And after you're done…we want you to write that obituary *again*.

Don't groan, this is our own twist on The Obituary Test and we think it's really the key to making it work - because this time, we want you to write your obituary the way YOU would like it to read. In other words, *don't* write it based on how your customers currently perceive you – but, instead, based on how you *want* to be perceived by them.

Let's use some make-believe obituary headlines as an example of what we're talking about. Let's say you're an investment consultant…and maybe, if your obit. was printed today, it might read:

LOCAL FINANCIAL PLANNER DIES; SERVED CLIENTS FOR 23 YEARS

But maybe you'd like it to read…

LOCAL FINANCIAL PLANNER SAFEGUARDED AND GREW CLIENTS' FORTUNES FOR DECADES

You can see the difference. The first headline is just a description; the second headline *tells a story*.

Here are a few other examples of obituary headlines that would reflect a lifetime of successful StorySelling:

CEO BATTLED CHILDHOOD POVERTY TO BUILD SUCCESSFUL BUSINESS

INTERNET MARKETER MADE CLIENTS INTO MILLIONAIRES

INNOVATIVE DENTIST USED CUTTING-EDGE TECHNOLOGY TO HELP PATIENTS

REAL ESTATE AGENT'S CHARITY WORK BONDED HER TO COMMUNITY AND CLIENTS

You see what we mean? These headlines differentiate their subjects and make them *more* than just another professional. They're known for something *specific* and *beneficial* that they accomplish.

So go ahead. Work on that second obituary. When you're done, go back and take a look at the first one you wrote and compare it with your second one. If they're pretty similar, you're in good shape; if they're very different, however, you're looking at the distance that StorySelling will need to transport your Celebrity Brand.

Now, many of you may have had difficulty coming up with that second obit. You weren't sure what to write – or aren't happy with what you ended up writing. That's not unusual. If you are having trouble coming up with your logline, let's drill a little deeper and see if we strike oil.

DEVELOPING YOUR LOGLINE

Your logline can focus on one of several different aspects of your personal and professional life, depending on what works best for your Celebrity Brand. In this section, we're going to ask you some questions – six of them to be exact. Your answers will hopefully help you identify the key points that make you stand out – and that will attract others to your story.

• **Question 1: What have you done?**

Personal stories of overcoming hardship and/or outstanding accomplishment are always valuable to a Celebrity Brand.

Fans of the legendary motivational speaker and author Zig Ziglar, who recently passed away, knew and loved his personal story: the 10th of 11 children whose father died when he was six and only realized his potential when a supervisor motivated him to greatness in his salesman job.

Similarly, Dan Kennedy, a direct marketing legend, has exploited his background as a copywriting genius who took on the advertising establishment with his famous "No B.S." approach. He tells his "herd" that he's the living proof that there's more than one way to sell successfully.

And, by the way, some people use elements of their backgrounds that don't really have anything at all to do with their current professions. For example, one of our clients is a real estate investment expert in Canada who used to be a policeman; he now positions himself as "The Wealthy Cop," in spite of the fact that law enforcement has precious little to do with buying and selling homes. It doesn't matter though – because people (a) remember who he is because of that nickname and (b) trust him more because he was a policeman.

• Question #2: Who are you?

We're looking for more than your name here – we're looking for personal qualities you possess that make you stand out from others *like* you.

Think of President Ronald Reagan's old nickname – "The Great Communicator." His "brand" was his ability to convey complex information in simple terms everyone could understand and relate to. Think of legendary soul singer James Brown's designation as "The Hardest Working Man in Show Business" – meaning you knew that when you went to see his show, you would see a *show*.

So - what about you makes you distinct? And remember, it could be as simple as something you wear (remember Larry King and his suspenders night after night?).

• Question #3: What's your title?

When Michael Jackson was at his peak, MTV desperately wanted to have him on an awards show. He said, "Sure – if you agree to call me 'The King of Pop' every time you refer to me." MTV shrugged and said, "Whatever" – they didn't care, as long as he showed. Result? People began to call him "The King of Pop" everywhere he appeared and that's how he was referred to in the press when he died.

Even though it's a title *he created for himself!*

So, we guess, the real question here shouldn't be, "What's your title?" – but, "What do you want your title to be?" If it actually fits your situation, as it did with Jackson, you can make it stick. Another one of our clients, Richard Seppala, helps small companies realize more money from their marketing, so he calls himself "The ROI Guy." That's *his* title and that's how people remember him.

- **Question #4: How is your product or service different?**

Another compelling logline you may be able to write could have to do with an innovative product or service that sets you apart from the competition. For instance, we know who Colonel Sanders was because his KFC chain used his "top-secret" chicken recipe to StorySell their authenticity and food quality; similarly, entrepreneur Wally Amos used his personality and his delicious cookie recipe to StorySell his "Famous Amos" cookie line (and what's interesting about both men is that they both sold out to other companies, who continued to StorySell them even after they were no longer involved!).

So how is your product or service different? Is it faster (think of the 5 Minute Car Wash)? Is it bigger (Burger King is "Home of the Whopper," after all)? Is it just simply better ("It's not TV. It's HBO.")? If it really stands out, you're the person who *made* it stand out – and that makes you more impressive in your logline.

- **Question #5: What's your attitude?**

In 1911, Thomas Watson was tired of sitting through uninspiring business meetings – so one day, he just got up, walked over to the easel and wrote the word, "THINK" in big letters on the paper. Three years later, when he started IBM, he remembered that moment and made that word a single word slogan that is still used to represent the business machine giant today (their company magazine is called *Think*).

Almost a century later, when Steve Jobs was ready to take over Apple again in 1997, he wanted a similar impactful statement to define his company – so he launched a multimillion dollar campaign around *two* words: "Think Different." Many saw it as a direct response to IBM's *one* word.

Whatever the case, both men used their basic philosophy – *or attitude* - as the underpinning for their loglines. Even Nike's modified Gary Gilmore line, "Just Do It," is all about attitude. Maybe your particular approach makes you memorable – if so, tap into it.

• Question #6: What do you promise?

FedEx pledges that they'll deliver to "The World on Time." The U.S. Postal Service, in contrast, says, "If It Fits, It Ships." Meanwhile, UPS insists that nobody's better than them at "Logistics." Three different delivery systems all focusing on different benefits - or *promises*.

Many successful brands and businesses have been built on promises – such as the Domino's Pizza chain, with their guarantee that deliveries would come in "30 Minutes or Less" and Wal-Mart with "Always Low Prices, Always."

So - what promise can you (or do you) consistently deliver on? Is it strong enough to be a part of your logline?

These are the main crucial areas you can explore to create your own logline. Some of these areas overlap and you may end up tapping into more than one of them for your final composition (as long as you keep it simple!).

Again, only you can decide what is the right logline for your Story-Selling narrative. Again, however, it's useful to do a reality check by showing your choice to friends and associates, as well as any branding consultants you might employ, to ensure your logline is both authentic and impactful. Remember - just because it works for you doesn't necessarily mean it will work for your customers, so feedback is essential.

Once you've decided on your logline, consider it the foundation of your "brand story." Use it in some fashion in everything you do from a marketing perspective. Legends like Richard Branson and Donald Trump always make sure that everything they do represents their brand; it helps them to continue to convert every new undertaking into a success.

So why shouldn't you?

About Nick

An Emmy-winning director and producer, Nick Nanton, Esq., is known as the top agent to celebrity experts around the world for his role in developing and marketing business and professional experts through personal branding, media, marketing and PR to help them gain credibility and recognition for their accomplishments. Nick is recognized as the nation's leading expert on personal branding as *Fast Company* magazine's expert blogger on the subject and lectures regularly on the topic at major universities around the world. His book *Celebrity Branding You* has also been used as the textbook on personal branding for university students.

The CEO of The Dicks + Nanton Celebrity Branding Agency, an international agency with more than 1000 clients in 26 countries, Nick is an award-winning director, producer and songwriter who has worked on everything from large-scale events to television shows with Bill Cosby, President George H.W. Bush, Brian Tracy, Michael Gerber and many more.

Nick is recognized as one of the top thought leaders in the business world and has co-authored 16 best-selling books alongside Brian Tracy, Jack Canfield (creator of the "Chicken Soup for the Soul" series), Dan Kennedy, Robert Allen, Dr. Ivan Misner (founder of BNI), Jay Conrad Levinson (author of the "Guerilla Marketing" series), Leigh Steinberg and many others, including the breakthrough hit *Celebrity Branding You!*

Nick has led the marketing and PR campaigns that have driven more than 600 authors to best-seller status. Nick has been seen in *USA Today, The Wall Street Journal, Newsweek, Inc., The New York Times, Entrepreneur Magazine* and FastCompany.com and has appeared on ABC, NBC, CBS, and FOX television affiliates around the country, as well as on FOX News, CNN, CNBC and MSNBC, speaking on subjects ranging from branding, marketing and law to "American Idol."

Nick is a member of the Florida Bar and holds a J.D. from the University of Florida Levin College of Law, as well as a B.S./B.A. in Finance from the University of Florida's Warrington College of Business Administration. Nick is a voting member of The National Academy of Recording Arts & Sciences (NARAS, home to the Grammys), a member of The National Academy of Television Arts & Sciences (home to the Emmy Awards), co-founder of the National Academy of Best-Selling Authors, and an 11-time Telly Award winner. He spends his spare time working with Young Life and Downtown Credo Orlando and rooting for the Florida Gators with his wife Kristina and their three children, Brock, Bowen and Addison.

About JW

JW Dicks, Esq. is America's foremost authority on using personal branding for business development. He has created some of the most successful brand and marketing campaigns for business and professional clients to make them the credible celebrity experts in their field and build multi-million dollar businesses using their recognized status.

JW Dicks has started, bought, built, and sold a large number of businesses over his 39-year career and developed a loyal international following as a business attorney, author, speaker, consultant, and business experts' coach. He not only practices what he preaches by using his strategies to build his own businesses, he also applies those same concepts to help clients grow their business or professional practice the ways he does.

JW has been extensively quoted in such national media as *USA Today, The Wall Street Journal, Newsweek, Inc.*, Forbes.com, CNBC.com, and *Fortune Small Business*. His television appearances include ABC, NBC, CBS and FOX affiliate stations around the country. He is the resident branding expert for *Fast Company*'s internationally syndicated blog and is the publisher of *Celebrity Expert Insider*, a monthly newsletter targeting business and brand building strategies.

JW has written over 22 books, including numerous best-sellers, and has been inducted into the National Academy of Best-Selling Authors. JW is married to Linda, his wife of 39 years, and they have two daughters, two granddaughters and two Yorkies. JW is a 6th generation Floridian and splits his time between his home in Orlando and beach house on the Florida west coast.

CHAPTER 15

PLANNING IS THE FOUNDATION FOR RETIREMENT

BY JOSHUA CUMRINE

INTRODUCTION

Congratulations on making it to retirement!

You've worked hard to get here. You've scrimped and saved and done what you were supposed to, and now it's time to relax and enjoy your golden years, right?

Maybe not.

Your advisor has run extensive simulations showing how you can comfortably spend your nest egg without running out. Life will be good; you've got nothing to worry about, right?

Maybe not!

Maybe you've been told that you have an 90% chance of making it through the next 30 years of retirement on the savings you have accumulated. Sounds pretty good, right?

It isn't!

Believe it or not, your retirement years may not be as great as you've been led to believe.

Let me put it this way. Let's say you've been looking forward to seeing Paris your whole life and now you have an opportunity to go. Upon boarding the plane, the captain announces that he expects a smooth ride, with an *90% chance of arrival*. How secure would that make you feel? How many people do you think will stay on that plane? Will you stay on the plane? I bet you wouldn't be able to get off fast enough!

Similarly, your retirement should not be left to chance. What if the stock market crashes? What if we go into another recession? What if the European crisis doesn't improve? What if inflation skyrockets? What if your health takes a turn for the worse? What if you run out of money? If you aren't prepared with a plan that protects you against these things and more, you could end up in a blue vest greeting shoppers at everybody's favorite discount supercenter. But that's not what you signed up for.

"What If." These two words have never brought so much uncertainty and worry. And you wonder why you aren't able to sleep at night.

How about this "What If": What if your retirement plan *eliminated* the "what ifs" and gave you a 100% chance of success during retirement? What if your plan gave you guaranteed income with no chance of loss? What if your plan provided you with a hedge against inflation? What if your plan protected you against market risks and volatility? Would that have any appeal to you?

If you said "Yes," then I urge you to continue reading.

In this chapter, you will learn that it is possible to create retirement security in any economy, eliminating the "what ifs," so you can sleep well at night once and for all.

MEASURING UP YOUR ADVISOR

One of the first things you must do to put yourself on the road to success is align yourself with the right advisor. You might be saying, "Well, I have a great advisor and he's done a terrific job helping me accumulate money." I applaud you for that and I offer my congratulations on making it to the top of the mountain. Now, though, I would ask you, "Does your advisor have a plan for getting you back down the mountain safely?"

You see, many advisors are what we call Accumulation Specialists, whose goal is to get you up the mountain by helping you pick investments and other financial vehicles that will grow your fortune in anticipation for retirement. His is the "buy and hold" strategy – buy an investment and let it grow over the long term. If he's successful, you will end up with enough assets to sustain you through your retirement.

But the trick then becomes how to transition from a "buy and hold" strategy to a "preserve and spend" strategy without destroying all that you've worked so hard for. This is where the Preservation and Income Specialist steps in. His goal is to help you have safety of principal and efficient distribution of assets, thus providing you with an income you can depend on, protection against inflation and market risk, and ultimately peace of mind and a quality lifestyle for you and your family throughout those golden retirement years.

Most people don't realize how critical it is to have safety of principal during their retirement years. Unfortunately, the advisor whose sole focus is on Accumulation cannot provide you with the safety and efficiency that you should have during retirement. If your advisor has built a plan that is based on a "chance" that everything will work out right, that nothing will change, and that nothing bad will ever happen, you might want to think about getting another advisor!

MAKING THE TRANSITION TO INCOME

During retirement, the key to achieving financial security in any economy is to have a dependable income without putting your money at risk.

If you're like most retirees or pre-retirees, you probably have some money saved up in a 401(k) or IRA, some kind of a Social Security benefit for you and possibly your spouse, and, if you were lucky enough to find an employer still offering it, you may even have a pension benefit of some kind. All added up, your accounts might look like a fortune on paper, but the problem now facing you is, "How do I generate income from my accounts without putting the principal at risk?"

Most people would say that you are safe to withdraw a little bit less than what you expect to earn in your account. For example, you may estimate your accounts will conservatively earn 5% per year, so you decide to only withdraw 3% per year, leaving the excess 2% in the account to offset future needs, market volatility or inflation.

But let's consider a few of our "what-if" scenarios again: What if the markets experience a 10% loss the first year you retire? What if inflation rockets up to 10% three years down the road? What if your taxes permanently go up because our government can't get its fiscal problems under control? Could you afford to continually withdraw 3% per year from your account, if one or more of these very possible scenarios actually occurred? Probably not.

What this creates is an "income gap" that somehow needs to be filled.

So, how do you bridge this income gap?

BRIDGING THE INCOME GAP

When building a home, what is the first thing your construction crew builds? The foundation! Without a strong foundation, your home would constantly shift, settle and sink until one day it all comes tumbling down.

So it is with your financial plan. Without a proper foundation to your portfolio you become much more susceptible to the risks of market volatility, inflation, taxes and the various other eroding effects of the economy. This financial foundation is your "safe money" - the critical portion of your portfolio that must be shielded from the aforementioned risks.

A few options for this type of safety include CD's which are backed by banks and the FDIC, fixed annuities which are backed by life insurance companies and some state guaranty funds, and government bonds which are backed by the government.

Now, please understand that there is a direct correlation between risk and return, so in the interest of full disclosure, due to the safety features of these instruments they will often provide a lower rate of return and less liquidity than your traditional investment portfolio. But keep in mind that this safe money is strictly designed to fill the income gap between your current income and desired retirement lifestyle, not provide growth.

So how do we know how much is necessary to place into these "safe money" accounts? That's what your Preservation and Income Specialist is for. He will analyze your existing assets and determine how much needs to be placed into your "safe money" accounts in order to bridge the income gap.

At the end of the day, the objective of retirement income planning is not to beat some kind of market benchmark, but instead to meet your goals and to do it within your comfort level. It's about providing you with a guaranteed income, while at the same time protecting your principal and guarding against the financial threats that may arise in the future.

GUARDING AGAINST FINANCIAL THREATS

Once you have bridged the income gap, you can then shift your focus to the portion of your plan designed to provide you with a hedge against the threats of inflation, rising taxes, market volatility, and more.

In order to protect yourself against the above threats, we need to be aware of what is hindering your performance. Among these threats are expenses within the investments. There may be costs associated with what you currently own, or have previously owned, that can be avoided by simply being aware of what they are and why you're being charged for them.

Surprising to most, market loss is not the only way you can lose money. There are usually many other expenses that you are paying just to own an investment. You may not be able to control the changes in the market, but you can control the investments you own, and thereby control – albeit indirectly – the expenses that are involved in your portfolio.

By reducing or possibly even eliminating these sometimes hidden expenses, you further improve your chances for success.

Take, for example, a popular balanced fund from a large mutual fund company with a good reputation. Looking at the prospectus for this fund we can learn that the expense for this fund amounts to .59% annually. Included as part of this expense are management costs and marketing expenses. However, what isn't being shown are the transaction costs, which are the costs incurred to buy and sell holdings in the fund. With this particular balanced fund, according to personalfund.com, the transaction costs amount to 1.32%, bringing the total expenses of the fund to 1.91%, more than three times the advertised cost shown in the prospectus!

Customers often wonder why their portfolio didn't perform as well as the market did, or why it ended up losing more money than the market did. This is often the reason why.

In addition to these "invisible" fees that are charged, there are other restrictions on the performance of mutual funds in general. We've mentioned the prospectus. A mutual fund's prospectus contains the objectives, investment strategies, fund management, expenses and risks associated with a particular fund. It serves as the governing document for the fund and its managers so that you, the investor, know how your money is being allocated within the fund.

DO YOU WANT A PROSPECTUS WITH THAT?

While having a prospectus is a definite benefit in terms of full disclosure for customers and in maintaining the integrity of a particular fund, you could experience potential problems because of the restrictions that a prospectus puts on the managers of a mutual fund.

Let's say that the market starts trending downward and you have money in a particular mutual fund. In the real world, you can usually move some or all of your money out of the fund into a cash account in order to mitigate potential losses to your overall portfolio. However, the fund managers for the fund don't have that same luxury. They are restricted by the objectives and allocations stated within the prospectus, which usually limits the amount of cash that can be held within their fund, thus hindering their ability to insulate the fund and its portfolio against the inevitable losses.

THERE MAY BE ANOTHER WAY

Most of you reading this may have never known that there is another way to invest besides going to your local broker and putting money into mutual funds or stocks, as described above. This is not to say that you were wrong for doing so. But it's important that you know that there are alternative ways of achieving growth of your money without the expenses, restrictions and risks that are inherent in mutual funds.

One particular strategy we often use is professional management of money, similar to that of mutual funds but with some important differences. One, there are no prospectuses that limit the ability of the manager to invest for both growth and protection. Second, you no longer pay the transaction expenses associated with moving holdings in and out of the portfolio, thus hindering the portfolio's performance. This allows the portfolio managers to be more proactive than the mutual fund managers because the cost of trading is drastically lower. And if a particular holding isn't up to par, it gets taken out of the portfolio and won't be held like it might be in a mutual fund.

When utilizing this type of proactively- and professionally-managed portfolio, a retiree's objective is not to hit home runs of 15-30% per year. Rather, the objective is to stay consistent at hitting singles and doubles in the ballpark of five to six percent annually. This allows you, the retiree, to keep up with inflation while eliminating a lot of the eroding factors that constantly eat away at your money. Not a bad trade-off when considering the risks associated with a full-fledged mutual fund or stock account, especially when you're in retirement and can't afford to suffer huge losses and additional expenses at every turn.

When making the transition from accumulation to preservation, believe it or not, there are investment strategies utilizing the market that may accomplish your goals and objectives without diminishing your hard-earned principal through fees and market volatility. You also could have your portfolio insulated in the event that market conditions get worse, allowing your money to be divested from its various holdings and moved into cash.

You're probably thinking, "Why haven't I found this type of strategy before now?" Chances are, this type of strategy was available to you, but you just didn't know where to find it.

CONCLUSION

When it comes to planning your finances for retirement, nothing should be left to chance. However, when using the wrong financial specialist or the incorrect strategy, that is exactly what you are doing. Most advisors are not going to tell you to leave them to go find a good Preservation and Income Specialist, but in many cases this is a necessary step that needs to be taken in order to "get down the mountain safely," as I mentioned at the beginning of the chapter.

It is up to you to educate yourself on all of the available options, and find that right advisor who will help you eliminate all of the "what if" scenarios and put together a properly-tailored plan designed to provide guaranteed income and efficiently preserve your principal against the risks of the market and unnecessary expenses.

Once you are able to do this, you will be able to relax, enjoy your retirement, and most importantly, sleep well at night once again!

About Joshua

If you have entered into retirement and are still using the same financial plan that got you to retirement, then you may be in big trouble! This is one of the core philosophies surrounding Joshua Cumrine's retirement planning practice. A veteran of over nine years in the financial industry, Joshua Cumrine founded Cumrine & Company in Loveland, Colorado in 2009 and has guided many retirees in developing sustainable financial plans to help them live their ideal lifestyles throughout their golden years.

A retiree's income should not be left to chance through the hope that the stock market will perform favorably over time. As a result, Joshua Cumrine specializes in creating and tailoring innovative financial plans designed with the retiree in mind to create a peace of mind that often does not exist in many post-retirement plans. As an Investment Advisor Representative, he feels it is vital to the families that he works to honor his fiduciary responsibility in always putting their needs and goals first.

Realizing that this particular method of retirement planning requires a paradigm shift in one's mind, Joshua Cumrine takes his select families through a process that allows them to develop an understanding of what the plan accomplishes, why they are making the decisions they make, and how it will ultimately benefit them. In turn, this helps to remove any doubt or confusion that is created through the typical financial plan by other advisors.

At a young age, he had wanted to enter into the field of either finance or law, and while studying Economics and Political Science at Brigham Young University, he developed a strong passion for the financial industry. Since shifting his focus to finance, he has never looked back and has become one of the most prominent retirement income planners in Northern Colorado.

Joshua Cumrine resides in Johnstown, Colorado, a small community north of Denver, with his wife and two sons. He is an avid softball and racquetball player, and enjoys supporting all professional teams in the area. If you would like to speak with Joshua about your retirement situation, he can be contacted at (970) 663-3211 or joshua@totalwealthmanagers.com.

CHAPTER 16

WINNING SMILE

BY KAREN L. ROYAL

[For J.D. and Colleen -- My greatest reason to smile.]

> *"Smile though your heart is aching,*
> *Smile even though it's breaking.*
> *When there are clouds in the sky, you'll get by...."*
> ~ Charlie Chaplin; "Smile"

He looked at me with a blend of pity, apathy and disgust.

I was surprised, hurt and confused.

We just stared into each others' eyes for what seemed an eternity. I wasn't sure what to do next. My feet were simply stuck to the floor and a heavy weight seemed to press down on my shoulders holding me in this moment of bewilderment.

The spell was abruptly broken by the sound of traders on the floor shouting out their bids and offers in a wave of activity. The crash of noise jarred me into movement as my body moved down the hall into my office.

Alone, slowly I sat down trying to absorb his statement. Thoughts racing through my mind as I desperately tried to hold onto one to no avail. Was it true? Have I been fooling myself? Was I really that naïve? Ignorant? Immature? What do I do now? Holy smokes! Where do I go now? All of these questions flew around my head like a tornado while I sat at the centre of the stillness as if viewing the whole interaction from somewhere outside of myself.

And then it happened again. "It" was uncontrollable. "It" held its own power over me and had done so all of my life. "It" is what I knew. "It" is how, or so I believed, I stayed sane, kept life simple and how I progressed. "It" was basic survival for me and "it" was my connection when I felt alone and distant.

Of the forty-three muscles in my face, some relaxed then others contracted. The crease in my worried young forehead smoothed out and there it was, cracking like ice on a river in spring.....the smile. Then the usual chuckle and the experience continued to the pit of my stomach where the clarity and healing lives in me. Whew! For a moment I'd thought it was gone, stolen out from under my eyes.

The time was 1987, Bay Street, Toronto. I'm employed at an interdealer Canada Bond brokerage firm. Young and female, this combination was rare for the times, the business was male dominated. The fellow who I had just met in the hallway was a colleague, he stopped me in my tracks, I with my usual sincere, happy good morning greeting and he with an expression of annoyance. His words were one's I will never forget. Words that remain a deep and great lesson for me. With a gruff growl he stated (as opposed to asked) "What's wrong with you? Why are you so happy?! Don't you know you have no life?! You're poor (compared to him I was)! You're skinny! You're a single mother! No one will ever want you! How can you possibly be so happy all the time??"

What he didn't know and I expect would not understand is that I took great effort everyday to stay positive and "happy." Although almost everything he stated was true, I was determined, against all odds, to not only make it, but also to make it happy.

> *"If you smile through your fear and sorrow,*
> *Smile and maybe tomorrow,*
> *You'll see the sun come shining through*
> *for you...."*
> ~ Charlie Chaplin; "Smile"

Now, don't get me wrong. We cannot walk around happy and delightful and positive all the time. That's just not realistic. And we sure shouldn't fake an upbeat attitude to the extent of annoying everyone around us under all circumstances and situations. We all know that life isn't a stroll through a pretty garden filled with chirping birds and warm sunshine.

However, what is wrong with us that we don't CHOOSE joy? That we refuse to see the positive side, because there are always two sides to everything in this life. Why are we so quick to stay in the misery? The judgmental, the dark side, in our daily life? Why do we choose not to see potential in our experiences? Why else are we here in the first place?

Here in Canada we are blessed with four seasons. Since childhood I could look down the same street from the exact same spot and four times a year see a completely different view. I think it comes a little more naturally for some of us to apply this phenomenon to our everyday lives. It is known that change will happen no matter what we think or how we feel, and we have no choice but to see things in a new light (and temperature!). Within each season is potential, new life and a new view.

Let's look at some successful folks who are well known for their happy, smiling selves. Some folks who see another view. Anthony Robbins has a killer smile. He radiates confidence and intelligence. Tom Hopkins expresses the most sincere, genuine and charismatic smile and even speaks of smiling in his sales champion training camps. The crucial importance of presenting ourselves with a smile, he warns of stepping into someone's personal space and beware the handshake and yet the smile is encouraged because it radiates friendliness and suggests everything's ok. Mother Teresa, wow, every crease that was etched on her beautiful face came alive with her smile. Take a photo of hers, there's plenty online, and cover her face with your finger, except for her eyes. Those are what my father called smiling eyes, a true smile. It deeply bothers me that some women won't smile to their full potential for fear of increasing the lines on their face. It has been proven that smiling makes us look younger! Mother Teresa preached that everyone we meet we should greet them with "kindness in your eyes, kindness in your face and kindness in your smile." With my family I recently watched the very popular movie "ELF" starring Will Farrell. My favorite scene is when he was confronted and asked why he was smiling, his response quickly and innocently was "Oh smiling? That's my favorite thing!"

Look closely at photos of your favorite athlete immediately after a win. Just look at that smile, elation through the pain! And what about the miracle of a baby's first smile, often and sadly the very first few are just gas pains (we should never point that out to new parents) however the muscles are priming for the real thing.

It's funny to me that the world will continuously challenge us and test us over and over again to choose, to smile or not to smile. Consider it theft should someone try to steal your smile. Misery does love comfort. (Speaking of misery, when it does come along get in it, sit in it and roll around in that mud. Taste it, smell it and feel it. Then get up and walk through it and know that you're amazing having learned a lesson and that more lessons will come, a new season awaits.) Stand firm. Protect it because it has a life of its own. Its attributes are both powerful and gentle. Why protect the corners of your mouth curling upwards? How can this make a difference? Why does it matter?

Thich Nhat Hanh, a Vietnamese Buddhist Monk teaches what he calls the Inner Smile and how to significantly reduce negative stress in the body with a simple smile. The man radiates peace with his smile. In his teachings he claims a smile immediately lowers blood pressure, boosts immune system, releases endorphins and natural pain killers and serotonin, lessens the stress of problems and increases the ability to solve these problems, and lastly, extends lifespan.

All of the benefits listed above are pretty substantial, however, I am most elated at the prospect of the effects of a smile on each and every person we meet as we go through our day. We have the power to make or break their day. If we hold a door for someone with a friendly smile, who knows where that'll go? Maybe just maybe that was the lift, the support, the acknowledgement that person needed to support someone else on that day – and they run off and share that little gift with someone who maybe will change the whole world for the better. Some even speak of the incredible effect on any individual who simply witnesses an act of good, of kindness. The witness receives the full benefit as if he or she were the direct recipient of the good deed. So who may be watching also counts in a massive way. Furthermore, in my travels around the world, I discovered that we are able to communicate in any and all languages with a smile. It is a greeting, the beginning of a new relationship and it is a farewell. Additionally, all ages understand that therein rests truth and honesty, all in a smile.

> *"Light up your face with gladness,*
> *hide every trace of sadness,*
> *although a tear*
> *maybe ever so near...."*
> ~ Charlie Chaplin; "Smile"

This is what I call in my sales training our "Natural Tools." These are our automatic and cognitive attributes to bring to the table without effort. They may be being an impressive speaker, fantastic grooming, or a calm demeanor with authority, to name a few, all with an authentic smile. Wow, combine these "Natural Tools" with learned tools and you are dynamic!

Learned Tools may be product knowledge, sales skills, attending seminars, studying successful folks who you look up to and wish to mirror their success and certain skills. Our options today to acquire this information are expansive for example books, CD's, DVD's, online, the information is endless. To enhance retention make sure you engage all senses and smile. A nice trick is to place a pencil or a chopstick in your mouth to engage your facial muscles into a mock smile. Amazingly and according to the Harvard Business Review, forcing yourself to smile can reduce stress. Heart rates of people who were recovering from stress were 7% slower if they gripped a pair of chopsticks in their teeth in such a way as to force themselves to smile, the study shows there are physiological and psychological benefits from maintaining a positive facial expression during stress.

I have worked with so many folks, sales agents mostly, who surprisingly really don't understand this concept of being a happy and smiling individual. Again, I stress not to be overly rambunctious. This actually can do more harm than good. It'd be like attempting a business transaction with the Disney character Goofy (we all have likely met one or two of these characters so you get my point).

Most recently, I've worked with a new sales agent who upon meeting was a very serious, non-smiling person. I made it my mission to earn his trust and initially mirrored his demeanor with sprinkles of upbeat words of support and optimism and of course lot's of smiles. Eventually he began to trust and open up. However, most importantly, he began to show more success in his closing ratio and a wonderful new skip in his step. Of the hundreds of sales people I've had the pleasure of working with over the years, my greatest gift has been not only seeing them succeed, but to also grow within themselves, increase their self confidence and hence the smile. The smile ultimately demonstrates their self confidence and their ability to open themselves up to the unknown. Everything is good and life is great says the smile. There is no hard sell, there is no pressure and there is no underlying desperation.

The following is a checklist of suggestions and reminders for you because sadly, most of us get so caught up in life "stuff" that we'll literally forget to smile as well as how to smile.

1. Keep with you at all times a pencil or chopstick, even write on it that it's your smiling tool. Place it side ways into your mouth everyday, preferably first thing in the morning and bite down gently for a few moments. You'll notice the effect immediately (mostly because you may have family members looking at you with concern over their breakfasts) as you laugh at yourself. It works and what a great way to start any day – however don't run with it in your mouth, better sit to avoid any mishaps!

2. Do a mirror test throughout your day. Smile big and with your whole face, get those eyes smiling. If you do telephone work keep a mirror handy, it's a great old trick to maintain positive energy while speaking with potential clients. If you are a face-to-face salesperson, before going into a presentation use your pencil/chopstick and be conscious of the difference in your initial meetings. It's just so refreshing to meet with a real professional exuding confidence and an original smiling face.

3. Smile instead of saying a word. Test this because it's fun. Smile and nod, smile and shake your head, smile with appreciation. See how you are able to communicate with your smile, we talk too much anyways.

4. Remember that your smile transcends you and everyone around you (and even someone who you don't realize is watching). It's a simple, natural way to help keep you healthy, calm and even better looking! And that we can all use a little more of!

5. Smiling and laughing is contagious. One of my sister's and I enjoy scuba diving. We are highly trained and she has extensive experience. This is definitely a serious sport and not to be taken lightly. That is until we're anywhere between 25 and 100 feet deep in an ocean somewhere around the world and one of us will undoubtedly get the giggles. Seriously, this is not recommended. I have had to look away and hold onto my regulator (breathing apparatus) because I could see her "smiling eyes" and that's all it would take to set me off. It's a sibling thing I

guess, the point is laughter is everywhere and again, I know it's contagious.

"That's the time you must keep on trying,
smile what's the use of crying,
you'll find that life is still worthwhile
if you just smile."
~ Charlie Chaplin; "Smile"

I want to thank all of the people who have made me smile. Some with pride, others through tears and still others through making me laugh 'til I just about "bust a gut" and lastly, those who have stolen my heart and just leave me with a quiet memory and a quiet smile.

Because, at the end of the day all I have is me and my smile. That's all I need.

That's all anyone needs.

About Karen

Karen is best known as an excellent educational and motivational speaker. With high energy, she is dedicated and engaged. She is often referred to as a real, down-to-earth visionary.

Karen's professional passion rests within the energy sector, she foresees a drastic shift as North Americans move into the new age of environmental and economical awareness. Overall, energy has become and will remain a hot topic that demands the attention, and in some cases the immediate action of businesses. It is her mission to clarify, educate and motivate these businesses throughout the region.

It is with a fresh approach Karen's firm moves to change the face of energy supply, generation and conservation. Through transparency, strong ethics and coherent options, Karen surrounds herself with some of the most brilliant minds in the industry to advise business owners so they may move into this new era with confidence.

To learn more about your business' specific market and options and Karen's speaking engagements, you may contact Karen and her team at:

www.NewAgeEnergyPartners.com

Or email: kroyal@newageenergypartners.com

CHAPTER 17

LEARNING AND PROTECTING THE VALUE OF A DOLLAR

KEITH W. ELLIS, JR. & DEREK L. GREGOIRE

Keith Ellis grew up knowing the value of a dollar. As a child, he used to collect baseball cards. Since he knew baseball cards cost money and that asking his parents for the money was not an option, he knew he had to work for it. It was not because they didn't want to give him the money or did not have the $1.50 for the pack of cards; it was because they wanted him to understand the value of work and how to earn money to purchase the baseball cards missing from his collection. It didn't take him long to realize that the cans and bottles scattered about the neighborhood would earn him five cents apiece. Selling bags of locally-grown cranberries to neighbors added even more money to his baseball card fund, and certainly, his toys from last Christmas were worth something; he sold those, too.

When he was 11 years old, he started a lawn mowing business along with his brother; they would push their mowers for miles to mow the lawns within walking distance. For those lawns that were too far to walk to, they had their dad who was always willing to drive them there – and wait in his truck until they had finished. Their parents taught them that each dollar earned mowing lawns was another dollar toward a financial goal they wanted to meet. Most importantly, they taught them that no lawn was too far, and for those that might have been, although they required assistance to get to, they were never out of reach. Through their hard work and parent's guidance, they started to watch the green grass they were cutting turn into the green in their wallets. They worked hard, and they had the baseball cards to prove it.

In the society Keith currently finds himself living in, parents are no longer driving their children to find work. They give their children the coolest toys and the sneakers that all of their friends are wearing – just so their children don't feel "left out." Gone are the days when the team that won the most games during the little league season is rewarded with a trophy; the losers win, too. Keith believes children are being raised in a Blue Ribbon Society and are suffering with Blue Ribbon Society Syndrome. Keith says if he had a trophy on his shelf for each time he lost a game, he'd have a hefty trophy collection. But, he would feel badly about those trophies; those would be the 'loser' trophies scattered amongst the trophies he was proud of – those that he deserved because he worked hard and he won.

Each person who Keith Ellis takes on as a client has lived a life of determination, hard work, and they have valued their dollars. They are people who are working toward achieving a goal or, have achieved it – Retirement.

Keith states: "It is my job to strategically construct the best plan specific to each of my clients in order to make their retirement work for them. I want my clients to feel like they have earned the trophy they have won."

Derek Gregoire grew up in a family of five in Southeastern Massachusetts. His parents were both hard working; his mother was a nurse, his father a plasterer. What he learned at a young age was to trust and obey God, to work hard, and to be disciplined in all matters.

It was the beginning of the summer, Derek was twelve years old, thirteen maybe. His mind was set on playing sports and getting together with friends just as he had done all the summers before. He was running out the door one day when his dad stopped him. His dad asked him what his plans were for a job. He thought to himself, "A job? During the summer?"

One morning his dad woke him up around 5:30 in the morning and asked him again, "Derek, what are your plans for work this summer?"

When he responded to his dad that he didn't have plans to work, he told him to get out of bed, get dressed and meet him in his truck. So, Derek got dressed and met him in his truck, just as he had requested.

His dad silently drove him down the street and pulled in to a nearby farm. He couldn't imagine what they were doing at the farm. His father told him to get out of the truck. "Get to work," he said. Derek knew he was serious, that he meant business, and that questions, gripes, or hesitation would not be tolerated. He went to work bailing hay in 97°F weather until twelve hours later, when his father returned. He went home that night with blisters on his hands and cuts covering his arms. He was completely exhausted.

He did not return to the farm the following day. Instead, he woke himself, got dressed and went out to obtain a summer job - on his own. He had learned a tough, but life-changing lesson that day at the farm; his father never had to question what his plans were for a summer job again.

Derek was always taught to work honestly and hard, to do the right thing, and just like the bible taught, treat your neighbor as you would yourself. If he wanted something, he had to work for it. His parents guided him in the direction he needed to go in order to "earn" the things he wanted, rather than "get" those things. He cannot thank his mother and father enough for the strong foundation they instilled in him early on in his life.

Derek Gregoire's dedication to his core values shines through the effort he puts in to personalizing each of his client's experiences with their own financial growth.

Keith and Derek began SHP Financial in the fall of 2003. Based on their core values and beliefs, they have built SHP Financial to what it has presently become.

In today's marketplace, we are seeing a shift in philosophy. People want to secure their retirement income; they want their retirement income to be guaranteed. People want to make sure they are taken care of for the rest of their lives. With pensions going the way of the dinosaur, it is now the working person's responsibility to create their own retirement wealth and income. So, now that this responsibility falls on the shoulders of the majority of Americans, people have to become creative in order to achieve the income that they desire; at least that is what they think. What people need to look at is the past decade. We are seeing a fundamental shift away from a rigged system, Wall Street, toward guarantees.

After 2002, Derek and Keith had people coming to their office who had enough of external circumstances; circumstances such as U.S. problems in foreign countries, Wall Street greed and problems within the United States of America. They had no control over these circumstances which were affecting their retirement, their assets and ultimately the income they would be receiving, to be able to cover living expenses once they did retire. They found themselves questioning people about why they were putting themselves in a position where they could lose so much of the money they worked so hard to make when they were so close to the finish line – Retirement.

THE BRAINWASH

It is the job of Wall Street's brokers to keep money on Wall Street and they are paid handsomely to do so. Many brokers do not want to talk to their clients about alternatives off Wall Street because they don't want to give their business to someone else, they want to keep it; to those brokers, you are a dollar sign. So, Derek and Keith ask their clients, "Is investing in Wall Street right for you? Or, for them? Are they lining your pocket with gains, or are they lining their pockets with commissions and sales charges?"

The people that Derek and Keith were meeting with in 2003 were brainwashed by the previous 20-year bull market run. This was a bull market run that was unheard of – and is something that had never happened before in the Stock Market's history. There is a great possibility that kind of market run will never happen again. American people lost huge chunks out of their retirement accounts; some had to go back to work, and many had to alter the amount of income they could draw from their retirement portfolios.

People are willing to gamble only so much of their money at the Wall Street 'casino' but, at the same time, they would pay even more for peace of mind over their future income, and that creates a major disconnect. Many people are financially uneducated. They have never been taught how to remove money from risk and place it in a vehicle that guarantees income. They have listened to their broker repeatedly tell them, "Don't panic. The market will come back." They are probably right in saying the market will come back; however, the issue is not if, it's when. How long can one wait? Income is the foundation of any retirement. The Stock Market and Wall Street definitely have their place but, Derek and Keith's philosophy is that you have to first secure your income for yourself, and if applicable, your spouse's future.

Through experience, Derek and Keith have learned that there are certain measures or steps that can be taken to give people the peace of mind that they are looking for in their retirement years.

Here are their top five tips on:

HOW TO MAKE YOUR RETIREMENT INCOME AND FUTURE STABLE AND SUCCESSFUL:

1.) Make sure your income is Guaranteed, Guaranteed, Guaranteed: If your current advisor is unwilling to guarantee your retirement income regardless of what occurs in the market, you should probably start looking for one who will. This cannot be stressed enough. Your income MUST be guaranteed. For example, in September 2008, they had a client who wanted their help in turning his current $1.5 million into $100,000 annually for both himself and his wife. They did better than that. They created a plan that would guarantee $102,000 annually for the couple. He left their office excited to implement their plan, but when he spoke with his financial advisor, that financial adviser convinced him to "ride it out."

In January 2009, three months after the market crash, he walked back into their office. This time, he came in with $1 million, a $500,000 loss from his first visit just a few months previous. His ultimate goal was to secure an income of $100,000 annually for himself and his wife but, because he "rode it out," he and his wife would only be receiving $75,000 annually; they were forced to take a $27,000 annual loss. When you plan for retirement income, you need a distribution specialist not an accumulation specialist. His current advisor had done a great job getting him to where he was financially, but the time was now to implement a distribution plan.

2.) Make sure you have a **spousal fallback** retirement income plan: If you are married, make sure the income plan that you establish will carryover to your spouse - not the account value, but the income – the account values will go to your heirs. Derek and Keith have seen so many retirees have a plan set in place that does not account for loss of income due to death, or the income will not continue to the spouse and there is nothing set up for that measure. They have had many clients within their own practice who believe that when their spouse passes away, the surviving spouse's income needs will be reduced – since the financial necessities will reduce from the needs of two people to that of one person. That is certainly a possibility, but, in their experience the income need stays.

3.) Make sure your income plan provides for Health Care. Raise your hand if you want Long Term Care Insurance!! What's that? …No hands? People do not want LTCI for different reasons. They do not want to believe that they could be in a position to have to use LTCI; it is expensive, what if you never use it, etc. However, for most people, it is the one true thing at this point in your life that can wipe you out. The cost of care is expensive and is not going to come down. As much as we all do not like to talk about it, for 60% of us it will become a reality. We have homeowner's insurance and car insurance, so why not Long Term Care Insurance? Why are people willing to risk it? I think a lot of it has to do with the insurance companies – what they have done and what they have to offer. You want to make sure that your retirement income plan includes Long Term Care protection. It is something that can help protect both the health of the 'well' spouse and the rest of your assets, so the 'well' spouse can continue living the lifestyle they were accustomed to living before the illness hit.

4.) Make sure your income plan has Inflation Protection. Keith used to drive his 1996 Honda Civic to college with a full tank of gas that cost him between twelve and fourteen dollars. Remember those days? That same tank of gas would now cost upwards of $60.00. What they are saying is that costs of goods and services that we all depend on and need consistently go up in price. Your income plan should reflect inflation and be prepared to deal with the cost of these goods and services rising. They have reviewed numerous income plans that do not account for inflation. That is a huge pitfall because if your income does not keep up with the cost of living, it is more than likely that you will have to adjust the way you live in the future – most importantly, your retirement years.

5.) Make sure your income plan benefits you and your heirs tax-wise both today and into the future.

Following these five simple steps will allow you to enjoy your retirement and will guarantee you the lifestyle you wish to live in the future. These, if followed correctly, are the steps that will eliminate the fluctuations in your income and allow you the ability to enjoy what you have worked so long and hard for – Retirement.

About Keith

Keith W. Ellis, Jr. has been with SHP Financial since 2003 as one of its founders. Keith earned his Bachelor's degree from Franklin Pierce University with honors. He is one of the managing partners at SHP Financial, and is responsible for all financial services, including their conservative investment solutions. Keith's philosophy on retirement is different than the traditional line of thinking. His conservative solutions have allowed his clients to enjoy what they have worked so hard to accumulate, and allows them to live a stress-free retirement.

Keith is a leading contributor for the *Money Matters* radio and television show. He can be seen regularly on WBIN, and heard on stations like WBZ, WXTK and WRKO. He also works with the Plymouth Council on Aging, Plymouth Area Community Television (PACTV), Cranberry Hospice/Jordan Health Systems and the Dana-Farber Cancer Institute.

Keith recently shot a segment for the new season of the Consumer Advocate, which will air on ABC, NBC, CBS, and FOX affiliates around the country later this year. He will also have upcoming publications in *Forbes* magazine, *The Wall Street Journal, USA Today* and *Newsweek* later this year.

Keith currently resides in Sagamore Beach, Massachusetts with his wife and two children.

About Derek

Derek L. Gregoire co-founded SHP Financial in 2003. He is one of the managing partners and currently serves as head of the Client Income Planning Committee. He is passionate about helping clients plan for their current and future income goals in a financially-conservative manner.

Derek graduated *cum laude* from the University of Massachusetts at Amherst. He is active in both the local Congregational church and the local community—working with organizations such as the Plymouth Council on Aging, Cranberry Hospice/Jordan Health Systems and the Dana-Farber Cancer Institute.

Derek is a current member of the Million Dollar Round Table, and he was recognized by *Boston Magazine* as one of their "Top Wealth Advisors" in February 2010. He also is a member of NAFA.

Derek is also a regular contributor to the *Money Matters* Radio and TV network. He can be seen regularly on WBIN, and heard on stations like WBZ, WXTK and WRKO. Derek recently shot a segment for the new season of the Consumer Advocate, which will air on ABC, NBC, CBS, and FOX affiliates around the country later this year. He will also have upcoming publications in *Forbes* magazine, *The Wall Street Journal, USA Today* and *Newsweek* later this year.

Derek currently resides in Lakeville, Massachusetts, with his wife and two children.

CHAPTER 18

HOLISTIC FINANCIAL DEVELOPMENT™ – BACK TO BASICS MAKING THE IMPOSSIBLE POSSIBLE!

BY MALIN CARLBERG

With failing bank structures, governments with short comings, and old fashioned, out-of-sync legal systems, the world DID seem to come to an end in the last years of finance and business. Many were those who saw their "normal" life go up in smoke, and suddenly they had to learn new ways to handle money, business and the economy.

Ironically, the different levels of financial disasters have also shone light on the sometimes less than favorable human character and the way we put legal and financial systems in play – just to maintain hierarchic power structures...

One and a half years ago, I got a request for certain high level connections, because there was some institution that needed a personal introduction to be able to give financial aid. To make a long story short, this became a very complex and difficult procedure for something that, on paper, seemed very straight forward. Financial aid was simply not supported legally or financially. Neither was it easy to put something new on the table when history rested as a shadow over every new idea or attempt – ringing ..."that cannot be done," ..."if I do something new I may lose face," ..."we have never done anything like that in this region before," ..."my great granddad's cousin was on the opposite side in 1829..." ... and on and on.

This was not the first time I ran into these types of problems while trying to bridge politics, the governmental sector, local councils, small business and humanitarian and community projects. It was like the going back in history and battling dinosaurs and cave animals... simply impossible! However big the need was, and still is, it is evident nothing could be done without a whole new way of thinking – whatever that would be...

Doing the math in Europe alone, it was about 24M small and often family-run businesses struggling, and about 20M unemployed, banks struggling. And there were emergency budgets going out to the social sectors from EU to several countries in the form of benefits – putting an enormous stress on all other sectors.

Technically, that meant that with just a <u>minor</u> adjustment and with the right type of help – if those companies could stay afloat and maybe even employ just one more person – the whole issue would go away.

Far easier said than done, it started the idea for something new – holistic financial development – going to the root of the actual problems instead of putting a band aid on it short term every time it is out of balance.

The list of obstacles was never ending:

- Accessing financial resources
- The average person's understanding and knowledge of finance
- Institutions capability and willingness to execute
- Politicians being more worried about their office than doing the right thing
- Bankers more concerned about their bonuses than what the projects were there for
- Lawyers either not knowing what they were really there to do or tied down by dysfunctional laws
- Business and asset owners too greedy to be concerned about how to be able to help
- Normal people unaware of how to even access resources and what to do with them

This list can go on forever and the sea of complications is without bottom and as complex as we could ever imagine. Dishonesty and empty talk become daily confrontations and disappointments. When you get to the bottom of things, the most evident problem is not lack of jobs or things that have to be done – but the lack of cash and the lack of mature management of it.

The second crucial component is the character and integrity of people. And the first usually one way or the other leads back to the second.

This topic can be a whole book in itself and the truth is we easily blame leaders of all sorts, but we all have the leaders we accept, tolerate and many times actively chosen. It is simply easier to follow than to be our true selves.

How we do ANY business is really OUR business. Everything counts, everything rubs off and everything comes back in one shape or another. When we start to understand this in real terms and our daily hunt to avoid responsibility or the guilt and shame if we fail that we give each other – it became painfully real how important this was. No matter what.

So where did we start? We started with product and service-based businesses that had a record of being stable small businesses, but had been (one way or the other), bought up by larger business groups, which, when the crisis hit, started to fall apart. Depending on jurisdiction, we talk foreclosures, bankruptcies, distressed finances, etc.

Secondly, we looked at how they got there? Or more importantly, WHO drove them there and who didn't.

The whole thing with holistic financial development is that behind each distressed situation there is a personal story and real people. Many times people for whatever reason intentionally or unintentionally end up where they ended up. Suddenly, they are let go or are offered half the packages they had before – and in a matter of minutes, whole lives have changed – but for someone else, it is just another statistic.

Life driven by guilt and shame is among the most painful to live, but also very often less productive than what it could be. Once you start trying it, it is quickly noticed that MONEY is not the biggest problem in the world – our psychological triggers are: value systems, beliefs, habits, integrity and self-discipline.

PRIMARY PROJECT FILTER: PERSONAL CAPABILITY - WORK ONLY WITH PEOPLE THAT ARE WILLING TO DO THE WORK AND BE HELPED

No matter the reasons, excuses, obstacles and hindrances – there are always people who will raise their hand and show up. They are honest with themselves, they are realistic with their situations and they never blame anyone one else.

That is our first filter – selecting who to collaborate with. Not what security they can offer, not how much they have in the bank or what they learned in school 20 years ago and won't remember any way. It is their capability and willingness to do what it takes today and tomorrow, ... to go through the tough times, ...to persevere, ...to keep learning and improve their responsibility and accountability. In other words – who gets things done.

Through this period, we sometimes comes across whole teams with these qualities. That is when it moves from a holistic and organic to level up to – development. A functioning team whose job has just been let down only on the financial side by possible weak senior management is the most rewarding to work with. Good solid workers who knows their craft and how to run what they do. All they need is a bit more financial security to be in play again, and more often than not they turn out to be are remarkable resources. And our communities are full of them...

If a team is identified then it comes down to primarily <u>five core principals</u> to evaluate if it is holistically possible to develop and what to develop:

1. FUNCTIONALITY

This is where we normally talk profitability. The holistic view is that all communities aim to have and provide a higher living standard than the minimum for survival. That in itself means there are certain functions and services we expect or wish to have mirroring those values. Obvious examples are clean water and safe roads. Other types can be free lunches and doctors for all children in school. That can be run as a profitable business or not – point is, it has high functionality in that community.

Under this point falls also the purpose of development and innovation. The conflict between the old and new becomes very evident if we, for example, look at technology. Many other things do not develop at the same speed. Those falling most behind are clearly integrating new communication with old systems for democracy. Sometimes development means letting something go or give it a new function. Embracing new and more ways to do something is the fastest way to new development, no matter if we talk football or community efficiency.

2. SELF SUSTAINABLE ECONOMIC MODEL

All financial restructuring is based on the fact that each project has a source of new finances – either independently or in collaboration with some other type of entity. Not only is this removing the risk factor, but it also engages the other party and allows the team to focus on WHY they do what they do and who they serve, rather than the paycheck or when to go home. It sets the groundwork for good leadership for both executed as well as nurtured. Another example is to have a business or financial model including different types with more or less passive incomes.

Many companies and communities today have many different types of assets unused. Not just people, but also in regards to inventory, property, patents and so forth. With a good alternative type of advisor, these can often easily bring in otherwise unaccounted for, income streams – instead of being neglected and lost.

3. PURPOSE

The right to have a meaningful day is rarely on the agenda anymore. A meaningful day for most people means a day's good work. Despite the economic burden of high unemployment, this means that even if we rely most on commercial jobs, a community should consider the overall type of activities, chores and tasks to be done.

This also includes the use and work of different art and communication forms. Making and nurturing creativity is easily neglected from an overall health aspect together with activities, reducing negative stress and worry.

To this category we also add the right to have the right person in the right place. Purposeful work doubles productivity and projects working with these issues are highly holistic on all levels.

4. TRUTH

The world has become very complex. Gone are the days when people were on the barricades fighting for their rights to vote and so on. In many places today, legally the rights are there, but we still live around old norms and measurements. Today we have to fight for our truth.

The management of funds is obviously the one we are most familiar with. In finance and business, there actually are many times during a transaction when this can be measured. There are also many different ways to handle it and different best practices around the world.

The need for transparency and honesty into all our different levels of financial institutions is crucial at this point. However, what is it worth if the legal system is running behind and will punish a new healthy behavior? Something very important to think about when setting new frameworks and bridging over from old to new generations – that change is positive and not a place to shame or make anyone feel guilty.

5. TOLERANCE

Tolerance in the context of finance refers not just to skin color and handling of minorities.

Primarily it focuses on ALL the things we are silently tolerating every day. Being paid by the hour vs. our input. Environmental impact and consequences. Dangerous environments. Low education. Corruption. Over-production vs over-consumption.

Everyday we are tolerating that things are not done 100% along the way. This principle is two-headed though. One half is what we are putting up with as a community and the other is what we put up with – with ourselves.

Being the most informed generation ever, as well as having the highest living standard and amount of money – how come we tolerate all this poverty and disadvantages? Going to the source, it starts with ourselves. After we feed ourselves, we become comfortable and truthfully a bit sloppy. I am no better than you – but if we want another new world and a new financial model, we have to dare to see and speak the truth – without judging.

A financially holistic project runs for a minimum of 2 to 5 years and with a goal to carry itself in all aspects after that. Constantly keeping an eye on our core principles profit is good, but not at the cost of something else equally important. Less loss is then a better motto at least during a developing period.

Holistic financial development on paper looks easily as some school-girl's idealistic dream, and turning dreams into reality, as we know, is never easy. With the first years of experience under my belt I can calmly advise – this is not something you start unless you have the guts and the courage to look yourself as well as your community directly in the eye.

When all the worse nightmares happen, and you have to face the systems, the institutions, the legals, suffering individuals – and when all those including yourself are under financial pressure, the truth suddenly steps in and unknown leadership talents rise, people come together, resources somehow last longer and magic suddenly happens. Just when you are so tired and think it can't be done. You have done everything you could and it didn't work. When you are beyond tired. Beyond finish. Beyond having any ideas left and you run out of all energy possible ...

Then it sparkles... Something within people – sometimes total strangers to each other – starts to give a helping hand, come together, work around problems, find unheard of solutions, and give encouragement and moral support. Suddenly when you were ready to give it all up, it takes a life of its own and what seemed totally impossible is possible and even done –

Changing the world one project at a time...

....against all odds.

About Malin

Malin Carlberg is an award winning innovator for marketing and international sales management with IBM and former vice president for professional women in Italy, before heading up the Aspasia Group Of Companies and Foundation. She is a financial strategist known for her concepts of Holistic Financial Development™ and My Alternative Banking™, helping companies and organizations to rebuild new holistic and more sustainable financial structures. Her background as a negotiator and deal maker for large institutions, as well as wealth and asset management, gives her a foundation very rare in the business – combining humanitarian work and values with real day-to-day business finance and development, and making all her knowledge and resources available to the public. For case studies and contact please visit: www.aspasiacapital.com .

Ms. Carlberg was born in Sweden in 1973, but operates from Switzerland and works around the whole world. She speaks five languages and lives with her two daughters and enjoys outdoors activities like horseback riding and hiking in her spare time when she is not reading.

CHAPTER 19

BUILDING YOUR BUSINESS THROUGH TECHNOLOGY: IT SOLUTIONS THAT SAVE AND MAKE YOU MONEY

BY JAMAL ABBASI MILLAR

Technology has become increasingly powerful and increasingly easier to use. The hardware also continues to shrink in size to the point where the computing power we can carry in one hand (our Smartphones) is now greater than that used to put a man on the moon back in the 1960's.

It's amazing how much technology we now use in our everyday lives. Whether it's taking photos, finding directions or just playing online games, technology has assumed a prominent position in almost every human activity imaginable.

Even though we use technology constantly in our personal lives, however, many businesses (especially smaller ones) don't use it to the fullest extent possible to boost their bottom lines. They either think it will be too expensive or too much trouble to implement it.

But the truth is that there are many cost-effective ways to leverage technology today in ways that make a business, no matter what its size, run much more efficiently and profitably – as well as convert more leads to sales.

Our company, Delta Business Solutions, provides these cutting-edge technological tools to our clients – and they find it makes an incredible difference to achieving "Victory" in their profit pictures. In this chapter, I'd like to discuss a few of these tools and why you should consider making them a part of your operation, if you haven't already.

MANAGED IT SERVICES

To begin with, any business (especially a small or medium-sized one) should consider hiring an outside company to manage their IT services. Most businesses live and die by their informational systems – but many of them simply can't afford the day-to-day investment of staff and technology required to keep those systems properly maintained, updated, and backed up. Not only that, but when those systems need to be revamped or retooled, there is considerable risk if the right professionals aren't guiding the way.

For example, our clients have access to my staff of twenty-two experts should anything go wrong. Obviously, to put twenty-two experts on their payroll would be cost-prohibitive – but, by hiring my company, they can take advantage of their extensive experience and expertise at a very minimal cost.

Hiring an outside firm to manage your IT services also means you have access to a full menu of technological solutions for what is usually a flat monthly fee. Whether your company is having a good month or a bad month, your IT costs will remain stabilized and affordable, which gives you some peace of mind moving forward with the technology you need to grow your business.

What's really awesome is that you can have the technical power that Wal-Mart uses at a fraction of the cost – since you can affordably have access to the latest software, technology and IT expert minds. We enjoy providing businesses all across the country with this kind of service and we see firsthand how it helps them succeed.

RETAIL MANAGEMENT AND RESTAURANT TECHNOLOGY

When it comes to retail stores, dashboards can be invaluable to ensuring a healthy and profitable operation. If you're unfamiliar with business dashboards, they are online tools that show you, in real time, different aspects of your operation. In stores, dashboards can help you instantly track inventory, sales, customers and other critical information.

For example, let's say you own a chain of ten or twenty retail stores – and you needed to locate a popular item for a customer in one of those stores. Without a dashboard, you would have to call each store individually, wait for them to check their stock and get back to you – that could be a process of a couple of hours. With a dashboard, you would instantly be able to see which store had which products in stock (and how well they were selling in each store too).

That's just the beginning of how a dashboard can help a retail operation. You can also compare sales at certain times and certain days in different stores – and try to analyze why sales might be bigger at one location than another. With the kind of real time data a dashboard provides, it's very easy to do.

We also provide loss prevention systems that are integrated with surveillance video so you can keep track of your stock more thoroughly and accurately.

These kinds of hi-tech systems can also benefit restaurants. For example, if you make a reservation at a restaurant – or want to pick up delivery food – we provide online order systems so the food is ready when you get there. We also place kiosks in fast food establishments, so a customer can place a food order without the restaurant having to provide a dedicated employee to make that happen. The restaurant doesn't have to hire that order person and that can means savings of tens of thousands of dollars over the course of a year.

AUTOMATED CUSTOMER LOYALTY PROGRAMS

In any kind of business, the most important element is *the customer*. That's why setting up a computerized customer loyalty program can be an important step to not only cement your relationship with those who buy from you, but also to maximize potential sales to them.

It can be as simple as asking a customer for their cell phone number when they buy from you to enroll them. That gives you the ability to send them text messages offering special discounts and "two-for" deals that can bring them back more quickly for their next purchase. A real plus is the ability to, on a slow sales day, send customers a text message that contains a great "instant offer" that has to be redeemed quickly. That can sometimes boost sales instantly anywhere from 40 to 50% - just from one text that costs virtually nothing to generate, once the system is set up.

You can also encourage these customers to provide more information for your customer loyalty program by using "bonus points" that either trigger a discount or a free gift once a certain number of them have been accumulated. For example, they might earn 200 of these points if they clicked on your link to officially enroll in your customer loyalty program.

If you can motivate them to leave such information as their email address, birthday and maybe even their wedding anniversary date, if they're married, there are a number of ways you can use that information to benefit them as well as your business. For example, one restaurant client of ours sends out birthday cards with a coupon for a free dinner to its customers. Now, that customer is most likely not going to come in alone to eat – he or she will bring at least one guest and maybe several for their big day, who will have to pay for their meals.

With a customer loyalty program, you are also able to keep track of when your customers are buying from you. If they haven't made a purchase in some time, you can then send them a special "We Miss You!" offer with a discount or freebee designed to get them to patronize your business again.

THE MAGIC OF CRM SOFTWARE

If you want to take your customer engagement to an even higher level, consider adding CRM (Customer Relationship Management) Software to your technology mix.

CRM software enables you to do two essential things: (1) automatically capture lead information, and (2) automatically generate follow-up marketing to those leads (as well as the ones you already have in your database).

Why are these essential?

Let's begin by going into more detail about the first "essential." Traditionally, if a lead calls to inquire about a product or service, it's up to you or your support staff (whoever takes the call) to remember to ask for the lead's contact information, as well as to *enter* that valuable info into your database. Now, obviously, things can go wrong with both steps. Just ask yourself how many contact emails, addresses and phone numbers you or your staff has misplaced on hastily-scribbled Post-It notes that get lost in the office clutter. CRM software answers these kinds of calls automatically and gathers that information (from both phone calls as well as web forms and landing pages) without you having to lift a finger.

Now, let's move on to the second essential – follow-up marketing. The truth about marketing is that, most often, the sale isn't made on the first, second or even the third contact with a lead. Studies show that 80% of sales are made on the fifth to twelfth contact – and yet, most salespeople (90%) stop after those first three attempts. That means the most reliable path to sales conversions – repeated contacts – is not taken.

You can program your CRM software to make those twelve contacts automatically – through emails, mailings, phone calls and so forth – and ensure your best shot at sales success! CRM software will also automatically reply to leads emailing or calling about your business offerings – so, even if you're busy, those leads will be taken care of (and their information will be captured).

This kind of customer automation is incredibly powerful – and it works amazingly well for any small or medium-sized business. It takes a lot of all-important marketing tasks on all by itself and allows you to make sure you're not missing any sales opportunities.

Of course, you can also automate many of your *internal* tasks – such as your accounts payable, your payroll and so forth. Working with systems that can automatically handle these tasks will save you money on hiring extra personnel (or worrying about covering for them when they take a vacation or a sick day).

KEEPING YOUR DATA SAFE AND SOUND

As we have discussed in this chapter, technology can be all-important to growing your business, especially when your resources (and budget) are limited. The plain fact is that most of our businesses could not run without some kind of technology. Medical clinics and other professional offices require appointment systems and a client database to run smoothly. Restaurants and retail businesses need to keep track of inventory, order fulfillment and so forth – and of course, all of this is done today with computers.

It's wonderful to have these technological tools at our disposal – but, because we are so reliant on them, we must protect them in case the worst happens.

For example, many businesses in New York and New Jersey were hit hard when Hurricane Sandy battered the coastlines of those states in November of 2012. Their computers were destroyed, they lost their all-important data and found themselves unable to even operate once the storm clean-up was done. The same thing happened in Joplin, Missouri in 2011 when cataclysmic tornados hit that region.

That's why it's important to have a back-up and recovery plan in place, in case of fire, weather disaster or any other unforeseen event that could wipe out your on-site systems. This is another service with which we provide many of our clients – and, should something of this magnitude happen to them, we are able to have them restored and back in business within six to eight hours.

We are also able to update their back-ups on our servers online on a weekly basis and make sure the data is as current as possible. As you can imagine, this kind of back-up service is important also for public institutions, such as police stations and government offices.

It's also important to protect yourself from simple equipment failure. For example, if your office computer crashes for good, you could also lose all your data. We provide a special monitoring system that checks on hard drives every fifteen minutes and makes sure there are no problems developing with them. If there are, we can address them long before the problem becomes dangerous to the business operation.

As you can see from the many technological solutions presented in this chapter, you can run your small or medium-sized business at a high level if you put the right ones in place. Better still, if you go with the right managed IT services package, you will have access to whichever of these technologies you want – as well as being able to consult with IT experts on what will work best for your particular business. It's like you're at a buffet filled with things that can only mean great things for your bottom line – so why not take advantage of as many of them as you can?

Technology will only become more and more important to companies as time goes on. Working with managed IT services allows you to grow with that technology and have access to whatever cutting-edge innovations are taking place.

And that will certainly ensure your business "Victory!"

CHAPTER 20

THE FIVE INSIDER SECRETS TO GUARANTY YOU A SUCCESSFUL RETIREMENT

BY MATT GOLAB

We've all heard the phrase "you play like you practice." The idea was if you goofed off, got distracted, or didn't take practice seriously, the game would be miserable as the other team bullied you around.

I remember one scene in particular. One summer I trained very hard, conditioned, ran and fine- tuned my technique. My efforts paid off – being recognized publicly for my skills – and our team had a great season.

The next summer I needed jaw surgery. I had my mouth wired shut, not being able to eat I lost a lot of weight (a problem I could use today), and muscle was lost also. My energy level was shot and I couldn't train the way I had the previous summer and I missed the pre-season.

My first game back was against a team I had thankfully played well against the previous season. As I entered the game, the front line began their attack. The position I played was to support the attack and be the first line of defense. This involved a great deal of back and forth running. I quickly realized my lack of preparation would have serious consequences. I performed terribly, my ego suffered and so did my teammates.

The obvious question is, "how does this fit with retirement?" There was a time in our country's history that a person worked for the same company for thirty or forty years and then retired with a full pension, medical and dental, with Social Security to fill in the gaps. With that knowledge, saving over the years was virtually unnecessary.

Now jump to the current retirement landscape and all of the challenges that face those who want to retire with success. We've had two massive stock market drops, a housing tornado of destruction ripping equity and throwing millions into the streets – and pensions are virtually a thing of the past and those few companies that have pensions are so under-funded, they're trying everything, even paying people to leave.

We have switched from social security being a retirement supplement to being the necessary foundation because so many have planned late in the game. So how does someone succeed in retirement. What I mean by succeed in retirement is *stay retired*. After 2008, we heard so many stories of people who had to go back to work either part-time or full-time to pay their daily expenses. In my opinion, that is not retirement success.

Our firm is here to allow people to receive the necessary education they need to fill in the gaps in their retirement income plane. This gives peace of mind regardless of their decision because it was made after a thorough education. It also provides security knowing they'll be able to live their lifestyle throughout their retirement – no matter how long it lasts. Retirement success can be achieved through sound education even for those planning late in the game.

As one of the nations top retirement income planners, I believe there are Five Insider Secrets to Planning Retirement Income late in the Game.

SECRET #1 ~ KNOW YOUR SOCIAL SECURITY NUMBER

Many boomers pursued a degree through college, this often meant they didn't enter the work force until their upper twenties. With so many wanting to retire early and this later start, many have under 35 years for the Social Security Administration to work off. Why does this matter you might be asking? They'll take the most productive 35 years to base the Social Security check we receive through retirement. So if you only worked 31 years, those other four years will get zeros. If you earned an average of $35,000 a year, those four years with $0 will have a sharp impact on your Social Security check. I help those who sit with me to know their numbers so this fate doesn't happen to them.

The other important factor to consider is when to take social security, 62, 66, or 70. Social Security encourages us to defer our payment with a generous 8% guaranteed increase for a limited number of years. With sound planning we might be able to take advantage of this and the wait can be painless, beneficial and the type of additional security we all crave.

SECRET #2 ~ WITHDRAW 4% FOREVER MORE

The 4% withdrawal method has been pushed and peddled by advisors more aggressively than fake Gucci handbags in downtown New York. So many advisors promoted this idea as foundational retirement success until the stock market crashes of 2000 and 2008 exposed the weakness and downright dangers of this flawed wisdom. The 4% withdrawal rule says a portfolio of roughly 50% stocks and 50% bonds will be able to support a 4% withdrawal through a thirty-plus-year retirement.

The big problem, the 4% is determined based off the first day value of retirement. A consumer has $450,000 and needs to have $1,500 per month. Well, if the market decreases by 15%, do you take 4% off that new portfolio value or do you keep withdrawing $1,500 per month. In my many years of experience helping people plan their income through retirement, I've never had anyone tell me they want their income to be continually fluctuating each month.

So what happens if the portfolio is down 15%? The average advisor tells them to keep withdrawing the same 4% dollar amount as last year – which brings their portfolio down 19% for that year. That puts a large burden on the remaining balance to maintain the monthly withdrawal. Its like sending a train downhill, the erosion of the portfolio speeds up and when the market takes off upwardly, its like sending a train uphill with previous losses and monthly withdrawals holding it back.

My job is to make sure our clients have a 100% chance of success that their retirement income plan will succeed and KEEP them retired!

SECRET #3 ~ CASH IS THE KILLER

We've been told over the years that "Cash is King." I've seen the exact opposite so many times that actually "Cash is the Killer" of retirement plans.

When we first get started saving, our first goal is to build an emergency fund of a few months expenses. As time goes by, unplanned expenses, market crashes, layoffs and other unforeseen hurdles skew our perspective. In our practice we see many approaching or in retirement have two or three years' worth of expenses in liquid savings. This is how cash can be the killer, by having large amounts of a portfolio in cash because it's liquid. That puts that money at high risk of daily being worth less through the corrosion of inflation.

Most people in retirement need lots of liquidity when health care issues demand it. Most "illiquid" investment plans become liquid as unforeseen longer term medical expense arises. With our planning process, we show the select families we choose to work with how to stabilize their income, this allows more security and removes the fear liquid savings will need to be activated, allowing more of their portfolio to pursue higher stable returns.

SECRET #4 ~ PASSIVE INVESTING AND THE DESTRUCTION OF NEGLECT

No matter what transition we are in life, we will always shave assets invested in the market. The real challenge is how do we manage risk? For so many years we've been told to have a risk tolerance, my philosophy is focused on risk avoidance. I would rather avoid unpleasant circumstances rather than tolerate them. This is the approach so many of our clients value in their portfolio.

Passive Investing or 'buy and hold' (hope) are focused on a set percentage of stocks and bonds. The emphasis is on "set," a consumer may have a great Mutual Fund with an excellent Manager but there can be something handcuffing that manager. It's called the prospectus. Here's how it works in real life. In 2008, many people had a "balanced" portfolio of mutual funds split between stocks and bonds, say 50/50. When the market turned down and stocks dropped, the manager may have seen what was going on and wanted to move more money to bonds and cash.

But this didn't happen. Why? There was a legal document that kept that manger from making that decision. That's right, it was the prospectus, which said the portfolio must be 50/50. He's the smartest manager out there with the best technology, but your portfolio immediately loses its diversification because of a predetermined percentage that can't respond to the market.

The difference between 'buy and hold' versus building an expert team around your money (a team that is just focused on your money and the market) is one is stagnant and doesn't respond to the market, and the other protects your money looking for opportunities to increase growth and reduce risk. Passive investing balances on a set schedule not based in what's going on in your life or the broader market. Having a professional team built around your portfolio can dramatically reduce risk and increase potential returns. The focus is not however bulking up returns, but making the investment roller coaster more of a kiddie ride than a screamer – like so many experienced in 2008.

SECRET #5 ~ THE RIGHT ADVISOR AT THE RIGHT TIME

There are three transitions in our financial life. The years when we get our first job until about ten or so years before we retire. This is when we take the most risk and can add to our balance. Time is on our side and we anticipate risk will allow us to average better returns. This transition is known as our accumulation stage. It usually lasts about thirty years.

The second transition is the few years preceding our retirement. This is our slow down or preservation transition, like approaching a stop sign. We've all seen someone squealing up to a stop sign, wheels smoking, stopping well over the line. I see so many people a few years before retirement not knowing their portfolio is set up the same way a thirty-five-year-old's portfolio would be set up. The right way is to have your portfolio set up is when a sharp market downturn doesn't cause you to postpone your retirement, or even worse, put it off indefinitely. This is why this transition is so important, it makes sure we meet that retirement date we're aiming for.

The third transition is the distribution transition. This is the time when our portfolio is providing supplemental income throughout a retirement. In this transition, time is now working against us, where in the accumulation transition, time is working for us. This is because each of these two transitions last around or more than 30 years. A portfolio must be crafted very carefully to ensure the income and principal continues. Each of the three transitions with their widely different needs and dangers need very unique experts. A preservation or distribution expert has completely different qualifications and skills than an accumulation expert. The danger is finding you're with the right advisor at the wrong time, after the markets exposed him or her and it's too late.

Most people who retire have what I call "go-go" plans. These are the things we dream about when we're working. When I retire I'm going to "go" here and do this or "go" there and do that. It might be church activities, taking cruises, learning a new skill like piano or golf, or maybe it's getting that time back with the kids and grandkids. One thing that we want to make sure is that finances don't stand in the way of an active and enjoyable retirement. Poor planning and feeling like it's too late in the game can block your ability to stay retired. So plan well, even if it's late in the game. Choose an advisor who has an up-to-date perspective on how to get you retired and keep you retired, and wisely chose the right advisor at the right time. As a nationally recognized Retirement Income Planning Expert, I suggest you follow these Five Insider Secrets to guarantee you have a successful retirement, especially if you're planning your retirement income late in the game.

About Matt

Matt Golab is a Registered Investment Advisor and a licensed Insurance Agent. He holds a Series 65 license in stocks, bonds, securities and private placements. He is the author of many articles for Financial Magazines and Journals, and a public speaker, holding educational seminars open to the public on income, retirement and investment planning options.

Matt has been featured in *Senior Market Advisor Magazine, Newsweek,* countless national newspapers and many, many more. On his radio show, Matt has interviewed experts such as John Bogle – Founder of the *Vanguard Funds,* David Walker – former United States Comptroller General, Rob Russell – writer for *U. S. News and World Report,* among countless others. Matt is frequently featured in *The Wall Street Journal,* CNBC, MSN Money, *The San Francisco Chronicle, Newsweek, TheSmartRetiree, Burlington County Times* as well as ABC, CBS, Fox, NBC and USA Today.

Matt enjoys assisting his clients in achieving their financial objectives. He continues improving his knowledge base by attending several advanced planning industry meetings each year. He specializes in working with retirees and pre-retirees in developing investment, income and estate plans for all sizes of estates. He has helped hundreds of clients reduce unnecessary income taxes, Social Security taxes and estate taxes.

Matt and his wife Becky have four children. They love spending time together, whether it's visiting family, vacationing at the ocean or going to sporting events.

Matt Golab
Chief Advisor
Call: 916-509-7227
Website: www.aaronmatthewsfinancial.com

Investment Advisory Services offered through Global Financial Private Capital, LLC. An SEC registered Investment Advisor.

CHAPTER 21

PERSUASIVE COLLECTIONS – SEPARATING PEOPLE FROM MONEY

BY ERIC J. CHRISTESON, PhD

Debt collection is the art of persuading debtors to do what they are already legally and morally obligated to do – pay their debts. Most collectors are intelligent individuals who, when armed with a plan, can work independently to achieve excellent results. The key is a plan composed of modifiable components designed to persuasively separate people from their money.

Every collector and collections environment is slightly different; however, the goal will always be the same. With each of these proposed collection management techniques, choose to reject, accept, or modify the approach to fit your specific collections department. While the techniques here specifically target the collector, the collections manager's job will become simpler when he or she commits to organizing the collection area to keep telephone collectors focused on one thing – telephoning debtors to collect money.

A single-person collections department requires they wearing two hats: the hats of the collector and the collections manager. In this case, a collector must be mindful of which hat he is wearing so that he does not overlook his own collections transgressions, or forget to set goals for his *department* and himself as collector.

ORGANIZING THE COLLECTIONS AREA

Your collectors (if you are the collections manager) or yourself (if you are a one-person show), <u>should (a) telephone debtors to collect money, and (b) do very little else</u>. If you are a one-man show who deals with collections issues only a few days per month, then organizing your collections area to the collector's *advantage* is paramount.

Support people should bring data to the collector, take away data with the collector's instructions, assure timely follow-up by bringing back data to the collectors at proper times, and receive and handle incoming phone calls but refer difficult cases to the collector.

Why do some organizations collect well while others do not? Are other collectors smarter? No. It is because their collection area is organized in ways to let collectors do almost nothing but make one phone call after another; proper data is in the proper place at the proper time.

COUNSELING COLLECTORS –
BRINGING *IDEAS* TO THE TASK

Incorporate the acronym **"IDEAS"** into your collections program.

- **I – Intelligence**. Intelligence is the ability to read, listen, and absorb, then to utilize actively, when collecting, that which was absorbed.
- **D – Drive**. Drive is the desire to succeed as a collector. To succeed, action must follow drive. An engine revving in neutral gets nowhere.
- **E – Eloquence**. Eloquence is the ability to express intelligent thinking by way of writing and talking. Collections are only made in one of two ways, writing and talking.
- **A – Attendance**. Show up to the job both physically and mentally. No matter how good you are at collections, it does not count if you are absent.
- **S – Social**. Social is the ability to collect in full and not offend the debtor.

A collector can add value to his or her own performance every month by adding value and improving performance in one of each of the five "IDEAS" above. If you are the collections manager, ask that each employee (or yourself if you wear multiple hats) report on exactly how he or she added value to that area that month.

The collectors who understand the program and participate, make a statement about, and give the collections manager "ideas" about their future. Conversely, the same is true of those who do not go along with "ideas." Before sharing "IDEAS," all collectors need some standards of conduct as a framework to function.

STANDARDS OF COLLECTORS' CONDUCT

Collecting, when performed properly, is a highly professional skill. So, help your collectors establish high standards of conduct. Try the acronym **"DECK"** - Dignity, Eloquence, Competitive, and Knowledge.

DIGNITY comes in two packages: The collector's own dignity manifested by his/her ability to remain calm under emotional conditions, and the dignity of the debtor. The collector earns his/her PhD (preserve human dignity) by responding to colorful words and phrases with firm payment demands, none laced with invective.

ELOQUENCE is mastery of the language. Collecting utilizes only two skills: writing and speaking. By reading omnivorously and looking up words not understood, the Collector masters language and dominates without arrogance.

COMPETITIVE means the collector must be, and know that he/she is, the best of all those other collectors, from other organizations, contacting the debtor. The collection department's bottom line depends on the collector separating the debtor from his money *before* his competition does.

KNOWLEDGE means the collector will know his/her organization, will be able to solve any complaint with transferring the call, then collect in full.

Tell your collectors to strive for perfection, to reach for the stars. They may not quite get one, but they won't come up with handfuls of mud either. When collectors believe they're competent, they will then be competent. When collectors become competent, it shows on the collection manager's record. The collector's record materializes in the collection manager's income.

COLLECTION LETTERS THAT COLLECT

If the goal of the collections department is to keep collectors on the phone collecting, then collections letters are simply a tool to motivate the debtor to pay the collector. They should make the job easier and enable phone calls to take less time.

Plan the content of the collection letter with the acronym "SPRA":

Situation-Proposal-Reason-Action

Begin by describing the situation. Next, make a specific proposal to the debtor. Then give the debtor a reason (from the debtor's viewpoint) as to why he/she should do as proposed.

End your letter with a call to action, telling the debtor what to do as he/she puts your letter down. The action may duplicate the proposal, but write it anyway using different words. That is selling – selling and collecting are very much alike.

Based on SPRA, stick to these five maxims:

- Keep paragraphs to two sentences. This gives read-sized paragraphs. Ignore grammar. People do not respond to grammar.
- Use no more than 22 words to a sentence. Long sentences confuse people.
- Keep words to a minimum of three syllables, with rare exception. It has been done in this section with the exception of the word "situation."
- Begin no paragraph with we-I-my-our. Use any other word in the language, but not a selfish, first-person pronoun.
- Use only one sheet of paper for your entire letter. Why? People are busy and frequently will not read more than one page.

Look at an ad that attracts you. See if most of the foregoing principles are not followed there. Make your collection letter an ad. Make it sell. (Collect!)

Rewrite your present collection form letters to the formulae above. When you do, you will increase dollars collected with those letters.

Collecting with the Upside-Down Letter

This format collects money. Try it.

MR. SMITH, YOU MUST ADMIT…

…that we have been most patient with you. We have written and phoned about your past due balance of $567.89.

You have made excuses and you have made promises. But no check has been received.

Your credit with us no longer exists. But it should, and it can.

Clear the matter today. Mail your check in full.

When you do mail that check, your credit will again be in order. So we look forward to receiving the check and (more importantly) serving you again.

Jill Q. Jones

The worst reason for not trying a different approach is, "We never did it that way before," or "they will never go for it."

HOW TO SAY MORE IN FEWER WORDS

Kill the A-B syndrome. Do not say "Actually" or "Basically." Both words are disclaimers, and both tend to obfuscate a situation.

Kill the Y-K syndrome; meaning "You know." If I know, why tell me?

Eliminate redundant words and phrases. The remaining words and phrases will have more impact.

Examples of redundant phrases abound; "As a matter of fact," "by and large," "to be honest with you," "you'd better believe it," and "what I mean is this" top a list of several hundred more phrases that are useless in collections.

Make a drastic reduction in saying words ending with "ly." Most are value judgements that turn people off. You simply do not need "generally" or "specifically" or "theoretically."

Collection managers should cut a deal with some business friends. Arrange to interrupt each other on hearing these redundant words and phrases. The interruptions will get a few laughs and will strengthen the friendships. Speech will become crisp and succinct.

After implementing this simple word-reduction program, ask your collectors to do the same. Everyone will have fun interrupting each other and each will make shorter collection telephone calls. Shorter calls make time for more calls. More calls means contacting more debtors. When collectors contact more debtors, they collect more money, therefore, controlling the collections call means controlling collections success.

PLANNING AND CONTROLLING
COLLECTION TELEPHONE CALLS

The collection telephone call comes in three phases.

Phase 1 is "Statement."
The statement phase is what the collector says to the debtor. This phase has five simple steps:

Identify the Debtor

Identify the Collector

Ask for Payment in full today

Solve the Problem, when you cannot get a payment in full today

Follow up on time

Phase 2 is "Reponse."
Response is what the debtor says back to the collector; it is the reason why he/she cannot pay in full today. Examples: In consumer lending "I am unemployed" and in commercial collecting, "Our customers aren't paying us."

Phase 3 is "Rebuttal."
Rebuttal is what the collector says back to the debtor to circumvent the response. The payment proposals a collector will make here will come to him or her when they have extracted sufficient data on which to base them. Extract those data with questions beginning with any combination of the words: who, what, when, where, why or how. Such questions cannot be answered with yes or no. Any answer obtained will extract data.

When the collector has enough data, he/she will make the payment proposals using simple, declarative sentences. The words will be there.

All collectors are different. Collectors must experiment with the Statement-Response-Rebuttal approach, then, modify it, using this approach as a base for collecting in ways indigenous to that individual's personality. In the same way that a collector will apply his or her own signature style to the three-phase collections call, the collector can apply his own signature "voice" to the call.

DEVELOPING THE "SPECIAL" TELEPHONE-COLLECTION VOICE

You, the collector, are going to make a collection telephone call. You have reviewed antecedent data and planned the call. You are eager for results.

Many times, when phoning with a plan, the edge in completing the payment arrangement can be the sound of that special "collector" voice, the compelling voice of authority. Collectors should develop a special voice. Compared with the normal voice, the special voice has three features: it is slower, lower, and louder, but not offensively so.

For four evenings, five minutes per evening, try this: obtain a magazine and go to a quiet room to be alone. Read the magazine aloud in a normal voice for three seconds. Then, listen to the sound of your voice. Do this by jamming a finger in your ear so you will hear your voice as others hear it.

Let your voice improve; sounding better to you. It will. When you discern the improvement, remove your finger, and keep that newly improved voice through the balance of the five minutes.

Repeat the exercise each evening. Each evening, your voice will become slower, lower, and louder. The fifth morning you will simply order up that voice when phoning debtors. This exercise, especially the finger in the ear, is indeed corny and hammy – that's why you are alone in the room. But it works!

And you do have the time. And you cannot beat the price.

HELPING DEBTORS FIND THE DOLLARS TO PAY BILLS

Once the collector has reached agreement with the debtor that the right thing to do is to pay their bills, the natural next step will likely be suggesting ways in which the debtor can obtain the money to bring the debt current.

Collectors need to know all the places where and conditions under which debtors can obtain money to pay their bills. Debtors do not always know of these places and conditions.

Remind consumer debtors that money can sometimes be obtained from credit unions, friends and relatives, banks, ordinary (not term) life insurance policies, city, county,state and federal sources, and many others. Collectors must know specific names, addresses, and details.

Remind commercial debtors that money can sometimes be obtained from receivables, inventory, improved own-collections techniques, factoring, banks, and many others. Collectors must know how to explain in detail.

Collection managers should list these places and conditions and distribute lists to all collectors. Follow up to be sure that collectors absorb and apply this knowledge.

This project will require research, likely available on the internet, and a good amount of time. Once completed, however, collectors will have a leg up on keeping past-due dollars at a minimum. Do not make the mistake of spending money for outside consultants to compile this list, as the project is a better in-house matter.

Even when offering solutions to a debtor, he or she may have complaints about the service received or the collections department as a whole. How a collector handles complaints will determine how quickly the debtor pays.

HOW TO HANDLE COMPLAINTS

The collector must handle complaints, if the bill is to be collected. The collector will not transfer the call to another department. This builds peachy pen-pal files of endless memos between departments, but the bill grows older and older. Collectors can try this approach:

Listen to the complaint, without interruption. Make keyword notes in order to understand, not necessarily approve, the debtor's position. Do not express a position. The debtor is not ready for that. Instead, repeat the debtor's position without emotion. Then, ask the debtor if his or her position was described properly.

The answer will be yes. Now, the collector piggybacks on the yes by expressing his position. The collector must get as close to the caller as policy allows.

Use the acronym **SPRA**, as used previously in the collection letters:

• Express the **Situation,** relevant to company policy.

• Make a **Proposal** as to what the debtor should do now.

• Give the debtor a **Reason**, from the debtor's viewpoint, as to why to accept the Proposal.

• **Action** means obtaining a commitment from the debtor and making a commitment to the debtor. Normally, the commitment is the follow-up plan.

Finally, the collector follows up until both the commitments are completed.

THE KEY: The collector will improve cash flow by handling the entire matter--by having the authority to do so--not transferring the call, and multiplying the debtor's rage. Qualified collectors thrive when given wide authority to work independently and solve problems.

Qualified collectors share many traits. Qualified collectors frequently are college graduates with degrees in subjects that require mastery of language. They are resourceful and do things a bit differently than the norm. They are good listeners who can readily sell his or her talents in an interview and might demonstrate a bit of cockiness or braggadocio, both of which serve a collector well. Additionally, the qualified collector will be results-oriented, offering imaginative problem solving and bringing new ideas to the collections manager or to his or her department.

Sometimes, collections managers cannot easily supervise competent collectors because each has his own way of doing things. However, when they are encouraged to pursue their own entrepreneurial instincts within the structure of company guidelines, competent collectors will become easy to manage and make their department money.

The competent collector elevates debt collection to the art of persuading a debtor to do what he is already legally and morally obligated to do – pay his debt.

About Rick

Eric J Christeson, CPA, MBA, PhD, DBA founded Dynamic Interface Systems Corporation in 1982. As Chairman of the Board, Rick has spearheaded a team effort to cultivate strong sales and earnings growth while ensuring stability and long-term survival by acquiring or developing easy to use, affordable, technological-ly-advanced products to assist the financial lending industry.

Prior to leading Dynamic Interface Systems Corporation, Rick spent twenty years in senior financial and line management positions in both small and Fortune 100 companies. During his tenure as CFO of a troubled, high-tech electronics firm, Rick restructured and refinanced the firm that then regained its NASDAQ listing and subsequent acceptance on the American Stock Exchange (AMEX). His additional experiences include controller of the $400-million division of a Fortune 100 company and several years as a contractor with the U.S. Department of Defense.

While in the Air Force, Rick obtained a Top Secret Cryptographic "codeword" Clearance. He has a B.A. degree in Russian from Syracuse University, a B.S. degree in Accounting from San Jose State University, and an M.B.A. with a concentration in Marketing also from San Jose. His Ph.D. in Economics and D.B.A. in Marketing Management both were awarded from Canterbury Christ Church University near London, England.

Despite a work ethic and schedule that would make lesser men cry "Uncle," in 2004 Rick was met at the door by his wife and his son as he arrived home from the office. He was greeted with the words "Alex wants to join the Cub Scouts, Dear." Not one to shy away from a challenge, Rick began what he then-called his "second full-time job" as leader of a 160-kid Cub Scout pack for the Boy Scouts of America. Of his experiences in Boy Scouting, too numerous to mention, Rick says, "Scouting has changed my life forever, just as Scouting has changed the lives of boys everywhere forever."

As often happens when one excels at one's job, Boy Scouts soon asked Rick to build a district leadership team as District Chairman – comprised of finance, training, membership, advancement, OA, camping and many more committees. He recently received the Silver Beaver Award from the Boy Scouts of America. "The Silver Beaver Award is made for service of exceptional character to boyhood by registered Scouters, Cubbers, and Explorer leaders..." Rick sums up his Boy Scouting experience by stating, "Nothing is more rewarding than watching a group of kids coming up the trail with smiling, dusty faces."

In his free time outside of work and volunteering in Boy Scouting, Rick sits on the Board of Directors for several other organizations. He and his family have been quiet, contributing members of the Unity Church of Unity Village, Missouri for the past 12 years.

CHAPTER 22

VICTORIOUS FINANCIAL PLANNING REQUIRES WORKING WITH THE RIGHT ADVISOR

BY REID ABEDEEN

Planning your financial future is one of the most important steps you will ever take to protect yourself and your family. Your victory and success depends on your ability to achieve your financial objectives and protect your assets in the years to come. Helping people make critical decisions about wealth management and investment planning to achieve their financial goals, protect their lifestyle and gain peace of mind is what I have been doing for nearly twenty years.

Throughout my career, I have observed numerous transitions inside the financial services industry. While this profession has matured and become technologically advanced since its inception, I'm sure we would all agree it is less than perfect.

In my opinion, one of the broken components I find in this industry that can have severe consequences for an investor is the professional fragmentation at the consumer level. Let me explain. The breakdown occurs when the consumer has a financial advisor, an insurance agent, a tax professional and a lawyer who never communicate, creating a "professional fragmentation" in the overall picture of the client's long-term financial and retirement objectives. These consumers believe they are covering all their bases because they have numerous experts giving them advice. However, the sad truth of the matter is that the direction given by these well-meaning professionals is likely going to be detrimental to the objectives of their common client because the client is not receiving advice based on a coordinated strategy. These professionals typically don't communicate with one another, they simply advise their mutual client based on the limited information the client provides them. Important components of the client's financial portfolio are "piece-mealed" and often do not work in harmony with one another.

My philosophy and approach to financial planning is to eliminate this "professional fragmentation" by coordinating all of the professionals in their disciplines to make sure each of these components work together. There must be a specific strategy. That's why I refer to myself as a Strategic Retirement Advisor. It is impossible to have an effective long-term financial plan without coordinating the efforts and advice of all the professional advisors needed to create the plan. I like to tell people that my role is to function as the quarterback of the team, bringing together all the necessary professional disciplines to make sure the client's financial plan is executed with precision, congruity, efficiency, and effectiveness.

I take a more holistic approach. That's how I believe successful retirement plans are created. All of the components of a solid financial plan are interconnected and cannot operate separately. That is the only way you can have success in retirement. You can have the best investment in the world, but what good is it if Uncle Sam takes a big portion of it? You may be making a good return on your money, but if you're not able to keep it, spend it or enjoy it, your planning was a waste of time. If you can't transfer it to your loved ones or the charity of your choice, you have defeated the purpose of planning for the future.

You must understand that the economy is going to change. We will have catastrophic situations that will affect the economy globally, nationally and personally. If you don't have someone that is "quarterbacking" your financial plan, you will pay the price. It's not a matter of "if" you will experience negative consequences, it's a matter of "when" you will experience them.

YOU NEED A STRATEGIC RETIREMENT ADVISOR

When planning for your financial future, I strongly believe you should speak with a Strategic Retirement Advisor. These individuals should be Registered Investment Advisors or Certified Financial Planners™ (CFP®) who have a very strict fiduciary responsibility to their clients. They are held to the highest standards when it comes to client relationships.

Interestingly, in a recent survey, 74% of investors did not understand the different obligations required of Registered Investment Advisors versus Stockbrokers. Unlike Stockbrokers, Registered Investment Advisors have an obligation to act in an investor's best interests in all aspects of the financial relationship.

When I meet with a new client for the first time, I discuss with them the differences between a Registered Investment Advisor and a Registered Representative or a Stockbroker. Registered Representatives and Stock-brokers are governed by the guidelines established by the Securities and Exchange Commission (SEC) and they work with their clients on a commission basis. These individuals also must have a relationship with a Broker-Dealer. The role of the Broker-Dealer is to supervise the advisor and make products available to them to offer to the public. When a financial transaction is completed through a Registered Representative or a Stockbroker, a commission is paid to the Broker-Dealer and the Broker-Dealer pays the advisor. So the issue becomes one of representation. These individuals represent the Broker-Dealer. Registered Representatives can transact business using mutual funds, while Stockbrokers can transact business using stocks, bonds, as well as mutual funds. However, these advisors are limited to the financial products available to them through their Broker-Dealer and will have to transact business only using those products.

Let's consider this analogy. If you were to go to a bank and ask to buy a Certificate of Deposit (CD), the bank is not going to shop for CDs across the country to find you the one with the highest rate of return. No, they will sell you their CD because they are representing that particular bank. The same will be true for a commission-based representative. They will base their sales recommendations on the investments they have available to them through their Broker-Dealer. Unfortunately, the financial products they represent may not be the best product for the investor. Their representation is to the commission-based Broker-Dealer and not to the client. I believe whenever there is a commission involved, there can be a conflict of interest.

To resolve any possibility of conflict of interest concerns and to do what I think is clearly and objectively best for my clients, I have chosen to be a Registered Investment Advisor. With this designation, I can transact business utilizing any number of financial vehicles – including stocks, bonds and mutual funds. However, I cannot be paid a commission. My representation is to my client. I am paid an advisory fee regardless of the transaction or purchase. Again, my representation is to the client, not to a Broker-Dealer.

When I started in the financial services industry, I thoroughly investi-gated what licenses were available. In my quest for information, I had a discussion with a Stockbroker with whom I was acquainted. He said to me, "The more money my clients make, the less money I make. And the less my clients make, the more I make." I was confused by his state-ment and asked him for clarification. He responded, "If my clients are doing really well in their investments, I can't call them and tell them they should sell. But, if their investments aren't doing well, I can call them and recommend they sell and put their money into something that will get them a better return." In essence, he was telling me that if his client's portfolio was doing well, he was not able to generate any ad-ditional commissions. Conversely, if a portion of his client's portfolio is doing poorly, that is an opportunity for him to earn a new commission by selling one thing and buying another on their behalf.

In the fee-based investment advisory world, the very opposite is true. In my world, the better the client does, the better the advisor does. The worse the client does, the worse the advisor does. So, you can see, a Registered Investment Advisor has a vested interest in the client's suc-cess. The advisor does better because they are paid on a percentage of the clients assets. For example, if a client has a $100,000 investment, the advisor may charge them 1% of the value of the portfolio. If the ad-visor is instrumental in helping them double their money, now, instead of receiving $1,000, the advisor receives $2,000. It becomes a win-win relationship.

I often like to use this analogy when discussing this subject with my clients. If you were to go to a meat butcher, he will be able to tell you about all the various cuts of meat he has available and the best way to prepare your selection so it will be the most flavorful. He will be glad to answer any question you have and help you select a great cut of meat. He would never say to you, "Mr. Jones, you have been buying a lot of red meat from me and I'm getting concerned about how this is affecting your cholesterol and your overall health. Maybe you should stop by the fish market and the vegetable market and buy some of their products. I think you should cut back on your red meat consumption and have a more balanced diet."

Allow me to continue this analogy. If I were to go to a nutritionist, he would run a number of diagnostic tests, do some investigative work, analyze the data, then discuss with me his findings and make recommendations for my diet. He will make objective recommendations, based on his professional analysis, as to what is best for me. He is not going to sell me meat, fish, poultry, vegetables, or fruit, but he will give me a dietary plan so that I can receive proper nourishment and become as healthy as possible.

Here is my point. A lot of times when people get extra money they will call a broker and say, "Hey, I have an extra $50,000, what should I do with it?" They may think that they're talking to the nutritionist when they are actually speaking to "Louie the butcher." In very simplistic terms, that is the difference between a commission-based financial representative and a fee-based Registered Investment Advisor that has a strict fiduciary responsibility to the client. The Registered Investment Advisor will function much like the nutritionist by collecting data, analyzing it, and then make recommendations that will be the most beneficial to your financial future.

WHAT SHOULD YOU LOOK FOR WHEN SELECTING A FINANCIAL ADVISOR?

I strongly recommend that you seek out a fee-based Registered Investment Advisor and interview them as if you are going to hire them for a job. Ask them about their experience and background. If you want to utilize their services for something specific, such as retirement planning, make sure they specialize in that area of planning. Talk to other people who have used that person. If you don't know anyone, ask the advisor for the names of references you can contact. Do a background check on them. Contact the Better Business Bureau to see if there are any unresolved complaints. Make sure they don't have a criminal background. You can also go to the SEC website to see what licenses they hold and if there are any justified complaints against them. You can check with your state's Department of Insurance and Department of Corporations to do further background checks. Also, for a fee, the National Ethics Bureau will do a background check for you on a financial advisor.

BEWARE OF RED FLAGS

Your financial advisor should take a minimum of one hour to gather information from you regarding your financial picture. Communication with your advisor is vital and essential because the consumer is the one that will pay the price if a mistake is made in the planning process. If your advisor cannot communicate and under understand your objectives, they cannot help you. Your advisor should ask you about your current assets, income, investments, debt, taxes, estate plan, children, grandchildren, etc. The list will be extensive and should be a very thorough investigation into your life. If the advisor doesn't do this during his first meeting with you, that is a huge red flag!

If the advisor begins recommending a specific investment within the first fifteen minutes of your initial conversation, that's a red flag. Walk away from that relationship. That is like going to the doctor and having the doctor write a prescription for you before he does any testing or diagnosis to determine if a problem even exists.

Advisors will sometimes try to influence a person's investing decisions based on past returns. If an advisor promises you high returns based on the past performance of an investment, that's a red flag.

After the advisor collects the information you provided him in the initial meeting, he must take time to analyze it. I refer to this as stress-testing the portfolio. This must be done before any recommendations can be made. Once the stress test is completed, a second meeting must take place to discuss the advisor's findings and recommendations. This meeting should be educational in nature. You should learn about the analysis and the specific recommendations for your financial future. If the advisor is unwilling to take time to adequately stress test your portfolio and educate you on where you are at today and how you will get to where you want to be in the future, that is a red flag.

I always recommend a minimum quarterly review for my clients. If your advisor is not doing this, you as a client will pay the price. The economy changes by the minute, not by the year. Advisors typically do not sit down with their clients for a review often enough. Clients go through changes that are occurring not only with the economy, not only with their taxes, but also with their lives and their needs. Make sure the financial firm with which you are working has the infrastructure to be able to have that many meetings with you. If the firm is short staffed and does not have the infrastructure or time to meet with you quarterly, that's a red flag. It may be a sign the advisor is taking on too many clients and the service aspect of the relationship is in jeopardy. Who pays the price for that? It's the client, not the advisor or the firm.

BE CAREFUL

I'm sure you can recall your parents offering these words of admonition whenever you would leave the house, "Be careful." The same, simplistic advice is applicable when navigating the complexities of the financial planning world. However, I'm confident if you take the advice I have outlined in this chapter and put it into practice, you will find the appropriate Strategic Retirement Advisor to help you coordinate all the necessary professional experts and assist you in navigating your way to a victorious and successful financial future.

About Reid

Reid Abedeen, founder of Safeguard Investment Advisory Group, LLC, is a Strategic Retirement Advisor who has been helping retirees for over 18 years with issues such as tax planning, insurance, long-term care planning, financial services, asset protection and many other areas. Reid has a degree in Business Administration and has continuously sought out other training opportunities, through formal and informal educational venues, to stay up-to-date on all the current developments in his industry so he is able to help his clients during any financial climate.

Beginning his financial services career in the banking industry, Reid always worked with his clients to put their interests first and foremost. However, he believed he could better serve his clients through his own independent firm, so he established Safeguard Investment Advisory Group, LLC for that purpose. He is a Registered Investment Advisor with a strict fiduciary responsibility toward his clients. His primary focus is to fully understand his client's long term goals and what they desire to achieve personally and financially. Through carefully working together with his clients, he is able to help them achieve financial soundness as well as guide them through the important steps of legacy planning.

Reid and his firm are committed to the financial success and peace of mind of each and every client they serve. His mission is to safely and securely develop his clients' assets through personalized custom-made solutions intended to reflect each client's standards, goals and objectives. Based on his extensive knowledge and understanding of today's markets, he has an unwavering commitment to provide exceptional service to his clients and provide them with the most accurate, up-to-date and honest advice for their given situation – so they may obtain financial success and freedom.

In 2011, Reid was named "Five Star Wealth Manager of the Year" as featured in *Los Angeles Magazine* and was nominated again in 2012 and 2013. He has also been featured in *Newsweek* as one of America's PremierExperts® "Financial Trendsetters" - where he was showcased for his forward thinking and successful strategies in wealth management, retirement planning, and wealth building.

Reid is licensed through the California Department of Insurance and is registered through the Financial Industry Regulatory Authority (FINRA). He is a member of the National Ethics Association and the Better Business Bureau. He can be heard hosting his own weekly radio program on *AM 1510, Financial News and Talk Radio* covering the Southern California market.

Reid and his wife, Smyrna, are the proud parents of three children, Yusef, Leena and Adam.

CHAPTER 23

SURVIVING RETIREMENT

BY TODD KIM & GREG ROUMPOS

STORY OF SUE

In June of 2010, we were fortunate to add Sue as a new client. Sue isn't her real name, but the situation we describe is all too real for many retirees. Sue had worked for over 28 years with a local company in Salt Lake City, Utah that developed fine jewelry and beautiful awards. The company was very successful over the years and were generous with their employees. Sue had worked hard and had accumulated a large retirement nest egg. Combined with her husband's retirement, their portfolio was approximately $850k. Like many people, Sue looked forward to retirement with great anticipation. She had calculated that they had enough money to live a comfortable retirement and pay off some lingering debts. She took over $100k of IRA money to finish paying off the house and make some needed improvements. Her advisor told her that it would be alright since she had substantially more assets and that with a little time, her retirement plan should make up the differences. In 2000, at her retirement Sue and her husband Phil had just over $740k in their portfolio, they looked forward to many years of traveling to see grandchildren. Yet when she came to us in 2010 they had only $382k left. Sue was worried that she might need to go back to work and they were looking into a reverse mortgage on their home. Something had gone very wrong.

Digging deeper we discovered the problem. Sue had discussed with her advisor the need for additional income every month in order to subsidize social security and provide enough income for a nice but modest lifestyle. They also wanted to maintain some liquidity for any future needs. Sue's advisor recommended allocating the accounts into a diversified group of stock and bond mutual funds. According to her advisor, this was a "conservative portfolio," modeled after questions he had asked them regarding their tolerance for risk, the time horizon needed etc. All of the funds came from recognizable companies and since they represented various groups, she believed that she hadn't, "put all her eggs in one basket." Still, Sue had some worries, what if the markets didn't perform or there were big swings? Her advisor calmly reassured her saying that, 'Markets go up and down you just have to stay with it. They would be well-placed for weathering any storms.' Like many retirees, Sue and Phil were victims of bad advice. How did this happen?

PORTFOLIOS BUILT ON PRETEXTS: AVERAGE VS. ACTUAL RETURNS

The title might be harsh, but when it comes to your retirement nest egg you need accurate facts. In building portfolios to accumulate wealth, advisors use certain sets of assumptions. One of these assumptions is to project an average yield for the portfolio based upon its allocation into various financial instruments. These assumption's average yields may be high or low depending upon the risk in the portfolio. The problem isn't in the portfolio's asset allocation or its risk analysis; it is in the assumption of average returns. Let me explain by asking you a question: If you had an account that experienced a -50% return in Year 1, and a +50% return in year 2, what would your average return be? Well the AVERAGE return would be zero, Right? +50 added to -50 is zero. Zero divided by 2 is zero. The mathematical average for that question is indeed zero. However, what is the REAL return in that scenario? Let's look at an example: If you had saved $100k in your 401k and it suffered a 50% loss you would be left with $50k. Now let's take your remaining $50k and add a positive 50% return for the next year. $50k increased by 50% the following year does not get you back to $100k, it only gets you to $75k. That is a **25% LOSS!**

The majority of advisors offering retirement advice regrettably still focus their planning around maximizing yields using average returns. These disastrous strategies require the advisor to assume a multitude of *possible* outcomes. Unfortunately, the average yields used to construct these retirement plans and eventually retirement income withdrawals will never be accurate. The only way a projected average return comes close to the real return you receive in your portfolio is to completely leave out any negative years! In other words, for these plans to work, the stock market cannot go down. How realistic is that? Now, let's look at Real Market Returns vs. Average Market Returns.

Average vs. Real

Year	Average %	Real %
5	5.08	2.17
10	3.55	1.13
15	8.86	6.72
20	11.04	9.14
25	11.63	9.97
50	11.28	9.78

Sue and Phil were banking on consistent, returns of 6%-7% in their portfolio, they instead received just less than 1%. Unbeknownst to them, the plan they were given was flawed from the start. It was never robust enough to withstand the turbulence of the next ten years, and the faulty logic used in its construction ensured its eventual collapse. Now, let's ask another question: What happens when you compound these problems with the need for the distribution of income?

REVERSE DOLLAR COST AVERAGING: BUY AND HOLD OR BUY AND LOSE

We come to the second fatal flaw in the design of their retirement plan: Compounding withdrawals in flat or negative years. Much has been said regarding the strategy of dollar-cost averaging when buying shares of stocks or mutual funds. Indeed, this can be sound and prudent over time in accumulating more shares and increasing wealth. But what happens to a portfolio when markets are flat or volatile and you take out withdrawals for income? Let's look at the chart.

Without a constant positive market, the effects of volatility and systematic withdrawals create a downward slide almost impossible to escape. Dollar-cost averaging now works in reverse, negatively compounding against your portfolio and gradually increasing your chances for retirement failure. Regrettably for Sue and Phil, they entrusted their wealth to an advisor focused on accumulation and using antiquated techniques in planning strategies. First, the use of average returns that didn't perform, mixed with systematic capital withdrawals created a poisonous retirement cocktail. What was the third and final straw?

UNLUCKY MARKET TIMING

How many times have you heard, "You just have to stay with it, the markets always come back." That statement might have some truth, but will the markets always come back in time for you? Financial entertainers and the media like to surround us with this dogma or the rhetoric of short-term sizzle issues like the "fiscal cliff." However, it's more important to see things from a pattern and relationship perspective so that you can make sensible investing decisions now and for your future. Let's look at the following chart, which illustrates the Dow Jones historical trends for the past 115 years.

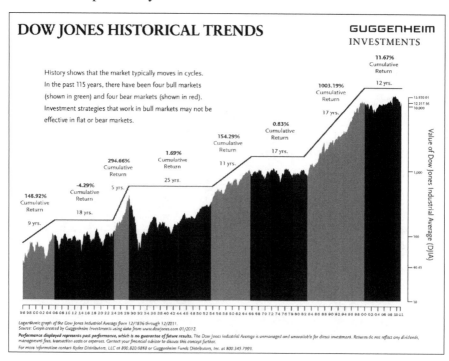

History shows that markets typically move in cycles. In the past 115 years, there have been four bull markets and four bear markets. Investment strategies that work in bull markets may not be effective in flat or bear markets. Let's view this chart and identify patterns that you can recognize visually. If you will notice, in years 1900 – 1928 the Dow Jones moved upward. From 1929 – 1942 the Dow Jones traded sideways or flat. From 1943 – 1966 the trend and movement of the Dow Jones was upward again. From 1967 – 1982 the Dow Jones traded sideways and flat. Years 1982 – 2007 the Dow Jones, once again, rose upward. From 2008 – present the Dow Jones is trading sideways. Are we seeing a pattern forming that projects the Dow Jones trading sideways into 2023 -2024? Possibly. The common denominators that created this interesting cycle of approximately 24 – 28 years of growth in the stock market, and then 14 – 16 years stagnation in the stock market are **demographics,** and more specifically, **baby boomer demographical patterns.** The question you now need to ask is; which 15 to 20 year cycle are you going to retire into? Unfortunately, we don't get to choose so, let's look at the main group of people that will continue to drive our economy.

The Baby Boomers are investors and consumers; they drive the economy and the markets. In the early stages, baby boomers are forming families, having children, spending on homes, furnishings, cars, and buying clothing for their growing families. As Baby Boomers mature, their spending and consuming continues so the economy grows. As companies earn more they are rewarded with their stock valuation increasing and the stock market in turn follows in an upward trend. You might have heard the saying, "The stock market is earnings driven."

So, let's look at one of the main economic drivers: home building, and the impact it has on the economy and stock market. How many people does it take to build a home? When you really think about the impact home building has on employment and the economy, the number is staggering. Who cuts the timber, transports the timber, cuts and shapes the wood into 2x4s and frames to shape the home? Who makes the drywall? Who weaves the carpet and creates the tile for flooring? How about the electrical parts, wiring, sockets, lights and canisters for the lights? How about home furnishings and appliances such as washing machines, dishwashers, stoves, refrigerators etc…? Home building is critical to the health of our economy. Jobs are created and employment improves. The more people employed and earning money means more people are paying taxes and spending on necessities and luxuries to make their lives more comfortable. The government (Federal, State, City and County), flourishes through the collection of more tax receipts. American companies earn more and their reward is a higher stock price. In essence, a ripple effect occurs in the creation of jobs and opportunities for employment in different industries and sectors. You can apply this same principle to the auto industry and ask the same question; "How many people does it take the build an automobile?" The answer again is in the tens of thousands. Edward Cheung, author of *Baby Boomers, Generation X, and Social Cycles* wrote: "Population growth impacts the size of society's work force and consumption. Society's consumption in turn impacts the level of production. Since consumer spending makes up approximately two thirds of GDP, demographics have a very large impact on the economy."

Let's view the demographic Baby Boomer cycles beginning with the turn of the 20th century, 1900 – 1929. With the turn of the century came a demographic group of baby boomers and spending that didn't take hold until 1919. After President McKinley's assassination in 1901, the panic of 1907 and financial crisis in the United States followed. The New York Stock Exchange fell almost 50% from its peak during the previous year and created alarm because this was a time of economic recession. There were numerous runs on banks and trust companies. The 1907 panic eventually spread throughout the nation when many state and local banks and businesses entered bankruptcy. Then our country entered World War I.

During this time, Ford Motor Company adopted the assembly line to mass produce the Model T. Henry Ford offered a $5 per day wage, which more than doubled the rate of most of his workers. The automobile industry had an amazing impact on employment and the economy. As you can see, after World War I, (November 11, 1918), the stock market began an upward trend continuing until it peaked in 1929. By no coincidence the market was descending at a time when this baby boomer group was transitioning from a consuming trend to a saving trend. The markets traded down violently over the next 14 years and struggled through the Great Depression until the next demographic baby boomer era started in 1942. This Baby Boomer generation cycle, called the "Bob Hope Era," ran for about 25 years, reflected in the chart from 1942 to 1967-1968. For approximately 25 years the stock market trended upward due to increased spending by baby boomer consumers. Subsequently, when large groups of the population pass their peak in spending they tend to save more; the economy slows down, the stock market trends downward and then flattens, becoming more volatile. This is reflected in the chart years 1968 -1982.

This now brings us to the amazing economic boom that occurred in our country from 1982 to 2007. This boom was brought on by the population growth in the 60s and 70s noted as the largest generation in our country's history. Baby Boomers had steadily been spending during that time. Consumption continued into the 2000s peaking in 2007, it was then that this group's behavior changed from spending to saving. The baby boomers are now dedicated to saving for retirement, and creating enough wealth and resources to sustain a comfortable lifestyle. Their focus is paying down debt, closing credit cards and transitioning from larger to smaller homes. These "Empty Nesters" now have children leaving the household and going off to college or getting married. This dynamic cycle now causes the baby boomers to do everything in smaller numbers. They are borrowing less and not upgrading or purchasing big ticket items. In contemplating the patterns we've identified in the Dow Jones Historical Trends over the past 115 years, one would have to consider that it is not a coincidence that stock market prices and the economy are impacted by population waves and their spending. These large demographic groups have a direct impact on the stock market and our economy.

Since the baby boomers are focused on paying down their own debt and saving, the economy will be challenged to grow. Also, the federal debt is approximately $17 Trillion, municipal debt $3 Trillion, and corporate and private debt are $40 Trillion. The government must face this debt burden or our next generation will be forced to carry a larger financial load. Today, our country's choice is be fiscally accountable or kick the can down the road. Greater taxation and reduced spending are economically painful and almost politically impossible. These two together will slow the economy and could greatly affect your retirement.

Has all this happened before? In a New York Times article dated October 16, 2010, Martin Fackler wrote about Japan's economic struggles. He wrote; "Few nations in recent history have seen such a striking reversal of economic fortune as Japan. The original Asian success story, Japan rode one of the great speculative stock and property bubbles of all time in the 1980s to become the first Asian country to challenge the long dominance of the West. But the bubbles popped in the late 1980s and early 1990s, and Japan fell into a slow but relentless decline that neither enormous budget deficits nor a flood of easy money has reversed. For nearly a generation now, the nation has been trapped in low growth and a corrosive downward spiral of prices, known as deflation."

Very interesting and non-coincidental in Japan's situation is demographics. Japan experienced a surge in birth rates after World War II which created a large baby boomer group. This group was responsible for Japan's economic rise and collapse after spending peaked, when paying down debt and saving become more of a priority. We can learn from Japan because what its economy experienced in 1990 is similar to what America is going through today.

CONCLUSION

Can you afford to use strategies assured to produce inaccurate results? Do you have an income plan with guarantees or will you be eroding precious capital? Are you **hoping** that you're lucky enough to retire during the right economic cycle, or will you be like Sue? We see the shaping of a potential retirement catastrophe for many current and soon-to-be retirees. Obsolete planning techniques combined with increasing volatility will prove disastrous to retirees relying on supplemental income. The need for a guaranteed income or a personal pension is of paramount responsibility. This should be the emphasis of those looking for peace-of-mind in retirement years and an advisor who can get them there.

About Todd

For over twenty years, Todd Kim has helped personal clients, business owners, professionals and financial institutions reach and maximize their financial goals. As a trusted financial advisor, Todd has worked with many retirees and pre-retirees in the construction and implementation of secure retirement income plans avoiding risks and maximizing full income potentials. Todd is considered a specialist in his field, coaching and training other advisors and financial and legal professionals seeking direction in the design and execution of well-crafted, defined benefit plans.

Todd takes a practical and personal approach with his clients by focusing on the fundamentals of wealth management and retirement income planning. This approach allows clients access to many of the top institutional asset managers along with state-of-the-art retirement planning vehicles and processes. Todd's goal is to maximize efficiency and growth, minimize expenses and reduce or eliminate unnecessary risks. His approach is unique in that he combines a high-end wealth management/income plan along with a platinum level service to his clients. Many of Todd's clients have been with him for almost twenty years.

Todd's career began as a stock and options trader at Fidelity Investments where he soon moved up to a bond trader on the fixed income team. Todd worked for six years at First Interstate/Wells Fargo bank as a financial advisor/planner on the Trust and Wealth Management Team. Todd spent seven years as a Financial Advisor and area Team Leader for Banc One/Chase Bank Private Client Services. Todd was an owner and co-founder of Intermountain Financial Advisors and then co-founded the Galileo Financial Group – which includes Galileo Capital Management and Galileo Financial Advisors. Galileo Financial Group is an independent financial services firm specializing in wealth management and retirement income planning. Galileo Financial Group constructs and manages the financial services/planning platforms for multiple banks and credit unions and has offices in Utah, Idaho and Arizona.

Todd graduated from Brigham Young University where he majored in History and received dual minors in Finance and Korean Language. Todd also has a Master's Degree in Science in Financial Services from the Institute of Business and Finance. Todd is Board Certified in Estate Planning and Mutual Funds and is a Certified Fund Specialist.

Todd grew up on a farm in Burley, Idaho and currently lives in Draper, Utah with his wife Heather and their four children. As a family, they love the Utah outdoors and enjoy camping, hiking, fishing and snow skiing. Todd is active in service work throughout the community and enjoys working with youth groups such as scouting, little league coaching and youth mentoring.

About Greg

For more than 20 years, Greg Roumpos has been helping his clients achieve their financial goals. Greg attended Westminster College in Salt Lake City, Utah, where he received his Bachelor's Degree in Finance and is currently striving toward a Master's Degree in Financial Services.

Greg began his career as a trader with Fidelity Investments and later relocated to Wells Fargo Private Client Services where he worked as a Senior Advisor and Trust Officer. He then became a Managing Team Leader for Bank One Investments, giving him the opportunity to work extensively in the field of Private Asset Management. Before taking the position as Senior Partner and CEO of Galileo Financial Group, Greg was a Managing Partner of Intermountain Financial Advisors, a financial institution partnering firm.

Greg is committed to providing his clients with superior service and personalized attention. His deep understanding of financial markets enables him to provide his clients with the best available investment products consistent with their needs and risk appetite. Greg is also sensitive to current fiduciary issues that drive his desire to establish trust and engender confidence from his clients.

Greg thoroughly educates his clients about the advantages and disadvantages of every financial decision they make and then helps them create and execute a material financial plan. This approach minimizes expectation gaps in his plan administration and investment advisory services.

Greg offers a wide variety of programs and services – which are individually tailored to each of his client's financial needs.

Greg enjoys spending time with his wife and three children. He and his family appreciate the outdoors and actively participate in sports. Greg spends most of his free time coaching his boy's youth baseball and basketball teams. Greg's passion for serving his family and his clients also extends to serving the local Salt Lake community and Greek ethnic community.

CHAPTER 24

YOUR FIVE-POINT PLAN FOR RETIREMENT

BY RON CAMPBELL

Hey, you are successful. You are a force to be reckoned with in your chosen field and the money is pouring in. Now what? Do you know how to manage this wealth? Do you have a plan or strategy in place to hold on to your wealth? Or are you just letting things "take care of themselves" because you believe your time and energies will have the best return by keeping focused on what got you this far?

I can tell you from experience it's much harder to hold on to your money than it is to make it. I'm always reminded of my Granny and how it's one of the reasons why I do what I do. She had an impact and influence in shaping my career choice. You see I grew up at a time where kids were to be seen and not heard. Well here's white-haired Granny who came to stay with us from time to time for months on end. I thought when you got old with white hair you could do whatever you wanted and she wanted to live with us every so often. I noticed that a certain time each month she got something called a Social Security check from the mail man. I also noticed that Granny, the daughter and daughters-in-law were in a good mood for that week and so were us kids because usually something was bought for us. And I used to think, "How cool would it be if Granny could get a check every week and be happy four times a month instead of just once." Of course as I learned later, Granny wasn't visiting us because she wanted to, BUT because it was my parents turn to put her up. Of course, with Granny came the Social Security check.

That vivid memory has stayed with me and drives me every day to help our clients' lives so they cannot only be happy EVERY week when they choose to retire, BUT also to enjoy the journey along the way.

Of course there are numerous hurdles to overcome in attaining this.

There are tons of things coming at you to get a piece of your money. The usual suspects are not only taxes, fees, expenses and risk, but also death, disability, divorce and lawsuits, just to name a few. But let's take a look at the two main categories.

Bill and Joann (prospective clients) were in our office recently. Bill asked me to expand on a statement I made in our workshop regarding who's after your money. So I asked him to imagine that we were looking at a big container full of their money. Uncle Sam is on one side and he has taxes, either now or later, plus penalties and restrictions on various accounts I may have. On the other side are the financial institutions. They're grabbing their share with various fees, charges and other expenses and the worst part is you're not aware of the total amount they are taking and the impact of that total on your bottom line.

You see, most people think they know what they are paying in fees and expenses. But according to a recent article in The Wall Street Journal, the hidden costs of mutual funds aren't reflected in a funds standard expense ratio. In what he calls "The Tyranny of long-term costs," Vanguard Funds founder John Bogle has written about how much costs matter. He illustrated that if we conservatively assume investment costs of 1½ percent per year and begin with a $1,000 investment that would be valued at $3.5 million today, with reinvested dividends BUT AFTER deducting those costs, the remaining value would be $1 million – some 70 percent less. This should be unacceptable, but sometimes we don't know what we don't know, and that includes the people sitting across from you giving you the advice. The key is not the fee by itself, but the value you are getting in exchange for that fee.

I said, "Bill, if 1 ½% in fees has a dramatic effect on your account; what do you think 30% in taxes is going to do? Remember the game of connect the dots. You were given a paper with dots and you connected them using a pen or pencil, and when finished you would have a picture of something that we were unable to see with just the dots. So if I said let's connect the dots on the following: if you go to the IRS website and see that income tax revenue is expected to be 75% higher five years from now and we have a reported 8-9% unemployment, and almost 50% of today's workforce in the US are ZERO liability federal taxpayers. What picture do you see when you connect the dots? Do you think the higher tax revenues are going to come from new workers or do you think it will come from people like us? Bill said, "People like us." "I agree," I said, "and that's why I'm personally planning to minimize the impact. I'm personally preparing for it coming from me."

Bill blurted out to me, "How do I do that; is it too late? Can you show me?" I assured him I could but we had more lessons to learn before we got to that point.

You see we have an aging population, a declining workforce and a government that needs money. All signs point to higher taxes.

Now his eyes were big and I thought he was going to hyperventilate, so I quickly assured him we had a plan to address these issues and that most of the time it would be similar to an oil change and tune up and not a complete engine overhaul. In other words, in most cases a client already has accounts that are good, and all we have to do is just modify and adjust a couple things to have a dramatic effect. With that he started relaxing a bit and I said, "Before I show you how our stress test review on your portfolio works, let's take brief look at risk. Bill, remember in the movie *Jurassic Park*, when Jeff Goldblum's character was against the premise of dinosaurs and man co-existing? He said to the founder of Jurassic Park that he was so busy figuring out if he COULD, he never stopped to think about if he SHOULD. You see the same goes for your level of risk. You could take a lot of risk with your money, but you need to think if you should; because if you lose 50% of your portfolio you will need to make 100% just to get back to even." A 25% drop will require you to make 33% to get back to square one. I told him Ron's #1 rule is to *not lose money*.

I didn't want to, but I had to ask if he remembered 2008. His expression changed again and he said, "Remember? I haven't gotten back to even." Then I said, "And yet you are still paying fees in those accounts even though you are still under water."

My industry has done a horrible job with helping Americans preserve their wealth and provide value for the money they're getting paid. It's like the golf industry. I'm an avid golfer and the similarities between golf and Wall Street are eerie. The last 20 years, in golf, have seen huge advancements in equipment from club heads and shafts to the golf balls, …right down to the shoes you wear- endless choices up and down the line. Yet with all of that technology the average golfer's score has improved by less than one stroke. Basically there's no improvement (value), which is what the golfing industry sells us (products). Wall Street and the financial community is the same. Fast trades, cheap trades, and endless choices for our money. But yet the percentage of people obtaining financial security has not changed. Some will say it's actually gone down with the lost decade in the stock market and a higher cost of living over that same time frame. Yet Wall Street promises easy riches and they get you to play their game with those promises – sometimes with truthful but misleading information.

Let me give you an example of how they have us conditioned. If I ask you, "What's the best way to choose a mutual fund what would you say?" Bill responded "Rate of Return." I smiled as I expected as much. Being in the trenches for over 30 years you get a good feel for people's perceptions.

I said, "Bill, we're going to do an exercise," while handing him a paper and pen. I said write +10, -10, +10,-10 vertically. He did and I said, "So what's the average rate of return?" Bill said, "Zero, right?" I agreed. So I asked, "If you had $100K in an account that averaged 0% for the past four years, you would have…" He quickly answered with "$100K". I said, "Good logical answer, BUT incorrect." Now handing him the calculator, I said, "Punch in 100,000 and multiply by 1.1 and give me the answer." Bill stated, "110,000!" I said, "Now multiply that by .9." He said, "The answer is 99,000." I said, "Now multiply by 1.1 again." "108, 900," Bill answered. Finally, I said, "Now multiply by .9 again." And Bill answered with "98,010." He finally looks up and I broke the ice by saying, "Incredible isn't it? Do you see how chasing rate of returns plays into Wall Street's hands because every time you buy and sell they get paid. And since you can't get the right answer starting with the wrong premise, continually chasing returns usually ends up in frustration and losses."

As he sat there, I said, "Just think, that is just a four year period and it doesn't take into consideration taxes, fees and expenses! Imagine the impact over a lifetime!"

We both agreed that a second opinion or 'stress test' was warranted and I collected a bunch of information regarding his accounts, taxes, and family information. We also discussed his concerns, dreams, desires, and intentions. Also, if time and money were not an issue, what would he be doing? I told him I felt good about ways I thought I could help, but only an analysis would determine to what degree.

Two weeks later Bill and Joann were back and I shared some good news with them. After reviewing his issues and concerns, (making sure that we were still on the same page), I laid out the recommendations. The bottom line was that he had a potential 34% risk in his portfolio, meaning if we experienced another 2008, his portfolio was at risk for losing $185K. After some repositioning and utilizing some guaranteed accounts for current income, his fees and expenses were reduced a little over $11,000 per year. Joann jested, "You just found my car payment" and we both chuckled as Bill shook his head. In addition, they will also save about $3K a year in taxes. With their new-found sense of relief and not having to worry about another stock market selloff, we agreed they could start enjoying life again and do the things they had been putting off. One last chore we had them do was to get back with their lawyer to update their legal documents and to also make sure their insurance coverages were up-to-speed. Although we still had things on their to-do list and Long Term Care needed to be addressed, Bill and Joann said they felt both relief and a sense of accomplishment. I said I was honored to be part of their solution.

WHAT ABOUT YOU?

Can you accomplish what Bill and Joann did? Maybe, maybe not – it all depends on your situation. But it's important to work with an advisor that can assist you in your own 5 POINT PLAN.

The 5 points are:

1) Your advisor should be able to direct you to the institutional side of the investment industry. This will allow you to be looked after by a fiduciary. This is someone that has to place your interests first.

2) He or she should be able to 'stress test' your portfolio against

taxes, penalties, risk, fees and expenses. This comparison needs to be done BEFORE implementing any strategy.

3) Their plan for you should reduce both the element of risk and taxes both now and into the future. We use what we call 'The financial GPS' or 'Guided Planning System'. This will become increasingly important as the Baby Boomers continue to age, placing more strain on an already fiscally-troubled system as they collect their entitlements.

4) Your advisor should be using a third party institution-style custodian to safeguard your holdings. (No Bernie Madoff surprises.) Our strategic alliance with Global Financial Private Capital helps us simplify the first 4 steps of this process.

5) The final thing that you should look for in an advisor is someone who will act as a Relationship Director or what my friend and colleague Chris Sleight likes to call a New Age advisor. According to Chris, your relationship director will act as the go between with you and the other pros needed to get the job done, i.e. money manager, custodian, attorney, CPA, etc. This way the advisor can guide and coach you and help you achieve what most of us wanted since we started or stopped working – a more peaceful and secure financial lifestyle.

Finding the right advisor will save you time, money and effort.

No matter where you are at financially, no matter your past financial experiences, it's not too late. You can do this. Financial security may be closer than you think. Remember, somebody is going to get rich off of your money; it might as well be you!

Comments or questions can be directed to ron@roncampbell.net. Investment advisory services offered through Global Financial Private Capital, LLC an SEC Registered Investment Advisor.

About Ron

Ron Campbell, CFP®, RFC®, is the founder and principal of Campbell Financial Services. He has over 35 years of "in the trenches" experience in the financial services industry. He has served as an adjunct faculty member for adult education in financial planning at various high schools and community colleges, and has also taught those same courses at several companies. Ron has served as host of radio's *Successful Business Hour* and has been quoted and published in various publications.

Ron was featured as part of America's Premier Experts TV Show "The Consumers Advocate" which airs on ABC, NBC, CBS and Fox affiliates. He has also been seen in *Forbes, Newsweek* and *The Suit* magazines. Ron has also been commissioned a Kentucky Colonel by the Commonwealth of Kentucky.

In specializing with retirees or those about to be retired, Mr. Campbell utilizes strategies that focus on guaranteed income and preservation of capital. What worked in the accumulation phase of one's life may not work as well during the distribution phase. Mr. Campbell believes when it comes to investing, there is more to be gained by avoiding losses rather than picking the apparent winners. With the changing demographics and our country's fiscal woes, Ron believes risk, taxes, fees/expenses, penalties and inflation need to be considered before implementing any investment strategy.

Memberships include The Better Business Bureau®, Financial Planning Association®, International Association of Registered Financial Consultants®, and Wealth and Wisdom®.

Ron regularly conducts educational events throughout Anne Arundel and surrounding counties. Ron resides in Linthicum, Maryland with his wife, Cheryl. They have four daughters, a son-in-law, and seven beautiful grandchildren.

To schedule a time to discuss your financial future, contact us at:
Ron@RonCampbell.net or call (410)766-0900 today!
7310 Ritchie Highway, Suite 700 Glen Burnie, MD 21061
Phone (410)766-0900 Fax (410)766-0908
www.RonCampbell.net

[Investment advisory services offered through Global Financial Private Capital, LLC an SEC Registered Investment Advisor]

CHAPTER 25

FROM THE GREAT DEPRESSION TO THE GREAT RECESSION: HOW A SAFE MONEY STRATEGY REAPS REWARDS AND LIMITS RISK

BY STEWART A. MILLER

Recently, I had a couple in my office who wanted to talk to me about handling their investments. They asked me, "What do you do differently than the other financial advisors?"

My response was, "My clients often tell me that due to the strategic planning where we focus on safety and contractual guarantees, they have peace of mind and are able to sleep at night."

They looked at me for a moment and said, "That's how we want to feel. That's why we're here."

After what the global economy has gone through the past few years, many people are understandably nervous about their money – they've seen what can happen very quickly should Wall Street circumstances turn unexpectedly. For example, did you know that America's total economic loss from October of 2008 through March of 2009 actually averaged out to an astounding $100,000 per household?

Sudden plunges like that are why I avoid stocks, bonds and mutual funds; I feel they're much too volatile – and, at the moment, I'm responsible for protecting, as well as growing, over a quarter of a billion dollars of my clients' money and assets. My low-risk Safe Money investment strategy (which I'll go more into detail later in this chapter) keeps that money safe and sound – and they can sleep as well as I do at night.

But it wasn't 2008 that convinced me to develop my Safe Money strategy –, it was actually 1929.

BUCKING THE BOOMING '90'S

I began my career as a financial advisor in the 1990s, a time when cautious investment advice wasn't really taken seriously. However, that was my approach even then. Others were making 14% returns on their investments, while mine were realizing 5% to 7% - but, of course, when those others found their double digit returns disappearing, my clients held on to their gains. That's why I tell my clients that they'll like me when the market is up – and they'll *love* me when the market is down.

The real reason for my insisting on a Safe Money strategy, however, was that I'm always anxious to learn from others – and many of my first clients offered me quite an education. They had lived through the Great Depression that hit the U.S. in 1929 and lingered throughout the 1930s – leaving our nation economically-devastated for over a decade.

Those old-timers had seen people lose everything – and many spent hours in line just to get a loaf of bread for their families. And they weren't about to forget – so they lived very modestly. I recall one client wore the same pair of wool pants every time I visited her at her home. If I happened to arrive close to lunch time, she generously offered to split their lavish buffet three ways – which consisted of a can of beans that she was heating up on the stove.

The kids of this "Greatest Generation" may have smirked at their thriftiness – but I personally saw how much wealth they had accumulated during their lifetimes, even with incomes that topped out around $25,000 a year. Many of them were still able to leave behind million dollar estates to their children – who felt a little differently about their parents' frugal financial habits when they saw the large amounts that were left to them.

TODAY'S RETIREMENT CHALLENGES

Even back in the 90's, retirement planning was easier than it is today. Now, few pension plans are offered by employers – and, in many cases, it's completely left to the individual to formulate a workable plan to ensure that there will be enough funds available for them to enjoy their sunset years beyond their meager Social Security payments (and let's not forget that this program continues to come under political attack). Added to this financial pressure is the fact that more of us are also living *longer* – well into our eighties and nineties – which means we need to save even more to cover those years.

Which brings us back to the "kids" I referred to earlier – the Baby Boomers, who are now closing in on retirement age, if they're not there already. They've had to learn the hard way that their parents and grandparents thrifty ways were justified – by dealing with more economic uncertainty than they ever expected to encounter as adults. Yes, their parents may have had to grapple with the Great Depression, but they also reaped the rewards of a huge postwar expansion of America's money-making power, as well as a steady upward economic movement that lasted most of their lives.

The Baby Boomers, in contrast, have seen unending volatility: the "Black Monday" crash of 1987, the tech bubble bursting in 2000, the market plunge after the tragic events of 9/11 and, of course, the most recent 2008 meltdown, have all made this generation incredibly cautious with their money.

Beyond that, they've seen the U.S. economy shift in a fundamental way; businesses and jobs that they once counted on to last forever continue to disappear, along with much of the middle class. Property values, which were also once thought to be largely invulnerable, still haven't recovered from the massive hit they took a few years ago. This has made them very leery of trusting anything or anyone when it comes to their money.

In the past we would have a short meeting discussing a little about what they wanted and how we could get them there. Before long we were having coffee and dessert and I had a friend for life.

EVERYTHING CHANGES

But, of course, nothing is going to dissipate the overall doubt people still feel about our economy. That means people are taking my Safe Money strategies seriously now – because more people actually share my investing philosophy than at any other time in my professional career. For example, a 2011 survey asked men and women ages 45 to 75 if they would rather invest in a financial product at a 4% rate of return with no risk, or buy a product with double the return but with some possible risk. A full 80% of respondents chose the guaranteed 4% return.

That represents a fundamental shift in how those approaching retirement age regard their money. They don't believe they will have the time or the opportunity to make their money back, should there be another 2008-style crash – so they know they have to make their investments in as safe a manner as possible.

Of course, the danger is that optimism is now on the rise because of a slowly strengthening economy. 2012 was a good year and people are beginning to believe the storm is over. And because some investors made money from Wall Street again, there's a sense that we should all jump back in and enjoy those higher returns. But, again, I'm reminded of those double digit gains in the 90's that ended up getting washed away with unexpected market downturns – which is why I still believe the average investor should take the profits and *run*.

That's how certain people not only survived the Wall Street Crash of 1929 – but actually made money. They came to the conclusion, even as the stock market was skyrocketing, that, ultimately, it was a dangerous bet. For example, Babe Ruth, one of the greatest baseball players of all time, cashed in his stocks and put that money in annuities, so he and his wife would have guaranteed incomes over their lifetimes. Joe Kennedy, father of future president John F. Kennedy, was also known as one of the shrewdest traders in the country, but he too took out his profits after a stock tip from a shoe shine boy. Kennedy and the Great Bambino, as a result, both made fortunes at a time when so many others lost theirs.

Don't be fooled - you can continue to make money in a down economy – when you pursue the right Safe Money strategy. My clients have done what few investors have managed over the course of what financial industry insiders have called the "Lost Decade." They've achieved above average returns and experienced no losses.

THE BIG CHOICE

Another challenge faced by those in this generation is what happens when the company they've worked for all their lives downsizes and lets them go. Since my company, Estate Financial Group, is located in Flint, Michigan, we naturally have many clients who worked for General Motors, which, as every American knows, has had many economic challenges in recent decades.

At one point, GM gave soon-to-be retirees seven weeks to make a decision that would profoundly affect the rest of their lives: they could either (a) receive a set-in-stone annual payment (after death, surviving spouses would receive 65% of the amount per year), or (b) immediately receive one large lump sum, with the agreement that there will be no further compensation from the company in the future.

Much of my current work involves working with these retirees who had to sort out the pros and cons of this very difficult life-impacting choice. On one side, you can see where a guaranteed annual payment for the rest of your life might provide a sense of security. However, the fact that that annual payout amount never changes could end up becoming a huge problem, should inflation heat up. In contrast, a lump sum, properly invested, gives you the flexibility to meet unexpected needs, as long as the principal is never put in jeopardy.

For example, GM offered one of my clients either $78,000 a year for life or the lump sum amount of $1,240,000. While the annual stipend was tempting, he had to consider that, if he died, his wife would only get 65% of that $78,000, which would take it down to about $50,000. He chose the lump sum, and I was able to invest it in such a way that they would receive $70,000 a year no matter who passed away first, and if inflation did happen to grow, that amount would grow with it. Not only that, but they should be able to leave their heirs a projected $1.3 million.

That, to me, is the value of a financial advisor; a good one should be able to help you come as close as possible to your desired retirement goals while working with your available assets. People all across the country are facing similar challenges, such as for example, what to do with their

401k accounts. My feeling is that you never want to lock yourself into set payments that can't grow. Life changes, your needs change, interest rates change, stock markets change, and inflation changes – and your investment strategy must have the flexibility to deal with those changes.

MY KEY RETIREMENT TOOL

To some people, the safest money strategy of all is simply putting it into a savings account – or even under your bed! The problem with this kind of approach is that you end up losing money. Interest rates on savings accounts are abysmal – and even if you just hide your cash in a drawer, you'll still lose money because of inflation.

I believe annuities provide some of the best options for leveraging your retirement nest-egg to the maximum advantage. But, with so many annuity options out there, it's easy to get confused.

Traditional annuities, including variable, immediate, and fixed annuities, all come with potential hazards. For example, variable annuities not only contain a lot of fees that can negatively impact the rate of return, they're also vulnerable to market fluctuations. Immediate annuities, though they promise upwards of a 9% payout, will hold on to invested monies if you should die prematurely. Finally, fixed annuities act like bank CDs, with no fees, but low interest rates.

Because choosing the right kind of annuity can be difficult, I often have people seeking me out through the Internet, asking me for my advice – and my recommendation is most often the relatively new hybrid indexed annuity.

Hybrid indexed annuities give their investors a lot more flexibility and a lot more control than other annuities – all while keeping the principal safe and sound. While they aren't tied to the stock market, their payouts do increase when interest rates rise – but if interest rates should happen to fall, the principal (as well as any gains made) remains untouched.

These kinds of annuities can be utilized to guarantee an income, almost like a pension (or the GM retirement option I wrote about earlier in this chapter) that will last as long as the retiree's lifetime, while also having the potential for more growth. There are also no annual fees for management of this annuity.

In addition, you also have the option of choosing from multiple exit plans – one of which provides for an annual 10% penalty-free withdrawal. Also, if you should face some unexpected expense such as a medical emergency, there is a long term care annuity, which provides extra income to handle those kinds of costs. Should the holder of the annuity pass away, many hybrid indexed annuities even wave surrender fees – which allow the heirs to inherit the money without charge.

The hybrid indexed annuity fulfills the requirements of what I call "Miller's Safe Money Philosophy" – "If all fails, it still guarantees them income they can never outlive."

Remember, at the beginning of this chapter, the question I was asked by a group of potential clients: "What do you do differently than the other financial advisors?"

I like to think that every financial advisor has their clients' best interests at heart. However, I also like to think that I take a few extra steps that maybe some do not to safeguard my clients' money against risk, as well as against unexpected changes in both their lives and the outside economy.

We cannot predict the future – but for now, I'm interested in helping my clients invest in safe places while the economy is still struggling. Should interest rates rise, should the market start performing strongly, whatever the case might be, I want to also make sure they have the option to change their investment strategies based on what's actually happening, rather than on what some economist might have forecasted years earlier (and probably would have been wrong about).

We're hoping for a Great Boom instead of another Great Depression or another Recession. But whatever the case, I want my clients to hang onto their money – and enjoy a relaxing and wonderful retirement. They've earned it.

About Stewart

Stewart Miller began working with retirees nearly 20 years ago. He has helped hundreds of hardworking Americans just like you protect over a quarter of a billion dollars with his Safe Money strategies. The winning strategies Stewart has applied to his practice have enabled his clientele to achieve above average returns and experience no losses. Many of his clients proclaim they rest much easier knowing they now have guaranteed income plans.

Stewart is a lifelong Michigan resident and resides with his family in Flushing, Michigan – although he has worked with clients all over the country. Stewart hosts a weekly radio program called "Safe Money Radio." Stewart has also been an expert guest speaker for many financial forums throughout the country. He is dedicated and passionate about protecting his client's financial future.

CHAPTER 26

MR. BUCKET LIST

BY JOHN JOCHEM
AND FAITH JOCHEM

I have walked on hot coals and on a glacier. I have eaten fire, broken wood with my hands and broken an arrow with my throat at a seminar. I have fed 150 alligators in a day and have been wrapped with an extremely large snake. I have zip lined over alligators in Florida and zip lined in Costa Rica. I have experienced the world's highest tandem sky dive, the world's tallest sling shot (a bungee cord event) and the world's highest thrill ride. I have parasailed and I have been on a sail boat. I have petted a dolphin and a dozen stingrays in a day and swam with the sting rays in the Grand Cayman Islands. I have seen the sun rise, while on an airplane and saw the curvature of earth, while flying into the sunrise. I have done America's only carousel on steroids ride.

I have interviewed sport superstars, like the Heisman Trophy winner, the heavyweight champion of the world and the gold medal winner, Gold Glove winner and the Golden Glove winner. I have been to a Super Bowl and a National Championship game and a heavyweight championship fights. I have had lunch with a President of the United States. I have co-authored multiple bestselling books and have multiple degrees. I have enjoyed a sunset cruise with my daughter. I have taken my daughter to Disney World for every A grade I earned in my masters program.

Have you ever bought somebody over a hundred roses at one time? Have you ever written a thousand love letters/emails/notes to the same person? Have you ever written somebody a hundred reasons why you loved the person or two hundred reasons or a thousand reasons? Have you asked what others want and do their bucket list with you, or a top 100 moments in the other's life?

Some things on your bucket list are easy. Safely driving 100 miles an hour in a car or being on the Daytona Speedway with an entire crowd watching you circle the track can be on your list. You just have to give consideration to the what and the how will come. Meeting Muhammad Ali was easy, but the fear of talking with the champ was something else. Going to the Super Bowl is a ticket. The courage and the time to go to the Super Bowl could be the challenge.

BUCKET LIST MENTALITY

I believe I can do things on my bucket list. I notice my bucket list items in real life. When I am having a bad day I may just attack my bucket list. I have woken up on a Saturday and jumped in the vehicle and went zip lining over alligators and then the world's only carousel on steroids and then sky diving the following day. A bucket list mentality is not an either or thing: you can do both. The bucket list mentality is you will find a way.

While doing bucket list items, magical moments happen. Parasailing and coming to the water and getting close to a sting ray; going to Sedona and seeing a two-ton plus elk in the middle of the road; seeing Winter the dolphin (without a fin on the dolphin tale in Disney movie Dolphin Tale) and petting a dolphin; magical moments just happen when you do bucket list items.

When you start doing your bucket list, you start getting brave and you add to your list and you do your list and live your list.

MY DAD AND HIS ADVENTURES

My dad had a conference call and he asked me what he should tell people about himself. I told him to say he was awesome. That weekend, we went to Orlando and stayed at the Nickelodeon Hotel. We did an airboat ride and fed about 150 alligators. Daddy wanted to go sky diving, but I'm afraid of heights. Instead, we did a helicopter ride and saw all of the parks in Orlando. Later we had a special dinner and we saw knights fighting with their swords on their horses. Next day I got 'slimed' at the hotel. We went to Gatorland. Daddy wanted to zip line over alligators, but I didn't want to. The following day, we went to Disney World. This is just one weekend with my dad.

While we were in Orlando, we saw a billboard for Winter, the dolphin. Winter was the dolphin, in Dolphin Tale, without a fin on the tail. The two of us went to Clearwater Beach, FL to see Winter. I got to see Winter, pet a dolphin and then pet a dozen sting rays. Daddy took me on seven boat rides. We raced with dolphins and did something scary. The two of us went parasailing. While we were being pulled in the air by a boat with the parachute holding us up, it sounded like the ropes were ripping. I screamed and daddy said it would be okay. As the parachute came close to the water, it looked like we were going to land on top a sting ray. Later that night, we did a sunset cruise on a pirate ship.

My dad went zip lining over alligators and skydiving without me. My mother does not want me to do those things. My mom does not want me to feed alligators, either, but feeding alligators is fun.

My mom does beach trips and camping. My advice to dads would be to take your kids to see Mickey Mouse. I want to go to Hawaii and Australia and Paris. I want to go to Key West and on a cruise.

My dad will actually ask complete strangers about their bucket list or scary things they have done. I have heard being surrounded by sharks with bloody bait in the water and train jumping, and rollercoasters which go upside down.

BUCKET LIST DATE

My ideal bucket list day is a bunch of things which I have already done. I want to start my night off at the Kennedy Space Center, in FL. In the morning, I want to watch the sun rise over the water. Then I will do the world's highest tandem sky dive, while looking at the Atlantic Ocean and the Kennedy Space Center. Then I will drive to Orlando and experience the world's tallest sling shot; being shot up into the air inside a ball. The ball is held with bungee cords between two tall cranes. You are flung straight up with massive speed and come down with excitement. Before leaving, I would do the world's only carousel on steroids. I would jump into the car and go to Clearwater Beach, FL, which is next to Tampa. The next adventure is parasailing 800 feet in the air, behind a boat on the Gulf of Mexico. After parasailing, I would have a romantic sunset cruise in the Gulf of Mexico. Then I would hold her hand on the beach at the hotel and tell her how grateful I am to be with her and experience life to the fullest. This is my ultimate day, which I have not accomplished in one full day, yet.

I didn't get to do my ideal day. Instead, I went on a G-Rated date and was chaperoned. Not only did my daughter come, but the date's two nieces came. We went to Disney World. The first night, Faith and I did the World's Tallest Sling Shot and then the World's Tallest Sky Coaster. We had the Disney experience and more. Playing dad and having fun is a great date.

GIVING IT AWAY

Imagine buying a family a Christmas. Imagine buying somebody over a hundred roses. Imagine arranging for all of the money to fund an orphanage. Imagine buying lunch for somebody; then buying groceries for a family. Imagine buying a plane ticket for somebody who couldn't afford to fly. I don't have to image it anymore. The Christmas of 2004 was the first Christmas I played Santa Clause for another family.

One year, my mother couldn't afford a Christmas Eve party. A father said it was the one event which his four children looked forward to every year. The father gave my mother a check for four figures. I put it as a goal to buy a family a Christmas. Tony Robbins bought Thanksgivings for people. I put it as a goal to buy a college degree/education for somebody and I prepaid my daughter's college. My father constantly gave funds to his church. When I arranged for an orphanage to be paid for, it was a goal. Giving it away is part of the bucket list.

On my bucket list, I wrote about buying a person a vacation. Giving it away is part of the bucket list. I wrote on my bucket list about buying a person a seminar and motivational DVDs and CDs and books. I wrote about making other people's dreams come true. I wrote about being about to give freely. Items were put on my bucket list, which didn't make any sense.

HOW I STARTED MY BUCKET LIST

My first great paper was called LUV 101, which listed 101 reasons why I loved a person. Then years later, I wrote LUV 202, which was 202 reasons why I loved a person and at the end I said I accept (marriage). Each year for my anniversary, 101 reasons were added. A paper called LUV 505 showed up to my wife's work with two dozen roses. Then I started 101 things I wanted to do with my wife, which was my first bucket list.

I actually stopped the LUV 101 papers. Later, my wife would not give me the time of day, but would only read romance books. The answer was obvious: I wrote her a romance book. In the book I listed over a thousand things I loved about the female character, which was my definition of my ideal person. I listed everything, which I did with the female character, which was my extreme bucket list. I listed everything I did in the book with my ideal female person and I listed a section, called I promise. "I promise" was a section listing ways I could be a better and ideal husband. My first wife had mentally left me by the time I was writing her the romance book.

I became the person who I was writing about: I got the master's degree and did doctorate work and taught college online. I co-authored best-selling books. I went out and did bucket list items and many of the bucket list items with my daughter in real life and in the book. I surprised people with over a hundred roses, just like I did in my romance book. In real life, my wife attacked me and left. I became dedicated to living life to the fullest and living the dream. I owe so much to my first wife. We enjoyed more good years than bad. Today, our daughter is enjoying the bucket list, which was written years before.

Before I started the extensive romance book with a bucket list, my father told me to stop chasing the millions and start living life. My father got cancer and lived like he was dying for over a decade. Things my father did, which I look forward to doing, are the Great Barrier Reef, the Great Wall of China, eating in Japan, a safari in Africa, staying at the Ritz's, going to the French Mediterranean, Paris…and the World Series.

NEXT

The bucket list is different to goals. Goals are dreams with a date. The bucket list is something you want to do. I want to go to the summer and the winter Olympics. I want to eat at the White House with the President of the United States. I want to watch the sun rise and set over large bodies of water in the same day. I want to jump off the Stratosphere in Las Vegas. I want to go in a submarine and swim with the dolphins. I want to see the green water of the Indian Ocean meet the blue water of the

Atlantic Ocean at the cape in South Africa. I want to take a two-week Alaskan cruise. I want to go on a hot air balloon ride. I want to fly in a Mig. I have a desire to eat dinner with the President of the United States in the White House and to dine with royalty.

When you go out and share your bucket list and do your bucket list, people help you to achieve more items. People also add things to your list. I have not yet done the Macy's Thanksgiving Day Parade, jumped in a Lear jet to Detroit and watched the Detroit Lions play on Thanksgiving Day and then jump onto the Lear jet to fly to Minneapolis to the Mall of America for Black Friday shopping. I have had my sister invite me to New Orleans for Mardi Gras and the Super Bowl. I have had people get me interviews with sports super stars. I acted as though there was a conspiracy of other people trying to help me achieve my bucket list.

Living your bucket list makes you cool. You have a fulfilled life. You start believing in yourself and others start believing in you. Others start helping you to accomplish more. In order to achieve your bucket list items, you develop a team and delegate more. When you become a bucket list person, success starts to become easy. Excuses start disappearing and results start appearing.

BUCKET LIST AND SALES

The major challenge with sales is the salesperson does not ask for the order. If you have the courage to jump off the Stratosphere in Las Vegas, then you have the courage to ask out the girl on a date. If you have the courage to jump out of a perfectly fine airplane at 18,000 ft., then you probably have the courage to ask for the order.

If you take action on your bucket list, then your self-image starts to improve. If you are worthy to travel to London or take a great cruise or see the Niagara Falls and the Grand Canyon, then you can be worthy to ask for the order. If you are worthy of the limo and the room on the ocean than you are worthy of the new account.

Some people work 80 hours a week and forget about living. One person believes living is taking breaths. Another person believes living is in the moments which take your breath away. You decide. Live your bucket list; have courage; and ask for the order.

About John

John Jochem is a bestselling author. He has co-authored books with Jack Canfield of Chicken Soup for the Soul, Tom Hopkins, who wrote *How to Master the Art of Selling* and Brian Tracy, who wrote *Goals*. John's books are *The Success Secrets, In it to Win it, The Victory,* and *Counter Attack.* John is a certified Zig Ziglar speaker and trainer, a success coach and a consultant. John has spent months on the road with Tony Robbins and has been mentored by Jack Canfield and Brian Tracy. In 2000, Tom Hopkins named John #1 out of a hundred thousand students, whom he trained. Corporately, John worked for 5 of the top 10 diabetic supply companies, and his best month in sales was 1,250 individual transactions. John did corporate acquisition for three of the top four diabetic supply companies; the biggest was about $25,000,000. His largest advertising budget was $62,000,000. He has worked with the number two power wheelchair company and helped to establish the number two respiratory wholesale company in America. Educationally, John's highest level is doctorate work. He has an MBA from the University of Phoenix and an undergraduate BBA with dual majors in marketing and finance from the University of Miami. As an undergraduate, John was on the National Dean's list, which is in the top 0.5% in the nation in grades. As a Master's student, John was the top of his class.

John was born with a speech impediment, was dyslexic and couldn't read for about two decades. He actually failed out of college, but collegially, people know him for his achievements. John was published before he was 20 years old. John was homeless and unemployed, but some know of him for increasing his net worth by a million dollars in one day. John has failed and succeeded and is best known for his successes. John has had books hit the Best Seller's List in 2011, 2012 and 2013; thus, he was been inducted into the Best Selling Author's Hall of Fame. He has taught college students business concepts in management courses.

Faith Jochem is an Honors student and a great daughter. She is probably an honors student because she has tutors and works harder and longer. She is probably a great daughter, because she has joy built inside of her and joy radiates out of her without conflict. Faith is known for selling 750 cookies for Girl Scouts and has been in the Scouts since Pre-K.

To contact John for consulting or coaching, email him at johnfjochem@gmail.com.

CHAPTER 27

GREAT RELATIONSHIPS WILL PUT YOU IN BUSINESS AND KEEP YOU IN BUSINESS

BY VANESSA NUNEZ
& BRIDGET SHOEMAKER

I believe that connecting with your clients is the single most important task, if it can be called a task that is, in any business. The manner in which this is done is the make or break for anyone that has a product or service to offer. Following these simple guidelines is my suggestion for longevity in success.

1. BE YOURSELF

In today's world everyone seems to want to be someone else. The easiest thing to do in life is to be yourself, being true to who you are. Your personality is so much of who you are, and how you are perceived in the world around you. Constantly I say, I am good at being "me." If you are requiring something other than that, it simply is not something I am interested in doing.

The most important realization in this concept of being yourself is to really embrace that you are a unique individual and you are not a carbon copy of anyone else. This means that at times you will be questioned and pressured by peers, clients, society, family and so forth to change who you are. Believe in yourself enough to know you are exactly who you are meant to be. That does not say you cannot learn and adjust behaviors and acquire new philosophies, it simply means always remaining true to your core essence.

As you continue on the path of being yourself, understand that does facilitate scenarios where you must be prepared to say it like is…not always a popular concept but one that is respected. If I had a dollar for every time I heard, "Did you just say what I think you said?" And I happily reply, "Why, yes I did." I would be a billionaire. This is because keeping it real is the path I choose – along with the philosophy that I would rather beg for forgiveness than ask permission.

2. KEEP IT REAL

Take the time to really observe 'the who', 'the what' and 'the how' of the people around you. So much can be said about the conversations to follow if the time is taken to evaluate these simple behaviors. It is in all of these little innuendos that speak without words. Inspire those you are in conversation with through your persona. The image of who you are in your mind is so much of who you are in person. As this becomes a natural technique in your everyday skillset, you can then seamlessly adjust your character – not your personality – to match the environment and culture you are in.

Mimic the body language of the people that are around you. Usually a calm, a familiarity comes from the energy of this, it also allows you the ability to be yourself. People like to respond to the familiar, and by keeping it real and in the moment, this is how you become a magnet for yourself and the people who are in your sphere.

There is no sugar coating in keeping it real; allow that personality to be in the moment. Embracing you for you is the most gratifying trait anyone can portray to themselves and those that they encounter. This allows you to be comfortable in your environment and to allow others to do the same.

3. FIND OUT ABOUT THEM

Knowing 'who' your client is, is the single most important thing you can determine. Watch them. How do they move? How do they use their hands when they speak? Do they look at you or away from you when speaking? Understanding the mannerisms of your client is the first step to connecting.

As you start observing this and practicing what the person in front of you is doing or saying, the energy that is being exchanged can allow so much data to be interfaced between the lines, that the interruptions become seamless between the two of you and knowing the customer is as easy as knowing yourself.

Another key is paying attention to details in their dress, down to what style it is. Are they wearing jewelry? ...Is it bodacious or understated? These are all clues, which give you insight into the customer's inner self and can give you a glimpse of how they view themselves.

Did you notice when they entered the room, did they just meander in with little attention drawn to them? ...Or did they stand out as if they were on fire? This is a very important step in knowing who client is, because this is how they see themselves through the eyes of others. All of the questions above run through my mind in a split second just prior to shaking hands and introductions.

When you meet your client, notice how they walk up to you. Is it timid, authoritative, or enthusiastic? This is also a direct window into how the customers see themselves; it is how they will set the tone in the exchange of conversation.

How are they speaking to you, and what's their choice of words? ...Do they use their body to speak as well? Tone of a conversation is so much more than just the verbal exchange, it is set long before the first word is spoken. The verbal exchange is just the finale to the rest of the engagement.

4. GETTING TO KNOW THEM

The next step in the process of getting to know your client and making a true connection is probing for their interests, hobbies, and philosophies in life. All this is easy to know by just simply asking the right questions and, above all, listening to their responses. Finding that common denominator that binds you and them together. Personally, I love making references to books, movies and asking their history.

Here is an example of what and how to do it. Out of the blue, an Internet lead (that lives in another state) that I had been working with for sometime came into town. As I met the mother and daughter, we started chatting. Before we knew it, I found out that they had family where I was born. As our conversation continued, I asked more about them and as they told me about their family and where they grew up, I asked them by telling them about my family that still lived in the area they had told me about. The mother actually knew some of my aunts and cousins. You never know who you will meet and how you can tie yourself to them. This can only be done through really wanting to know who your client is and fully engaging in their stories they are telling you.

5. GENUINE INTEREST

When asked what it is I do as I tell people I am a professional social-izer, yes, I am a realtor by trade, but what is it that is the true center of what we do as human beings? We socialize…that is the key. Just meet people! That is the secret. When people feel you are genuinely inter-ested in 'who' they are, that is when the connection is really set in stone and truly it is what everyone, including ourselves want – for someone to take the time to really connect.

You may be asking how is this so? It is the 4 key elements that are com-bined that create a genuine interest.

1. Use of body language

2. Eye-contact

3. Pitch of your voice

4. Making them feel warm and familiar like an old friend would.

Many times I find by hugging my clients as I greet them and when I leave them. Of course, this is after we have made that initial connec-tion. When we speak on the phone, I want to know how they are doing in their personal life, not just the transaction in which we are involved. One of my clients that I have never met face to face felt close enough to me that we are now friends on Facebook and we chat via text because we have common fitness goals – so we exchange kudos on our achieve-ments. She refers relocations to me now. Finding that true heart-to-heart in a bond with a client is what will separate you from the rest.

6. PERSONALIZE IT

Now that you have all this information that the client has shared with you, it is time to personalize all your interaction with them. Tailor it spe-cifically to them to make it familiar and interesting. Your client should feel that it is all about them. Constantly refer back to references in their 'likes.' It is important to make sure they always have a reason to come back and use you as their personal reference and their professional of choice. Make sure you have input that is valuable to them, that way they always have reason to come back around to you.

All my initial interaction is based around them and everything they have told me about themselves. When I speak I keep it real, no sugar coating here. Clients will call you first because they know you will want the best for them, even if they call to ask your opinion on their next room color, or who they should use for insurance, or how they should go about something. For me, I always make sure that if they are going to use the home warranty company that we selected at closing, to call me first, so I can put them in touch with the local rep that will stay on top of the claim. This small token has been an invaluable tool. It gives them a reason to reach out to me and for me to have reason to reach back out to them and ask if the situation was fixed …and to simply ask, how are you?

7. MAKE THEM FEEL LIKE A FRIEND

The one thing I know about myself is that all my clients are my friends. I want to know about them every time we speak. I ask how are they doing, what's going on in their world. Just like when I call an old friend. It is important to include them in the interaction; it should be a real conversation that is two-sided. The conversation should have spontaneity and flow that is stimulating a real bond in friendship. There should never be a 'good-bye' or finality in your dealings – always have a reason for you to contact them and them to contact you.

Another story that I can share to reiterate the importance of them calling you to assist their needs is my client that purchased a duplex – and he is an owner occupant. As we were hunting for the perfect duplex, I found an expired listing that was willing to sell. However it would need some TLC so as we negotiated the contract, he asked me if I would help in the design process. Being that I have a strong background in architecture and interior design, I was thrilled. As each stage of renovation approached he called to consult and we would collaborate ideas and come up with a design plan that worked. I have assisted him through the entire evaluation process of each step of remodeling his home and his rental units, now that it is time to lease it out, who do you think he called to consult and list it.

The unit was listed and rented at the absolute top of the rentals in that area and in record time. First thing he said was, 'Thank You" and "You were right in guiding me in what I needed for my best case scenario." This is a client for life now, because I took the time to get to know him as a real person, so, I am the first person he calls to consult on what I think, and I help to evaluate the scenario in a pro and con to best get the results he was wanting and needing.

8. NOT ABOUT THE HOUSE OR THE PRODUCT

This brings me to the most important factor; it is not about the house or product. It is all about the people that you meet and how you choose to make them feel. The true connection and bond that becomes a real point of why they chose to work with you and refer you to their sphere of influence, is the basis to the entire bond that is established. The house or product is the commodity, not the person purchasing the home or product.

Human connection is what we all strive to do everyday at its simplest form. Keeping it real and from the heart is what clients will appreciate and that will be their reasoning to refer you and keep coming back. That is the goal to have longevity in any business. Think of yourself as a doctor of real estate or whatever your product is. If you have a doctor with a horrible bedside manner, you are most likely inclined to avoid going to them or you will find a new one. However, if you have a doctor that greets you by name, asks you about your kids, your dog, your hobbies and specifics in your life, you are more inclined to look forward to that appointment and refer him or her to your friends and family so they can have the same experience. Right?

Well then, get going, it really is that simple! Become that social butterfly that is a breath of fresh air everywhere you go and begin connecting with people. It is the connections in life that will bring you continuously back around to who and where you need to be in life. Keep a smile on your face and enjoy each and every interaction with the people you meet.

It really is that simple.

About Vanessa

Vanessa Nunez studied architecture and interior design at the University of Louisiana at Lafayette. Upon graduation, she moved to St. Thomas, USVI and had much success in high-end jewelry sales and as an entrepreneur in the restaurant business with her ex-husband. Returning to the states, she was ready, willing and ripe for her long-time passion in real estate. She quickly made her mark in the Austin Real Estate market, establishing Austin Board of Realtors "Rookie of the Year" 2011 in just a short 7 1/2 months from obtaining her license.

She has been noted by many colleagues for her tenacity, drive, focus and loyalty she delivers to her clients, peers and partners in business. Vanessa is seen as an inspiration to many for her constant rally to motivate herself and others around her.

In her second calendar year, Vanessa was nominated for Austin Business Journals prestigious award: "Power in Profiles" – featuring the top women in business in Central Texas; nominated for Platinum Top 50; and nominated for Austin Board of Realtors Salesperson of the Year 2012. Vanessa also shared her 'secrets' in her success on Top Producer panels including Texas Association of Realtors Convention 2012. She is eager to share her knowledge with anyone who has the desire and curiosity to learn.

Vanessa is noted by many partners in the real estate community to be an admirable ambassador with a rare combination of raw talent and incredible drive with a servant's heart, she does this all the while producing high volume, managing her 8-year-old son and competing in figure competitions twice a year.

Vanessa recently began her own company brand, Lifestyle Properties of Austin with her co-author Bridget Shoemaker. Since collaborating and writing the chapter Vanessa and Bridget found that they were both very driven individuals that shared the same philosophies in the real estate business and branched out on their own. They created their own unique brand because they both feel strongly that they sell lifestyles. Hence no better name than Lifestyle Properties of Austin.

About Bridget

Bridget Shoemaker believes that all successful real estate transactions come about as result of clear and open communications, particularly regarding the needs and expectations of her clients and the market conditions. Bridget is aware that every client has unique requirements and circumstances, and that the journey to achieving a successful transaction will be tailored to fit their goals and ultimate desires. Her ability to be flexible and provide a high level of responsiveness to changing needs is essential to her to success as a well-rounded and solution-providing agent.

With Bridget… "what you see is what you get." Each and every detail of her business model will be laid down in ink; leaving out unknowns or ambiguities before, during, and after the transaction cycle. All of this is secured by years of work applied to developing a massive front-end and back-end system, which in turn transforms home buying /selling into the enjoyable and seamless experience that it is ultimately meant to be.

While some agents may encourage a client to make a quick decision, Bridget always urges her clients to take time and carefully reflect before making their final move. She's also quick to discourage a choice if she sees any conceivable issues ahead that would adversely affect her clients' welfare in the future. Experience in foreclosure markets and investment properties have also given her a keen ability to identify accurate values for all ages, makes, and styles of homes. She too has owned many herself and knows all that goes into the process.

In 2010, Bridget was honored to have won the "Outstanding Achievement in Lifetime Connection & Program Excellence in Relevant Social Media Communication" award from Max Avenue. Also in 2010, Bridget was nominated for the Austin Board of Realtors' Community Service Award. Bridget founded and served as Vice President of "Austin Angels" - a non-profit organization focusing on helping members of the community in need. More recently, Bridget was nominated amongst the Platinum Top 50 Finalist Realtors® in Austin, Texas in late 2011. She has also obtained her CNE (Certified Negotiation Expert) and her ALHS (Accredited Luxury Home Specialist) designations. Each of these merits in combination with her championed success as a REALTOR® are what sets Bridget apart from her competition, and ultimately provide proven results to buyers and sellers in the greater Austin area.

Bridget prides herself in her level of expertise and customer service. She believes she is not in the Real Estate business…She is in the business of building relationships and selling lifestyles!

www.Bridgetsellsaustin.com

CHAPTER 28

SEVEN STEPS TO COMPLETE YOUR RETIREMENT INVESTMENT PLAN

BY JOHN CONVERY

Victory! We all want that in all aspects of our lives, don't we? How do you have victory in your financial life? How would you like to know and achieve being able to thrive in your retirement and not just survive?

A very prominent Wall Street Investment banker has taken a little time to retreat to a sanctuary from all his international travel and private equity transactions. On this day, he is enjoying a secluded ribbon of sand beach down in a verdant area of Mexico on the Yucatan Peninsula. As he raises his eyes up onto the beautiful turquoise and azure waters he can't help but notice a wooden canoe with outriggers bobbing out in the ocean, three Mexican men aboard working hard to harvest fish. At first, it is just an innocuous glance, but eventually he finds himself entranced as he watches their system of casting and running in a figure eight pattern a series of nets in unison to pull the fish together and harvest an abundant amount. It is something truly amazing to watch. Later, when he sees them come in to the dock, he decides he has to go over and have a conversation with them, with the spring in his step for a potential new opportunity.

He reaches them and begins a friendly conversation by asking, "What do you plan on doing with the fish that you've caught, and why did you come in so early? At the rate you were going you probably could have caught fish all day."

"Oh, senor, we most certainly could have," they answered, "but we only want to catch enough fish in our nets to feed our families. Then we can take our mid afternoon siesta, enjoy a lovely fish dinner and fine wine with our friends and family and play some music with our amigos. That's really our joy in life."

The investment banker, looking perplexed inquired, "Why wouldn't you continue to fish the rest of the hot afternoon and sell your fish to the fisheries? Eventually you could become profitable enough to open your own cannery, then look at creating joint ventures for international distribution lines and some of the unique fish to these waters could be shipped internationally."

The Mexicans look at each other, contemplating, and then ask, "Then what would we do?"

The investment banker answers, "Then you basically become so successful that some of the big food companies would want to buy you out or you take your company public through an IPO, and once you did that, you'd be multimillionaires."

The Mexicans then ask again, "Then what would we do?"

"Then you could return to the Yucatan, retire, enjoy fish with your family and friends, drink fine wine, and play music with your amigos."

"AHA and ouch!!"

And so it is for so many pre-retirees or retirees who've worked their entire lives toiling to save to educate their children, to pay their taxes, to fund their 401(k) retirement plans, only to arrive at the gateway to what presumably will be a stress-free retirement so they can enjoy eating fish, drinking fine wine, and playing music with their friends. Alas, in these tumultuous times it isn't so easy. Many folks find themselves more consumed by just trying to monitor their investment positions, and trying to figure out how to put together an overall strategy that will give them the peace of mind that they are looking for in a less-stress retirement lifestyle. It can be had. In fact, there are methods you can use to thrive, not just survive, in retirement. The key, though, contrary to what most people think, is not your balance sheet or price per share at the close of the business day of the stocks you own, but rather cash flow and the ability to manage the longevity risk – so that no matter how long you live you will always have an inflation-adjusted abundant retirement harvest. That's what I find my clients are genuinely most passionate about.

Many folks are calling this day and age the new normal, with market disparities and so on and so forth. As a matter of fact, a national magazine published a report that said from 1998 to 2008 the unmanaged S&P 500 for every $100 invested in a 401(k) adjusted for inflation ten years later at the end of term was only worth $73.52. Yes, most people have actually gotten poorer during that period of time. Consider this is what a major Wall Street executive had to say: "The longer we live, the greater stress that puts on our ability to pay for our retirement-income goal - an inflation-adjusted income stream that lasts as long as we do," says Tom Idzorik, chief investment officer at Morningstar Inc.'s Ibbotson Associates Unit. "We need to go beyond the universe of mutual funds and exchange-traded funds and consider longevity-risk products." (Source: Wall Street Journal, "Investing for Retirement. Making the Case to buy an annuity." ~ March 8 2011). That being said, it is important to know though, that today with most people, my experience is they don't really have a prudent plan for managing their investments. Rather, they have a wild assemblage of investments and oftentimes redundancies, and are overpaying taxes as well as subjecting themselves to so much correlated and systemic risk. This is what we typically see and even people that profess themselves to be conservative at age 70 years old oftentimes have about 70% of their money in equities with no underlying guarantees.

To combat these potentially harmful situations, we've developed a proprietary seven step numeric model for figuring out your investment plan and it starts like this. The seven steps are: (1) gather, (2) diagnose, (3) select and prioritize objectives, (4) consider alternatives, (5) decide, (6) implement, and (7) monitor.

1. **Gather**: It seems obvious, but investment solutions can't suitably be made or recommended without first stepping back to look at the landscape and it starts with gathering appropriate information. In the case of investments, a properly-balanced plan cannot be curated without first reviewing, at the least, the following information.

   a. Client Goals, timelines and risk tolerance

   b. Current investment statements

   c. Insurance policies and illustrative ledgers

   d. US1040 tax returns and corporate returns, where appropriate

As amazing as it seems, in my own anecdotal experience in my practice, I find that most clients referred in from broker dealers tell me they've never been asked for some of this documentation for review, particularly their tax return. I always tell them that the tax return is a seminal document because for instance if you're retired you have what's called a provisional income or MAGI (Modified Adjusted Gross Income). For instance, if this number is over \$34,000/year for joint filers husband and wife, 50% of your Social Security Benefits will be reported on line 20b and subject to your ordinary income tax rate. Some people would be outraged and argue that since Social Security was a FICA or payroll tax, that's double tax and I tend to agree. While for the most part there is very little you can do of consequence to affect your line items from line 16a and beyond, your early line items from lines 7-15b should be scrutinized as you can influence these amounts. The reason for that is, to some degree, these reported amounts of dividend income, interest income, tax exempt income, etc. can be influenced as it is a direct reflection as it correlates to the investments you've selected. For instance, if your interest income is on line 8b it is tax exempt and you pay no Federal taxes, however if it's on line 8a and correlates to CD's you may have with banking institutions, that must be reported on a Schedule B if over \$400 and will increase your adjusted gross income. Strategically, you may want to consider allocating more money "tax free" if you're concerned about paying tax on Social Security, which can only really be discovered and prudently addressed through review of the tax return.

2. **Diagnose**: I've tipped my hand by my comments gathering information but configuring a masterful plan for any individual's financial victory requires a holistic approach where you look to balance:

   a. Growth Orientation

   b. Tax Savings

   c. Risk Management

   d. Income Planning

   For example, let's say a client has a significant whole life policy, with paid-up additions whereby no future premiums are required to maintain the face amount/death benefit of coverage. This may diminish that client's need to pursue purchasing growth stocks in the hopes of leaving a "stepped up" basis or tax friendly transfer of wealth to their children or grandchildren at death because of the following. Life insurance will mature at death and let's say it's a $100,000 policy tax free under Section 101(a) of the IRS code and therefore in all likelihood may be greater than could be achieved in appreciating shares in a short period of time. Therefore, this client may want to consider eliminating the redundancy of having both a whole life policy and shares of growth-oriented company's common stock to achieve the same common objective of transferring wealth tax-free to their family. What they may want to consider is transitioning some of the stocks through conversions at low capital gains tax rates into income-adjusted inflation-protected investments that can deliver greater cash flow, and from that greater cash flow live the abundant life now while they are presumably healthy enough to enjoy it, and if they prefer, gift money tax-free under the annual allowances to children and grandchildren and see them enjoy the fruit on the tree now while they can appreciate the smiles on their faces warmly and give this some thought.

3. **Select and prioritize objectives**: Oftentimes, folks take more time to plan a vacation, which can be forgettable but resident memory in short order, versus selecting time to prioritize their financial victory. In order, though, to do this, you need to look at selecting and prioritizing your objectives. For instance, in my

practice, I always give a list of financial characteristics that you can ascribe to any type of financial instrument or investment.

a. Principal Protection

b. Aggressive Growth

c. Tax Reduction

There would be a dichotomy here though, if the person says they are primarily concerned about principal preservation, but 70% of their holdings are in aggressive growth stocks. This is an incongruence that would need to be addressed through better alignment in creating their overall strategic plan. Another example is, if on line 15b IRA distributions are noted and you can extrapolate that the withdrawal for the Required Minimum Distributions (RMD's) for persons over age 70-1/2 is significantly less, you may want to modify the amount of future distributions from the IRA to create "tax reduction." Of course, to provide for the offset in lowering of income, you want to look at how to increase cash flow while reducing taxes at the same time through careful attention to the MAGI that I had mentioned earlier.

4. **Consider alternatives**: Let's say congratulations, you've gotten to this point. Now it's a matter of ethically prioritizing your objectives and looking at alternatives. Alternatives need to be grouped into their respective categories. For instance, if you're looking at safe money strategies, this may include things such as:

a. Treasury securities

b. Bank CD's

c. Fixed annuities

You want to compare and contrast the attributes of each in the given market environment. For instance, as of my present writing of this chapter, the ten-year treasury note has a 1.75% yield to maturity which means that you get 1.7% / year and have to wait for the face amount of your money to mature in ten years and get all your money back and walk away. There is an interest rate risk in that if interest rates go up and you want to sell your bond prematurely, you may actually receive less. Conversely,

CD's, which are FDIC insured, are certainly taxable and may yield the same or a lower percentage on a five year basis, but if the penalty for premature withdrawal savings is less, this may be a better pursuit than taking the interest rate risk associated with a longer term to maturity (ten years of the treasury security).

5. **Decide**: Ahh, decision time. It all comes down to the rubber meeting the road. Don't let 'paralysis analysis' get you here – which would say, "Okay, stand at the marksmen's line, point your firearm and ready aim, aim, aim aim…" You have to aim and then fire. Fortunately, if you've carefully gone through the steps outlined here, you will be prepared, and not because of being nonchalant, but because of having the confidence of going through the process and better understanding yourself through the introspective discovery that invariably comes out of the journey.

6. **Implement**: Get 'er done. Get 'er done. Obviously implementation speaks to itself. You have to follow the proper plans and procedures to inaugurate your plan and really move towards harvesting the benefits thereof.

7. **Monitor**: I believe it was Tony Robins who said you need to establish an "evidence procedure," to use his vernacular. Specifically, this is the way to determine the score card. In major league baseball, there's a score card capped in individual metrics such as batting average, RBI's and bases stolen for each individual player – to let you know how are they doing against their own individual performance and against their peer group or competitors. It's no different in the investment arena. We need to know what do we want to measure and how often. For instance, if you're in a portfolio of diversified securities you want to review the same with your advisor at least quarterly. However, if you are invested predominantly in safe money strategies of a non-correlated nature with some principal assurances, you may more likely be able to monitor the same on an annual basis. Again, you need to establish before you start down this journey of monitoring what you're going to measure. Are you going to measure appreciation and price per share, or income over the last quarter, etc. – so you know if you're on target, exceeding your expectations, or if some further adjustments are in order?

Victory. It sounds so easy but is yet so elusive. However, I wholeheartedly believe that if you follow the seven steps enumerated in this chapter, you'll discover a number of things about yourself, who you are and what's genuinely most important to you at your core value level. Additionally, you'll become more educated and holistically begin to see the inter-relationship between the strategies that you've used financially to achieve your best result.

My best wishes and wholehearted congratulations to you for working through this chapter and my audacious hope is that you'll inaugurate this strategy to live the abundant victorious life.

About John

John Convery is the President at The Educated Wealth Center, LLC. He has 27 years experience in the fields of retirement income, wealth preservation, wealth management and estate planning. John graduated *magna cum laude* from the Commonwealth of Pennsylvania's East Stroudsburg University. John is a proud member of the National Ethics Bureau, with which he has an impeccable reputation. John is recognized by his peers and was bestowed the Bronze Eagle Award, as presented by AXA Financial Group, recognizing him for his excellence and professionalism in the marketplace.

John is constantly sought by the local and national media. On the national level, he has authored articles for CNBC, MarketWatch, Reuters, Yahoo Finance, Fox Business, *Newsweek, The American Chronicle* and has appeared in *US News and World Report* as well as on the national television network WE TV. Additionally, he was recognized as a "Financial Trendsetter" in the December 24, 2012 last paper edition of the national publication *Newsweek*.

CHAPTER 29

WARNING: Don't Even Think About Selling Your Home Until You Read This Chapter and…

"DISCOVER HOW TO SELL YOUR HOME FOR MORE MONEY…AND IN LESS TIME" … IN THIS NEW DIGITAL ECONOMY!

The Fastest and Easiest Way to Expose Your Home to Thousands of HOT Qualified Buyers Using Breakthrough Technical Advances… And How You Can Put This System To Work For YOU!

BY SASHA MILETIC

If you are planning on selling your home in the next two years for TOP dollar while avoiding the hassles and pitfalls that go along with the real estate process, then this chapter is IMPORTANT TO YOU.

I have laid out THE MOST ADVANCED techniques I know for exposing your home to the greatest number of highly motivated and qualified buyers. We will discuss how to price your home competitively at the highest perceived value, preparing your home for sale with the least amount of effort and choosing the right agent in your market. But before I dive right in, here is a quick background:

HOW IT WAS IN THE BEGINNING

Prior to 2000, selling real estate was fairly homogeneous amongst real estate agents. Here were the primary means of exposing, advertising and marketing a property:

- Local newspaper;
- Specialty real estate magazines and papers;
- Cable and Television;
- For Sale Sign;
- Open houses.

Overall, there wasn't that much of a difference in the level of service you were receiving from one agent to another. One could argue that top agents would have experience with negotiating offers and reviewing contracts. However, many would stockpile listings and homeowners would rarely hear from them after the listing agreement was signed.

Back then, and even today to some extent, an agent would sit at a prospective client's kitchen table and elaborately present what they would do to sell a home. This typical 30 minute sales tactic itemized the sale strategy, but the irony is that every agent followed similar steps and just didn't bother to tell you.

The bottom line back then was even if you used your Aunt Betty or a top-producing agent, the marketing exposure to qualified buyers would be virtually the same.

WHAT YOU'RE UP AGAINST

I want to share with you some hard facts and averages that will shock a lot of you. Take a look at what is happening in my marketplace for residential sales:

In 2012...

- The average agent SOLD 5.84 Units*;
- Only 54% of all listings end up selling;
- And they sold on average in 74 days.

In 2011...

- The average agent SOLD 5.58 Units*;
- Only 51% of all listings end up selling;
- And they sold on average in 76 days .

In 2010...

- The average agent SOLD 5.63 Units*;
- Only 49% of all listings end up selling;
- And they sold on average in 75 days.

In fact, you can go back 20 years and the numbers won't fluctuate much. Surprisingly, from 2010 – 2012, the market went up as home prices rose from $163,346 to $175,581, a 7.45% increase, yet the average number of homes an agent sold remained the same.

The average agent does not sell a lot of homes per year and I bet this is throughout all of North America.

WHAT DO PEA PODS HAVE IN COMMON WITH REAL ESTATE AGENTS

In 1906, an Italian economist named Vilfredo Pareto observed that 20% of all pea pods in his garden contained 80% of the peas. This is now known as the Pareto Principal. If you look at virtually any sales field, you'll find that 80% of all sales are done by 20% of the salespeople.

Here's what this has to do with you. The first and most obvious thing is if an agent isn't selling much, they typically lack certain sales and negotiating skills. If an agent is a low producer, there is not much money left that is required to invest in and run a business. So at the end of the day, their listings will be exposed to fewer qualified buyers, which lead to lower demand for the listings. This results in a lower sales price.

DIRTY LITTLE INSIDER SECRET REVEALS HOW REAL ESTATE AGENTS CAN MAKE MONEY OFF A HOUSE EVEN IF IT DOESN'T SELL

"Why do so many listings expire?" Half of all of the houses on the market will NOT sell because they are overpriced. Why do agents take these listings? Because they can make money even if it doesn't sell! A listing gives an agent exposure, which generates phone calls or leads. If they never had the listing, they would lose out on the opportunity for more clients.

HOW THE "FALLACY OF TIME" CAN BE HAZARDOUS TO YOUR WEALTH

Nine out of ten homeowners today believe that to get top dollar, your home can stay on the market indefinitely until you find the right buyer. I call this the "Fallacy of Time."

The reverse is true. The less time a home is listed for sale, the higher the price. Fact is, homes that sell for above market value almost always sell quickly and ones that sell beyond the average days on market go well below what they are actually worth.

Studies show the highest level of interest on a property is within the first 30 days. After that, it drops dramatically. Once your home is listed, it will be marketed to qualified buyers looking for similar properties. Buyers narrow their list once they've viewed several homes. If your house doesn't appeal to a wide majority of buyers, then it sits. A house that doesn't get offers is soon considered "stale." Unfortunately, as a homeowner, the only parameter you can control is the price and not what buyers think.

By now you're probably wondering what all of this has to do with selling your home in this new digital economy, right? But in order for you to grasp what needs to be done, you need to understand the current situation and what brought us here.

THREE DEADLY MISTAKES MOST HOMEOWNERS MAKE... AND HOW TO AVOID THEM

1. **Lack of Preparation:** Owners who do the research and prepare their home to sell, make the most money... Period! Unfortunately, most homeowners neglect performing their due diligence and interviewing multiple real estate agents. Furthermore, they totally lack knowledge in:

   • How to market and attract qualified buyers;

   • What questions to ask an agent during the interview process;

- The importance of pricing and the dangers of overpricing a home;
- The sellers role in the sales process;
- Preparing the home for Sale;
- The Brokers role in the sales process;
- Timing and whether to sell first or buy first.

It's sad to see that most home owners neglect to protect what will probably be the largest investment of their lifetime. Hopefully this chapter can shed some light on what to do and more importantly what NOT to do when you sell YOUR home.

2. **Overpricing Your Home:** If you price your home too high, it won't sell. Note that real estate agents do not determine your home's value, the market does. Yet over and over, homeowners select an agent that encourages them to list at a higher price. When this happens, price reductions are necessary and increases the time your home is on the market. In half of these situations, your listing will expire. Keep in mind that the role of a successful agent is to sell your home, not to price it. That is your job based on the information provided to you by your agent.

3. **Lack of Exposure:** Advertising and marketing are different. Advertising uses media (i.e. newspapers, cable, magazines) to sell something, while marketing is a targeted message. Most agents are completely clueless when it comes to marketing. Anyone can write an ad and place it somewhere but marketing is a different story.

As mentioned, 90 percent of buyers start their home search online. The Internet gives buyers information, pictures, video tours, feature sheets, school reports & demographics INSTANTLY and a lot more than you can fit in a 15-second commercial or in a 5-line ad.

Today, it's easy to put a house on the Internet, but you need to generate:

Traffic! Traffic! Traffic!

It doesn't take a rocket scientist to figure out that you'll have a better chance of selling your house if thousands of qualified buyers looked at it than only a few. So here are the...

3 KEY METHODICAL STEPS YOU NEED TO TAKE TO SELL YOUR HOME FOR MORE MONEY... AND IN LESS TIME!

STEP #1: You Need To Ensure That Your On-Line Exposure Is Maximized:

Contrary to what anyone tells you, an agent's job is to get the greatest number of qualified buyer eyeballs looking at your house and the owner's job is to sell the house by presenting it properly.

✓ **Does The Agent Have Their Own Web Site?:** Creating a web site takes effort. Agents who have their own site as opposed to using their office site gives you double the exposure. For sellers, this is a win-win. I always look for this when sending out referrals to other agents in North America.

✓ **How Connected Is Their Web Site With Social Media?** People around the world spend on average one hour a day on Facebook alone. Here are the most highly ranked sites as far as Internet traffic:
  1– Facebook
  2 – Google (g+)
  3 – YouTube
  10 – Twitter
  14 – LinkedIn
  23 – WordPress
  36 – Pinterest

Make sure that you see "share" links on the pages of the agents site. It means that page is viral, maximizes traffic and increases SEO.

✓ **Are Videos Posted On YouTube or Their Web Site?** Your home video should be on both the agents site and YouTube with share links.

✓ **Does the Agent Have Facebook and a Facebook Fan Page Account?** Take a look at my Facebook account at: www.Facebook.com/MileticSasha and my Fan Page at: www.Facebook.com/RealEstateWindsor . The difference is that Facebook is more personal and a Fan Page is more for business.

✓ **Does the Agent Use LinkedIn and Twitter?** These are hugely important to share information and stay connected.

✓ **Does the Agent Utilize Kijiji and Craigs List?** Market your home on Kijiji and Craigs List on a rotational basis with a link back to a video tour on the agent's site.

✓ **Is the Agent Working For a Local Independent Company or Part of a Franchise?** National franchises spend millions of dollars on marketing & SEO. Unfortunately, independent brokers cannot compete. If you'll be paying a full service commission, why not benefit from all of this extra traffic?

✓ **Locally, How Optimized is the Agent and Companies Web Sites?** SEO is crucial because it's a key driver to getting local on-line traffic. Surprisingly, you'll notice that individual agents generate a lot more local traffic than most large major brokerages within their city.

If you were to look for real estate locally, what would you type in Google? Let's try Windsor, Ontario

- Windsor Properties
- Windsor Real Estate
- Windsor Homes

You can simply substitute **Windsor** for your home town. Those sites listed consistently on page 1 are the highest ranked as far as search results and get the most web traffic. Sellers take note.

✓ **How Often Does The Agent Publish New Content On Their Site?** Agents that blog daily will have a higher ranking and get more qualified buyers to their site than someone who doesn't.

FOR SALE BY OWNERS (FSBO'S) ARE GIVING AWAY MONEY FASTER THAN A HOLLYWOOD BREAKUP

According to a 2011 study by the National Association of Realtors, FSBO's only accounted for 10% of the overall market and, a typical FSBO home sold for $150,000 compared to $215,000 for an agent-assisted home (30.23% less).

Furthermore, most qualified buyers are already working with an agent under contract so if they buy privately, they would be liable for the commission. That means that the serious FSBO is hoping to save the other 3-4% by going alone. Sometimes it works, but in most cases they either sell it undervalued or they get frustrated and hand it over to an agent after they've exhausted their time and money. They cannot match the exposure of an accomplished agent.

STEP #2: Price Your Home Competitively

Prices are driven by supply and demand PERIOD! Supply is determined by how many houses you are currently competing with in your area and demand is when you look at recent sales. Every month there will be sales in your neighborhood as well as new listings. If your home was valued at $200,000 three months ago and currently there are eight other homes similar to yours averaging $187,000, you'll be overpriced. The reverse is true as well. If there are currently three homes for sale averaging $225,000, you'll shortchange yourself drastically if you asked $200,000.

DO NOT RELY ON AN APPRAISAL, HOME ASSESSMENT OR AN OPINION OF VALUE TO DETERMINE YOUR HOMES PRICE

The supply of homes changes month in and month out so an appraisal from 4 months ago is useless today.

Also, different areas sell better than others at given times. Listing inventories fluctuate and you need to determine what the absorption rate is in your area. This is a measurement of how many months it will take on average to clear the listing inventory. Most agents won't have a clue what this is, but if your house was worth $200,000, take a price range of $175,000 - $225,000 and pull up all of the sales over the past 12 months. Let's say there was 38 sales, now divide that number by 12 and it will give you the absorption rate of 3.17 which means that a little over 3 homes sold per month in your area over the past year. If you look at the number of listings currently for sale in that same price range (18 currently for sale) and you divide it by the absorption rate of 3.17, you can see that the market softened up a bit and now it will take 5.68 months to clear the current listing inventory in your area.

STEP #3: Do Your Homework:

Be realistic and understand that if you purchased a home in most markets throughout North America over that past 5 years, and if you are thinking of selling now, chances are likely that you'll be at a loss. Even in Canada where we've experienced a real estate bubble, many markets are flattening out and stabilizing. There are local agents that do over-the-net home evaluations. Take advantage of this service. Once you fill out the form, they should send you a list of sales in your area. Although this is not 100% accurate, it's a great starting point. Here are some other things you may want to consider:

- ✓ **Do you go with an individual agent or a team?** Individual agents often work 100 plus hours a week to maximize their profits. A team works with others to divide their jobs and responsibilities.

- ✓ **Do you know what you are signing?**

  - Consider the length of the contract, which is usually 6 months. Agents spend time and money marketing a home and they want to increase their chances of selling it when the market swings. But cancellation options should be offered if an agent doesn't do as promised.

  - Commission: Don't go with the cheapest agent. How many people work harder if you give them a reduced pay cheque? How can they fund a marketing program while working at a discount? Remember, you can always negotiate commissions when you get and negotiate an offer.

- ✓ **Your role in the selling process:** Keep the home show-ready. I offer a 4 page report on what your role as a home seller is. If you want a copy, send me an email at: info@sashamiletic.com. Type in the subject: Victory, Client's Role.

- ✓ **Buy or sell first?** Ask yourself this: Do you want to own two homes at the same time? What if you buy a home and can't sell your own? Or what if you get an offer that is well below the listing price? A Guarantee Sales Program works best in these situations.

WANT TO KNOW THE TOP 2 REASONS
WHY A HOME DOES NOT SELL?

1. It's Overpriced. No one wants to pay for an overpriced turkey. Overpriced listings have a negative impact on the final sales price.

2. Lack of Exposure. It's simple. If buyers don't know about your home, then you won't get showings.

Real estate is an ever-changing and evolving business. A few years ago we didn't know about Facebook or other social media. Today, it's a game changer when selling homes. The Internet? Ninety percent of buyers turn to this before even contacting a real estate agent. A real estate agent that is keen on these changes and looking toward the future understands that it takes more than a "For Sale" sign in the front yard. Sellers must understand that a home must be exposed, priced properly and show-ready in order for it to sell quickly and for TOP dollar.

My website contains all of the latest real estate information to answer any questions you may have. Subscribe to my daily blogs, access the free reports and toolkits and see all that my team has to offer by going to: http://www.SashaMiletic.com. If you have specific questions, I am always available at: info@SashaMiletic.com.

*Total units sales were divided by total membership count for 2010-2012.

About Sasha

Sasha Miletic is a 25 year veteran of real estate sales. He was born in the former Yugoslavia. In 1971, when he was five years old, he moved with his family to Canada. His strong work ethic came from his parents. His late father, Steve, worked at Chrysler before getting his real estate license in 1975 and his late mother, Zee, worked as a registered nurse. Together, in 1980 they started Prime Realty, Inc., and Zee said goodbye to nursing and obtained her real estate license.

Sasha's first job was janitor at Prime Realty where he worked through high school. During the summer after Sasha's graduation from Riverside High and prior to university, Sasha successfully passed his courses for his real estate license and joined the Windsor Essex County Real Estate Board one year later as a real estate sales representative.

Sasha dabbled in real estate during the summer months while in university. After being awarded a B.A. in 1990 from the University of Western Ontario, he quickly jumped right into sales to become one of the top listing and selling agents in Windsor and Essex County.

In 1996, Sasha left sales to train, recruit and manage his family's business, Prime Realty Inc. During that same time, Sasha served as a director for the Windsor Essex County Real Estate Board either chairing or co-chairing various committees which included the revisions of the Board's By-laws, Policy and Procedure manuals & Rules and Regulation committee, Standard Forms committee, Computer & Technology committee, Public Relations committee, as well as various others.

In 1999, Sasha ventured off to Palo Alto in Silicon Valley with a business plan. He managed to get a law firm and an accounting firm to invest in his project *pro bono*. Unfortunately, in 2000 the Internet bubble blew up and so did the project, but the knowledge and insight that he acquired was priceless.

With the overwhelming popularity and usage of the Internet, in 2004 Sasha quickly realized that national franchises have a massive competitive advantage in terms of capital and resources over local brokerages, so the Miletic family sold Prime Realty to RE/MAX Preferred Realty and Sasha went into Sales.

Today, Sasha's business is built on a strong foundation of experience in all facets of the real estate business. The lessons learnt in Palo Alto are the cornerstone of his business. Sasha's main function on his team revolves around marketing; managing social media, search engine optimization, blogging, tweeting and all other tasks to do with generating traffic and exposing his team's listings to the greatest number of qualified buyers – while other team members service clients.

Sasha is a Hall of Fame recipient with RE/MAX and his web site ranks as one of the highest in Google for organic searches, and generates more traffic than most brokerage companies in his city.

Sasha is currently married to Louisa going on 11 years and has 2 sons, Andrew and Steve who will be 9 and 10 in 2013. Sasha's favorite hobbies are reading and golf and is also an unabashed Detroit Lions football fan.

If you respectively would like a free Home Sellers Toolkit, visit Sasha's website at : www.SashaMiletic.com.

Or alternatively, you can contact Sasha by email at : info@SashaMiletic.com or call him directly at 519.962.9150.

Sasha Miletic is a Broker with RE/MAX Preferred Realty Ltd., Brokerage that is independently owned and operated. It is located at 6505 Tecumseh Rd. E., Windsor, ON N8T 1E7 -- Office Phone: 519.944.5955.